T0210965

Communications in Computer and Information Science 1157

Commenced Publication in 2007
Founding and Former Series Editors:
Phoebe Chen, Alfredo Cuzzocrea, Xiaoyong Du, Orhun Kara, Ting Liu,
Krishna M. Sivalingam, Dominik Ślęzak, Takashi Washio, Xiaokang Yang,
and Junsong Yuan

More information about this series at http://www.springer.com/series/7899

Xin Wang · Francesca A. Lisi ·
Guohui Xiao · Elena Botoeva (Eds.)

Semantic Technology

9th Joint International Conference, JIST 2019
Hangzhou, China, November 25–27, 2019
Revised Selected Papers

Springer

Editors
Xin Wang (iD)
Tianjin University
Tianjin, China

Guohui Xiao (iD)
Free University of Bozen-Bolzano
Bolzano, Italy

Francesca A. Lisi (iD)
University of Bari Aldo Moro
Bari, Italy

Elena Botoeva (iD)
Imperial College London
London, UK

ISSN 1865-0929   ISSN 1865-0937 (electronic)
Communications in Computer and Information Science
ISBN 978-981-15-3411-9   ISBN 978-981-15-3412-6 (eBook)
https://doi.org/10.1007/978-981-15-3412-6

This Springer imprint is published by the registered company Springer Nature Singapore Pte Ltd.
The registered company address is: 152 Beach Road, #21-01/04 Gateway East, Singapore 189721, Singapore

Preface

This is the second volume of the proceedings of the 9th Joint International Semantic Technology Conference (JIST 2019) held during November 25–27, 2019, in Hangzhou, China. JIST is a joint event for regional Semantic related conferences. Since its launched in Hangzhou in 2011, it has become the premium Asian forum on Semantic Web, Knowledge Graph, Linked Data, and AI on the Web. In 2019, JIST returned to Hangzhou, and the mission was to bring together researchers in the Knowledge Graph and Semantic Technology research community and other related areas to present their innovative research results and novel applications. This year's theme was "Open Web and Knowledge Graph."

The proceedings of JIST 2019 are presented in two volumes: the first one in LNCS and the second one in CCIS. The conference attracted high-quality submissions and participants from all over the world. There were 70 submissions from 8 countries. The Program Committee (PC) consisted of 52 members from 13 countries. Each PC has been assigned four papers on average and each submission was reviewed by at least three PC members. The committee decided to accept 24 full papers (34.3%) in volume 1 (LNCS) and 22 other papers (31.4%) in volume 2 (CCIS). In addition to the paper presentations, the program of JIST 2019 also featured three tutorials, three keynotes, one special forum on Open Knowledge Graph, and poster presentations.

We are indebted to many people who made this event possible. As the organizers of JIST 2019, we would like to express our sincere thanks to the PC members and additional reviewers for their hard work in reviewing the papers. We would also like to thank the sponsors, support organizations, all the speakers, authors, and participants for their great contributions. Last but not least, we would like to thank Springer for their support in producing these proceedings.

December 2019

Xin Wang
Francesca A. Lisi
Guohui Xiao
Elena Botoeva

Organization

General Chairs

Huajun Chen	Zhejiang University, China
Diego Calvanese	Free University of Bozen-Bolzano, Italy

Program Chairs

Xin Wang	Tianjin University, China
Francesca A. Lisi	Università degli Studi di Bari, Italy

Special Session Track Chairs

Kewen Wang	Griffith University, Australia
HakLae Kim	Jungang University, South Korea

Local Organizing Chairs

Qingpin Zhang	Zhejiang University, China
Wen Zhang	Zhejiang University, China

Industrial Forum Chair

Haofen Wang	Leyan Tech., China

Poster and Demo Chairs

Kang Liu	CASIA, China
Chutiporn Anutariya	Asian Institute of Technology, Thailand

Workshop Chairs

Yuan-Fang Li	Monash University, Australia
Xianpei Han	ISCAS, China

Tutorial Chairs

Xiaowang Zhang	Tianjin University, China
Jiaoyan Chen	Oxford University, UK

Sponsorship Chair

Jinguang Gu   Wuhan Science and Technology University, China

Proceeding Chairs

Guohui Xiao   Free University of Bozen-Bolzano, Italy
Elena Botoeva   Imperial College of London, UK

Publicity Chairs

Meng Wang   Southeast University, China
Naoki Fukuta   Shizuoka University, Japan

Program Committee

Carlos Bobed   everis and NTT Data, Spain
Fernando Bobillo   University of Zaragoza, Spain
Huajun Chen   Zhejiang University, China
Wenliang Chen   Soochow University, China
Gong Cheng   Nanjing University, China
Dejing Dou   University of Oregon, USA
Jianfeng Du   Guangdong University of Foreign Studies, China
Alessandro Faraotti   IBM, Italy
Naoki Fukuta   Academic Institute Shizuoka University, Japan
Jinguang Gu   Wuhan University of Science and Technology, China
Xianpei Han   ISCAS, China
Wei Hu   Nanjing University, China
Ryutaro Ichise   National Institute of Informatics, Japan
Takahiro Kawamura   National Agriculture and Food Research Organization,
                               Japan
Evgeny Kharlamov   Bosch Center for Artificial Intelligence and University
                               of Oslo, Norway
Martin Kollingbaum   University of Aberdeen, UK
Kouji Kozaki   Osaka Electro-Communication University, Japan
Weizhuo Li   Academy of Mathematics and Systems Science, CAS,
                               China
Yuan-Fang Li   Monash University, Australia
Juanzi Li   Tsinghua University, China
Francesca A. Lisi   Università degli Studi di Bari, Italy
Kang Liu   Institute of Automation, CAS, China
Yinglong Ma   NCEPU, China
Theofilos Mailis   National and Kapodistrian University of Athens,
                               Greece
Riichiro Mizoguchi   Japan Advanced Institute of Science and Technology,
                               Japan

Trina Myers	James Cook University, Australia
Jeff Z. Pan	University of Aberdeen, UK
Guilin Qi	Southeast University, China
Guozheng Rao	Tianjin University, China
Edelweis Rohrer	Universidad de la Republica, Uruguay
Tong Ruan	ECUST, China
Floriano Scioscia	Politecnico di Bari, Italy
Wei Shen	Nankai University, China
Jun Shen	University of Wollongong, Australia
Umberto Straccia	ISTI-CNR, Italy
Thepchai Supnithi	NECTEC, Thailand
Hideaki Takeda	National Institute of Informatics, Japan
Kerry Taylor	The Australian National University, Australia, and University of Surrey, UK
Xin Wang	Tianjin University, China
Meng Wang	Southeast University, China
Zhe Wang	Griffith University, Australia
Haofen Wang	Shanghai Leyan Technologies Co., Ltd., China
Shenghui Wang	OCLC Research, USA
Zhichun Wang	Beijing Normal University, China
Tianxing Wu	Nanyang Technological University, Singapore
Gang Wu	Northeastern University, China
Guohui Xiao	Free University of Bozen-Bolzano, Italy
Bin Xu	DCST, Tsinghua University, China
Xiang Zhang	Southeast University, China
Xiaowang Zhang	Tianjin University, China
Amal Zouaq	University of Ottawa, Canada

Additional Reviewers

Tonglee Chung
Shumin Deng
Michel Gagnon
Yuhao He
Zixian Huang
Natthawut Kertkeidkachorn
Bao Zhu Liu
Juan Li
Shutian Ma
Shirong Shen

Yulin Shen
Sylvia Wang
Kemas Wiharja
Kang Xu
Lingling Zhang
Wen Zhang
Leyuan Zhao
Qianru Zhou
Xiaoduo Zhou

Contents

Building a Large-Scale Knowledge Graph for Elementary Education in China

Wei Zheng, Zhichun Wang$^{(\boxtimes)}$, Mingchen Sun, Yanrong Wu, and Kaiman Li

School of Artificial Intelligence, Beijing Normal University,
Beijing 100875, People's Republic of China
zcwang@bnu.edu.cn

Abstract. With the penetration of information technology into all areas of society, Internet-assisted education has become an important opportunity for current educational reform. In order to better assist in teaching and learning, help students deepen their understanding and absorption of knowledge. We build a knowledge graph for elementary education, firstly, we define elementary education ontology, divide the knowledge graph into three sub-graphs. Then extracting concept instance and relation instance form textbook and existing knowledge base based on unsupervised method. In addition, we have acquired four different learning resources to assist in learning. At last, the results show that the procedure we proposed is scientific and efficient.

Keywords: Elementary education · Education ontology · Knowledge discovery

1 Introduction

Elementary education has laid the foundation for the entire educational undertaking. It is also the basic project to promote social progress, cultivate specialized talents, and improve the overall quality of the people. With the advent of the Internet-assisted education era, emerging educational technologies are used in classroom, massive shared educational resources appear on the Internet. For example, online education platforms such as Maker, MOOC, Netease Cloud Classroom[1], resource sharing platform such as Baicizhan[2]. However, due to the lack of a unified knowledge framework between resources, this knowledge cannot be effectively integrated into the process of teaching and learning.

In order to better provide personalized teaching services, researchers began to study how to organize knowledge in teaching resources. Most of the existing research focuses on concept map generation and subject knowledge graph construction. Knowledge in concept map is represented as concept, and knowledge is related through a learning dependency between concepts. However, in

---

[1] https://study.163.com/.
[2] http://www.baicizhan.com/.

© Springer Nature Singapore Pte Ltd. 2020
X. Wang et al. (Eds.): JIST 2019, CCIS 1157, pp. 1–12, 2020.
https://doi.org/10.1007/978-981-15-3412-6_1

actual learning activities, the representation of knowledge is diverse and not just a mere concept memory. Knowledge graph [17] was firstly introduced by Google in 2012 which contain large amount entities and their relations. Recently, knowledge graphs have been successfully applied in various domains. In this paper, we study how to build a large-scale knowledge graph for elementary education in China.

With high-quality education becoming the focus of education, China has developed a series of documents to regulate the implementation process of education. Among them, the Ministry of Education formulates compulsory education curriculum programs and curriculum standards to standardize the implementation of the curriculum. The curriculum standards clarify the educational value of the subject, determine the core literacy and teaching objectives of the subject, clarify the content and academic quality, and have a guiding and normative role in the preparation, teaching and evaluation of teaching materials. The above criteria are also the theoretical basis for the construction of Elementary knowledge graph.

This paper investigates the construction mode of knowledge graph in education field, and combines the status of elementary education in China, proposes a construction method and concrete construction steps of elementary education knowledge graph. The main work includes:

– The ontology of the elementary education knowledge graph is defined and divided into three layers, the three layers are linked together by a knowledge link to form a complete graph.
– Using the textbook catalog structure features, Wikipedia and other external data, based on unsupervised learning to extract knowledge objects, prerequisite relation, ISA relation, reduce the manual intervention in the construction process, to ensure the professionalism of the graph.
– The knowledge retrieval and knowledge analysis system is used to explore the application forms of the graph in the field of education.

2   Related Work

At present, the construction of knowledge graph in the field of education is mainly divided into two ways, based on ontology construction and automated construction based on knowledge extraction. The work in [5] creates a domain ontology to represent higher education concepts and assist specialized e-learning systems. The work in [7] develops a learning ontology model which integrates different kinds of learning entities like curriculum, syllabus, learning subjects, and learning materials based on a layered structure. Hu et al. [10] construct an ontology-based knowledge base for Chinese K12 education with high accuracy and efficiency. Zheng et al. [21] construct a high educational knowledge graph (HEKG) based on MOOCs.

With the development of automatic extraction technology, some researchers try to construct knowledge graph in an automated way. Liang et al. [11] model a concept in a vector space using its related concepts and measure the prerequisite relation between two concepts by computing how differently the two's related concepts refer to each other. Wang et al. [18] use textbooks to extract concept maps with explicit prerequisite relationships among the concepts. Duan et al. [9] combine priori knowledge from concept map with extended textual fragments collected from web sources to construct an expanded knowledge base named DKG, in order to expand the learning materials on MOOC platforms. Chen et al. [6] adopt the neural sequence labeling algorithm [8] on pedagogical data to extract instructional concepts and employs probabilistic association rule mining [1] on learning assessment data to identify the relations with educational significance.

3   Elementary Education Ontology

In 1956, Bloom [2] proposed a set of Bloom's educational goal classification theory. The framework in Bloom's theory is recognized and practiced in teaching work around the world. Knowing and understanding at the bottom of the framework which requires learners to memorize important nouns, concepts, and knowledge points, and to understand their meanings and relationships. The application, analysis, synthesis and evaluation on the upper level which require knowledge elements combine with specific application scenarios. Based on the above theory, this paper constructs the elementary education ontology to ensure the scientific of knowledge transmission and improve the efficiency of learning.

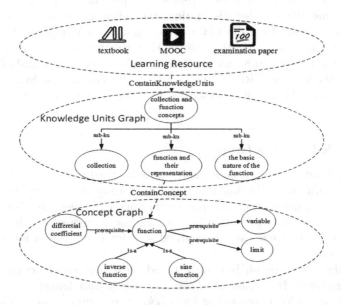

Fig. 1. Framework

As shown in Fig. 1, our entire knowledge graph is divided into three parts: leaning resources, knowledge units graph and concept graph. Learning resources are all resources that can be used for learning. In the teaching process, the curriculum knowledge is decomposed and classified, and finally decomposed into a series of knowledge units. Concept graph contains a series of basic subject concept. Through the analysis of learning resources, they can be associated and combined with knowledge units, then knowledge units linking with concepts, greatly improving the applicability of learning resources. In this section, we will introduce how the three parts are constructed in detail.

3.1 Concept Graph

In the concept graph, a node represents a subject concept. The core concepts are extracted from textbook outline, other concepts are from Wikipedia, covers various domains such as geographic information, people, companies, films, music, etc. Edge represent relation between concepts, the relations mainly includes prerequisite relation, ISA relation and other relations. Prerequisite exists as a natural dependency among concepts in cognitive process when people learn, organize and generate knowledge. A prerequisite is usually a concept or requirement before one can proceed to a following one. For example, in learning the concept of "function", we must first learn the meaning of "variable". ISA-relation is a basic semantic relation between concepts. For example, given two concepts, X and Y, there is the ISA relation between X and Y if the sentence "x is (a kind of) y" is acceptable. For example, "once function" is a kind of "function". Other relations we collectively call related relations, represent concept's related properties, including the founder, the nation, the religion, the region, and so on. Related relation from DBpedia's [3] infobox, infobox in Wikipedia describes all properties of entity, categorization information classifies an entity in a category, DBpedia extract this feature information, mapping them and translate to RDF statements. We get these RDF links as a part of relationships. Specific knowledge discovery methods will be described in detail in the Knowledge Discovery section.

3.2 Knowledge Units Graph

In knowledge units graph, a node represent a knowledge unit. Knowledge unit is the basic unit for delivering teaching information in the teaching process, including theory, principles, concepts, definitions, examples, etc. For example, a chapter in a course, a definition in a section, or a theorem can be used as a knowledge unit. A course can be regarded as a learning process for a series of knowledge units.

Knowledge Units graph is mainly based on expert construction and curriculum standards. It consist of a series of compound knowledge units and meta knowledge units, expressed as $ku = \{ck_1, ..., ck_n, mk_1, ...mk_n\}$. Compound knowledge units are composed of compound knowledge units and meta knowledge units. Meta knowledge units cannot be decomposed continuously, are basic

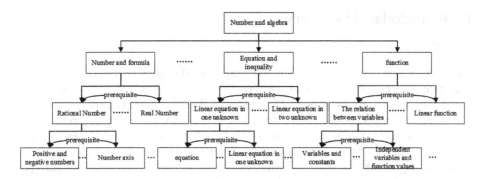

Fig. 2. Examples of knowledge units graph structure.

knowledge unit. Take Junior Middle School Mathematics as an example showed in Fig. 2, top level knowledge unit named "(number and algebra)", then the underlying knowledge units will be developed around this topic. Low level knowledge units are more detailed, and their prerequisite knowledge units are marked by experts. They also have links to specific concepts through knowledge unit content. For example, knowledge unit "number axis's" content is "The number axis is a straight line specifying the origin, direction, and unit length, where the origin, direction, and unit degree become the three elements of postoperative". Based on the content, this knowledge unit can be linked to the concept "origin" "direction", "unit degree" and "axis".

3.3   Learning Resources

According to the way of learning, we mainly have three kinds of learning resources: textbooks, MOOCs, examination papers. They provide different ways to learn knowledge, combining them to transfer knowledge is more effective to the mastery of knowledge.

Textbooks. In Chinese Elementary Education, textbook is a teaching book written according to the requirements of the curriculum standards. It is the main material for students to gain systematic knowledge and study in school, and reasonably reflect the logical order of each subject and the psychological order of students' learning.

MOOCs. Since the appearance of Massive Open Online Courses [14], a large number of courses has been generated. MOOCs are considered as important learning resources in our knowledge graph.

Examination Papers. Examinations are important in the teaching process. Through the analysis and study of examination papers, they can provide important feedbacks of the students.

4   Knowledge Discovery

4.1   Concept Linking

Some researchers have tested the coverage of Wikipedia-related [13,15,16]. Although the results show that Wikipedia does not include latest scientific knowledge in time, it also proves [13,16] that Wikipedia's coverage of elementary education is comprehensive. Therefore, if a Wikipedia title is closely related to a mention in the catalog, then the mention may be a core concept in the article. In the work of [4], documents are annotated with relevant Wikipedia concepts based on page-rank method. The method firstly constructs a mention-concept graph to implement global disambiguation, if there exists in the Wikipedia a hyperlink with the anchor text an and the target c, then exist an edge from a to c. Every node has a PR score, and each vertex distributes its page-rank score to its immediate successors in the graph. Thus after a few iterations, page-rank should tend to accumulate in a set of concepts that are closely semantically related to each other and that are strongly associated with words and phrases that appear in the input document. In addition, PM is the probability that, when a link appears in the Wikipedia with this particular subrange as its anchor text, it points to the Wikipedia page corresponding to the current annotation. At last, Score(c|m) combined local similarity calculation, representing the score of the mention m link to Wikipedia concept c. Take the above three indicators and extract the references that meet the above conditions as the core knowledge in the discipline. For the above three indicators, we set the appropriate thresholds through experiments. Finally extracting the mentions that meet the above conditions as the core concept in elementary education.

4.2   Pre-relation Discovering

A prerequisite dependency requires that learning one concept is necessary before learning the next. For instance, we need to have basic knowledge of "variable" in order to learn "function". Figure 3 show a more detailed example.

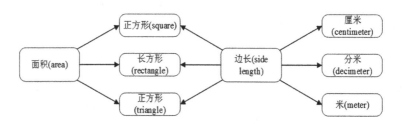

Fig. 3. An example of a prerequisite relation.

As the basis of experiment, we prepare the data set of Wikipedia page-link which includes 21.87 million data. It holds the Wikipedia entry links that exist in every article. Then we define the Wikipedia-based reference distance [11] as

$$RefD(A, B) = \frac{\sum_{i=1}^{k} r(e_i, B) \cdot w(e_i, A)}{\sum_{i=1}^{k} w(e_i, A)} - \frac{\sum_{i=1}^{k} r(e_i, A) \cdot w(e_i, B)}{\sum_{i=1}^{k} w(e_i, B)}$$

where $E = \{e_1, e_2 \cdots e_k\}$ is the entity space, $w(e_i, A)$ weights the importance of e_i to A, $r(e_i, A)$ is an indicator showing whether e_i refers to A, which are links in Wikipedia.

Specifically, the entity space E consists of all Wikipedia articles of entitles. $r(e_i, A)$ represents whether there is a link from Wiki entity E to A. For $w(e_i, A)$, we defined it as :

$$w(e_i, A) = \begin{cases} tf(e, A) * log\frac{N}{df(e)} & if \ e \in L(A) \\ 0 & if \ c \notin L(A) \end{cases}$$

As a result, RefD is expected to satisfy the following constraints:

$$RefD(A, B) \in \begin{cases} (\theta, 1] & B \ is \ probable \ a \ prerequisite \ of \ A \\ [-\theta, \theta] & no \ prerequisite \ relation \\ [-1, -\theta) & A \ is \ probable \ a \ prerequisite \ of \ B \end{cases}$$

Only the result of RefD is not enough to explain the prerequisite relationship in our data. Because of the order of catalog in textbook, we can use these orders to make our discovering more accurately. In our experiment, we added catalog distance (CatD) to verify prerequisite relationship. CatD is defined as

$$CatD(A, B) = \frac{lecID(A) - lecID(B)}{len(Cat)}$$

Where lecID(A) is the id number of current entity A, and len(Cat) is the length of the book catalog. We combine these two distances as following:

$$\begin{cases} RefD(A, B) \cdot CatD(A, B) > 0 & B \ is \ a \ prerequisite \ of \ A \\ RefD(A, B) \cdot CatD(A, B) < 0 & A \ is \ a \ prerequisite \ of \ B \end{cases}$$

Using this method, we predict prerequisite relation between concepts in textbook.

4.3   ISA Relation Discovering

Two methods are used to extract ISA relation in this section. First, we build some ISA patterns that can match Chinese Wikipedia data to acquire a group of relation instances and utilize category information to improve the accuracy of results. Second method according to cross-lingual links in Wikipedia, we translate ISA data with high frequency of Probase into Chinese.

Pattern Matching in Wikipedia. Every article in Wikipedia has a kernel subject, to explain and classify. We regard the subject as entity 1, and the noun, which can explain the subject as entity 2. Usually entity 2 appears in the first sentence of abstract, and in this paper, we restrict it to have entity linking. Taking "(equilateral triangle)" as an example, "(equilateral triangle)" is entity 1, " (triangle)" is entity 2 corresponding. They comprise Hypernym-Hyponym relation, demonstrate that "(An equilateral triangle is a triangle)" as we all know. We also call it ISA relation.

In term of their properties, subjects will be classified in category of Wikipedia. Hierarchical category generally contains its super-categories, sub-categories with high quality. As "(equilateral triangle)" belongs to "(polygon)", while it also the subclass of "(triangle)". Hence, we filter the entity 2 by guaranteeing the extracted entity 2 must be contained in category of its article, in order to improve accuracy.

In summary, we achieve ISA relation discovering as follow: (1) Acquire Wikipedia articles and label their abstract, distinguish nouns in the describing sentence have entity linking or not. (2) Determine ISA patterns. Moreover, use regular expression for transforming these patterns. (3) Extract relation instances matching patterns. (4) Check the extracted entity 2 whether belongs to category or not.

Relation Mapping in Probase. We propose an approach that acquire abundant ISA relations from Probase, by using cross-lingual links in Wikipedia. Microsoft built Probase in 2010, in order to make machines understand human being's communication better. Now it already has exceeding five millions unique concepts, twelve millions instances and eighty-five millions ISA relations [19,20]. These relations actually demonstrate the frequency of each ISA relation appears in billions of web pages, which were mined by Microsoft to learn general knowledge in real world. It is inevitable that these relations exist mistakes. Therefore, we quote the conclusion in [12], that a larger frequency implies higher trustworthiness, when the frequency of one ISA relation over 100, the accuracy is 100%. Based on it, we set 100 as a threshold, delete the relations has weak trustworthiness (Fig. 4).

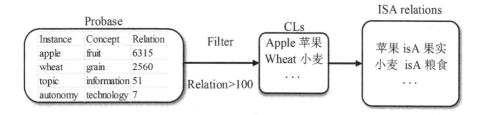

Fig. 4. Relation mapping in Probase.

Cross-lingual links contain articles explaining the same subjects in different languages. Therefore, we can derive a Chinese-English comparison chart from CLs, and then exploit it to finish ISA relations mapping in Probase.

5   Results

This section presents the results of our work.

5.1   Statistics

Table 1 shows the statistics of the built knowledge graph.

Table 1. Statistics of the built knowledge graph

Types	# resources
MOOC	3,367
Textbook	824
Examination	7
Concept	9,059
Prerequisite relation	7,882
ISA relation	9,474

5.2   Evaluation

Since the extraction of ISA relations are based on high-quality external knowledge bases - Wikipedia and Probase, the accuracy is close to 100%. Table 2 shows the evaluation results of the concept linking and discovered prerequisite relations. We marked 100 catalogs and 100 prerequisite pairs from mathematics and physics subjects for manual evaluation.

Table 2. Evaluation of concept linking and prerequisite relations

Discipline	Concept linking		Prerequisite relation	
	Precision	Recall	Precision	recall
Mathematics	89.4%	75.3%	71.2%	77.8%
Physics	91.3%	73.2%	73.4%	76.5%

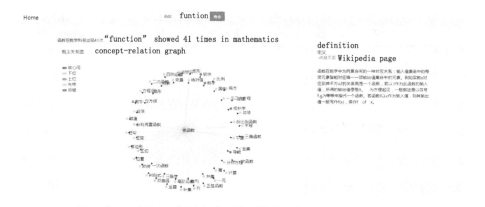

Fig. 5. The definition and relation graph of concept "function". (Color figure online)

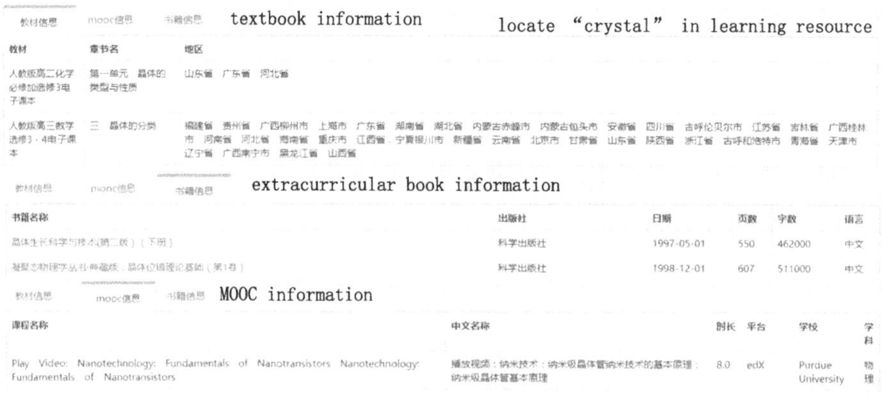

Fig. 6. Learning resources about concept "crystal".

5.3 System

In this section, we explore the application of knowledge graph in the field of elementary education based on a web application.

Knowledge retrieval is a basic function of knowledge graph, Fig. 5 shows the definition and relation about a concept "function". Its definition comes from first paragraph in Wikipedia, then visualizing the conceptual relationship in the form of force-directed graph which layout algorithm provided by JavaScript library D3. There are five detailed types of relationships for a concept, it's hypernym, hyponym, prerequisite concepts, subsequent concepts and related concepts, nodes in different relation type would be rendered in different color. Figure 6 shows the retrieved learning resources about a certain concept.

6   Conclusion

In this paper, we present our work on building a knowledge graph for Chinese Elementary Education. We first define an ontology for the knowledge graph of elementary education, and then propose methods to extract the instance-level data from various data sources. At last, we present a web application built on the knowledge graph.

Acknowledgment. The work is supported by the National Key R&D Program of China (No. 2017YFB1402105).

References

1. Agrawal, R., Srikant, R., et al.: Fast algorithms for mining association rules. In: Proceedings of the 20th International Conference on Very Large Data Bases, VLDB, vol. 1215, pp. 487–499 (1994)
2. Anderson, L.W., Sosniak, L.A.: Bloom's Taxonomy. University of Chicago Press, Chicago (1994)
3. Auer, S., Bizer, C., Kobilarov, G., Lehmann, J., Cyganiak, R., Ives, Z.: DBpedia: a nucleus for a web of open data. In: Aberer, K., et al. (eds.) ASWC/ISWC -2007. LNCS, vol. 4825, pp. 722–735. Springer, Heidelberg (2007). https://doi.org/10. 1007/978-3-540-76298-0_52
4. Brank, J., Leban, G., Grobelnik, M.: Annotating documents with relevant Wikipedia concepts. In: Proceedings of SiKDD (2017)
5. Bucos, M., Dragulescu, B., Veltan, M.: Designing a semantic web ontology for e-learning in higher education. In: International Symposium on Electronics and Telecommunications (2011)
6. Chen, P., Lu, Y., Zheng, V.W., Chen, X., Yang, B.: Knowedu: a system to construct knowledge graph for education. IEEE Access **6**, 31553–31563 (2018)
7. Chung, H., Kim, J.: An ontological approach for semantic modeling of curriculum and syllabus in higher education. Int. J. Inf. Educ. Technol. **6**(5), 365 (2016)
8. Chung, J., Gulcehre, C., Cho, K., Bengio, Y.: Empirical evaluation of gated recurrent neural networks on sequence modeling. arXiv preprint arXiv:1412.3555 (2014)
9. Duan, H., Zheng, Y., Shi, L., Jin, C., Zeng, H., Liu, J.: DKG: an expanded knowledge base for online course. In: Bao, Z., Trajcevski, G., Chang, L., Hua, W. (eds.) DASFAA 2017. LNCS, vol. 10179, pp. 376–386. Springer, Cham (2017). https:// doi.org/10.1007/978-3-319-55705-2_30
10. Hu, J., Li, Z., Xu, B.: An approach of ontology based knowledge base construction for Chinese k12 education. In: 2016 First International Conference on Multimedia and Image Processing (ICMIP), pp. 83–88. IEEE (2016)
11. Liang, C., Wu, Z., Huang, W., Giles, C.L.: Measuring prerequisite relations among concepts. In: Proceedings of the 2015 Conference on Empirical Methods in Natural Language Processing, pp. 1668–1674 (2015)
12. Liang, J., Xiao, Y., Zhang, Y., Hwang, S.W., Wang, H.: Graph-based wrong ISA relation detection in a large-scale lexical taxonomy. In: Thirty-First AAAI Conference on Artificial Intelligence (2017)
13. Okoli, C., Mehdi, M., Mesgari, M., Nielsen, F.Å., Lanamäki, A.: Wikipedia in the eyes of its beholders: a systematic review of scholarly research on Wikipedia readers and readership. J. Assoc. Inf. Sci. Technol. **65**(12), 2381–2403 (2014)

14. Pappano, L.: The year of the MOOC. New York Times **2**(12), 2012 (2012)
15. Rush, E.K., Tracy, S.J.: Wikipedia as public scholarship: communicating our impact online. J. Appl. Commun. Res. **38**(3), 309–315 (2010)
16. Schweitzer, N.J.: Wikipedia and psychology: coverage of concepts and its use by undergraduate students. Teach. Psychol. **35**(2), 81–85 (2008)
17. Singhal, A.: Introducing the knowledge graph: things, not strings. Off. Google Blog **5** (2012)
18. Wang, S., et al.: Using prerequisites to extract concept maps from textbooks. In: Proceedings of the 25th ACM International on Conference on Information and Knowledge Management, pp. 317–326. ACM (2016)
19. Wang, Z., Wang, H., Wen, J.R., Xiao, Y.: An inference approach to basic level of categorization. In: Proceedings of the 24th ACM International on Conference on Information and Knowledge Management, pp. 653–662. ACM (2015)
20. Wu, W., Li, H., Wang, H., Zhu, K.Q.: Probase: a probabilistic taxonomy for text understanding. In: Proceedings of the 2012 ACM SIGMOD International Conference on Management of Data, pp. 481–492. ACM (2012)
21. Zheng, Y., Liu, R., Hou, J.: The construction of high educational knowledge graph based on MOOC. In: 2017 IEEE 2nd Information Technology, Networking, Electronic and Automation Control Conference (ITNEC), pp. 260–263. IEEE (2017)

A Temporal Semantic Search System for Traditional Chinese Medicine Based on Temporal Knowledge Graphs

Chengbiao Yang[1,2], Weizhuo Li[1], Xiaoping Zhang[3(✉)], Runshun Zhang[4], and Guilin Qi[1]

[1] School of Computer Science and Engineering, Southeast University, Nanjing, China
ycb@kgtdata.com, liweizhuo@amss.ac.cn, gqi@seu.edu.cn
[2] Nanjing KG Data Technology Co., Ltd., Nanjing, China
[3] China Academy of Chinese Medical Sciences, Beijing, China
xiao_ping_zhang@139.com
[4] Guang'anmen Hospital,
China Academy of Chinese Medical Sciences, Beijing, China
runshunzhang@139.com

Abstract. Traditional Chinese medicine (TCM) is an important intangible cultural heritage of China. To enhance the services of TCM, many works focus on constructing various types of TCM knowledge graphs according to the concrete requirements such as information retrieval. However, most of them ignored several key issues. One is temporal information that is very important for TCM clinical diagnosis and treatment. For example, a herb needs to be boiled for different periods in different prescriptions, but existing methods cannot represent this temporal information very well. The other is that current TCM-based retrieval systems cannot effectively deal with the temporal intentions of search sentences, which leads to bad experiences for users in retrieval services. To solve these issues, we propose a new model tailored for TCM based on the temporal knowledge graph in this paper, which can effectively represent the clinical knowledge changing dynamically over time. Moreover, we implement a temporal semantic search system and employ reasoning rules based on our proposed model to complete the temporal intentions of search sentences. The preliminary result indicates that our system can obtain better results than existing methods in terms of precision.

Keywords: Traditional Chinese medicine · Temporal knowledge graph · Temporal semantic search · Temporal intention

1 Introduction

Faced with a huge number of TCM data, it is an urgent requirement that utilizes these data to provide effective services such as information retrieval.

This work was partially supported by the National Key R&D Program of China under grant (2017YFB1002302), the NSFC grant (U1736204), the Fundamental Research Funds for the Central public welfare research institutes (ZZ11-064).

X. Wang et al. (Eds.): JIST 2019, CCIS 1157, pp. 13–20, 2020.
https://doi.org/10.1007/978-981-15-3412-6_2

The early approaches stored the TCM data into the relational database and employed data mining and text mining methods to provide the services [2,3]. However, many TCM resources are scattered and disconnected so that low utilization of resources limits the ability of the above approaches and bring users bad experiments of the services. Knowledge graph as a graph-based form of knowledge representation obtains increasingly attention in the medical domain. Intuitively, a knowledge graph is a directed labeled graph composed of entities (nodes) and various relations (different semantic labels of edges) [1]. Benefited from their structured features and interpretability, knowledge graphs have been widely used in various knowledge-intensive industries.

Over the past decades, the studies of TCM knowledge graphs have received more attention. Gu [4] manually built a TCM knowledge model with the capability of rule reasoning using OWL 2. Yu et al. [5] integrated different data resources to form a knowledge graph with a semantic network as the skeleton. Cheng et al. Weng et al. [6] proposed a framework for automated medical knowledge graph construction based on semantic analysis. Wang et al. [7] proposed a knowledge graph enhanced topic modeling approach for herb recommendation.

However, most of them ignored several key issues when they built knowledge graphs for TCM. On one hand, temporal information is very important for TCM clinical diagnosis and treatment. For example, a herb needs to be boiled for different periods in different prescriptions, but existing methods cannot represent this temporal information very well. One the other hand, current TCM-based retrieval systems cannot effectively deal with the temporal intention of the search sentences, which leads to bad experiences for users in retrieval services.

To solve these issues, we propose a new model tailored for TCM based on the temporal knowledge graph in this paper. It can effectively represent the clinical knowledge changing dynamically over time. Moreover, we implement a temporal semantic search system and employ reasoning rules based on our proposed model to complete the temporal intentions of the search sentences. Compared with some existing retrieval methods, the preliminary result indicates that our system can obtain better results in terms of precision.

2   TCM Temporal Knowledge Graph

2.1   Temporal Knowledge Graph

The general theme of temporal knowledge is an old AI topic. *Temporal RDF* [9] introduces a temporal semantics for RDF, where time is modeled as a label on RDF triples, giving each triple a validity time. *Annotated RDF* [10] extends RDF triples into quadruples, and the fourth component is used for several kinds of meta-facts. *EventKG* [13,14] proposes a multilingual event-centric temporal knowledge graph based on the Simple Event Model (SEM) [11]. *PatientEG* [8] proposes a patient event graph representation to model medical activities and temporal information, and its data model is also extended from the SEM. However, the event model is too complicated to describe simple knowledge, which leads to very high query complexity. We are mainly inspired by *Temporal RDF* and *Annotated RDF*, and we believe that extending the RDF model is a more concise and versatile solution for representing the temporal knowledge of TCM.

In the RDF model, resources include *entity* (**E**), *class* (**C**), *property* (**P**), *relation* (**R**) and *literal* (**L**). We can define the triple $(\mathbf{s}, \mathbf{p}, \mathbf{o})$ as bellow:

$$(\mathbf{s}, \mathbf{p}, \mathbf{o}) = (\mathbf{E} \cup \mathbf{C}) \times (\mathbf{P} \cup \mathbf{R}) \times (\mathbf{E} \cup \mathbf{C} \cup \mathbf{L}) \tag{1}$$

Generally, the knowledge graph **G** is a set of triples, denoted as $\{(\mathbf{s}, \mathbf{p}, \mathbf{o})\}$. For TCM, we add a temporal dimension **t** to the triple, then the form of triple becomes $(\mathbf{s}, \mathbf{p}, \mathbf{o})$: **t**. **t** is a temporal label, and **T** is a set of temporal labels, which consists of a set of temporal properties $\mathbf{P_t}$ and a set of temporal literals $\mathbf{L_t}$, that is $\mathbf{T} = \mathbf{P_t} \times \mathbf{L_t}$. $\mathbf{P_t}$ is a set of special property defined in Table 1. $\mathbf{L_t}$ consists of a numerical value and a unit. We define $(\mathbf{s}, \mathbf{p}, \mathbf{o})$: **t** as bellow:

$$(\mathbf{s}, \mathbf{p}, \mathbf{o}) : \mathbf{t} = (\mathbf{E} \cup \mathbf{C}) \times (\mathbf{P} \cup \mathbf{R}) \times (\mathbf{E} \cup \mathbf{C} \cup \mathbf{L}) \times (\mathbf{T}) \tag{2}$$

The temporal knowledge graph $\mathbf{G_t}$ is a set of $\{(\mathbf{s}, \mathbf{p}, \mathbf{o})\}$ and $\{(\mathbf{s}, \mathbf{p}, \mathbf{o}) : \mathbf{t}\}$.

Table 1. The definition of $\mathbf{P_t}$.

P_t	Explanation
start-time	A fact starts at a certain time
end-time	A fact ends at a certain time
duration	The duration of a fact
time	Refers to all other ambiguous time types

Example 1. *Clinicians often describe the dynamic changes of symptoms in the medical records, such as "A headache occurred on August 1 and disappeared after taking Pulsatillae Radix (a kind of herb) for a week". In this case, we need to use* $(\mathbf{s}, \mathbf{p}, \mathbf{o})$: **t** *to describe this dynamic information as bellow:*

(mr, hasPatient, p)
(p, hasSymptom, headache):{[start-time, 2019-8-1#Date], [duration, 1#Week]}
(p, takingHerb, PulsatillaeRadix):{[duration, 1#Week]}
(PulsatillaeRadix, cure, headache)

We assume that the medical record **mr** *above belongs to the entity* **p**, *which is a patient. Based on the above symptom description, we get the temporal facts about* **hasSymptom** *and* **takingHerb** *as mentioned above.*

2.2 Reasoning of Temporal Facts

The raw data of the TCM temporal knowledge graph comes from the Classic Chinese Medicine Clinical Case Library. There are 7 types of entities including

Medical Record, Disease, Symptom, Prescription, Herb, Patient, and Doctor. As the clinical information is stored in a relational database, so most of them can be converted into the knowledge graph by *D2R* techniques [12]. After the base knowledge graph is constructed, we need to extract the temporal information for the facts. Fortunately, temporal information described in the electronic medical records is standardized so that it is not difficult to extract. We define several regular expressions manually to extract temporal information from the medical records. Based on these techniques, we construct a TCM temporal knowledge graph, containing **106, 139** entities, **603, 615** properties, **426, 744** relations, and **71, 656** temporal facts.

Table 2. The definition of temporal reasoning rules.

Rules	Conditions	Conclusions
Rule 1	{[start-time, o_1], [duration, o_2]}	{[start-time, o_1], [end-time, $o_1 + o_2$], [duration, o_2]}
Rule 2	{[end-time, o_1], [duration, o_2]}	{[start-time, $o_1 - o_2$], [end-time, o_1], [duration, o_2]}
Rule 3	{[start-time, o_1], [end-time, o_2]}	{[start-time, o_1], [end-time, o_2], [duration, $o_2 - o_1$]}

In addition, we try to get more temporal facts through reasoning. Since time is computable, we define three temporal reasoning rules based on the logical relationships among *start-time, end-time* and *duration*. The definition of the rules is shown in Table 2. *Rule 1* indicates that the start time o_1 and the duration o_2 of a fact can be used to calculate the end time according to the formula $o_1 + o_2$. *Rule 2* and *Rule 3* are similar. They state that *start-time* or *duration* can also be calculated by the other two.

Example 2 (Cont. of Example 1). *Given the original facts listed as bellow:*

(p, hasSymptom, headache):{[start-time, 2019-8-1#Date], [duration, 1#Week]}

we can get new fact with Rule 1 as bellow:

(p, hasSymptom, headache):{[start-time, 2019-8-1#Date], [duration, 1#Week],
[end-time, 2019-8-7#Date]}

With the help of above three rules, we have inferred **30, 103** new temporal facts from original ones in the TCM knowledge graph.

2.3   Storage of Temporal Knowledge Graph

We employ Neo4j to store temporal knowledge graph, which is an open-source and high-performance graph database supported by Neo Technology. Since Neo4j utilizes the property graph model, so we define a set of rules as shown in Table 3 about converting temporal knowledge graph into property graph.

Figure 1 shows a concrete example of the transition between temporal knowledge graph and property graph. According to mapping rules of Table 3.

Table 3. The mapping rules between temporal knowledge graph and property graph.

Temporal knowledge graph	Property graph
Entity	Node
Class	Type of node
Property	Property of node
Relation	Relationship
Temporal label of fact	Property of relationship

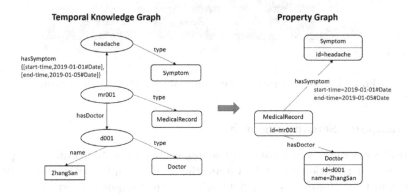

Fig. 1. An detail example of the transition.

3   Temporal Semantic Search System

3.1   System Overview

The TCM temporal knowledge graph extracted from the Classic Chinese Medicine Clinical Case Library records a lot of expert experience. Therefore, we construct a temporal semantic search system based on this knowledge graph that allows young clinicians to quickly retrieve treatment options. The system is divided into the online part and the offline part as shown in Fig. 2. The offline part is mainly about the construction, storage, and indexing of the knowledge graph, and the online part is mainly about the understanding, conversion, and execution of the search sentence. In this section, we mainly introduce the online part.

After the system receives a search sentence, it first identifies the *entities*, *properties*, and *relations* in the sentence by semantic analysis, and then matches the sentence based on the templates or other techniques. If the matching is successful, the values of the slots can be extracted from the search sentence. Then, the system combines our defined rules to generate the query statement of the knowledge graph. On the contrary, if there exists no match, the entities that are most relevant to the search sentence will be returned.

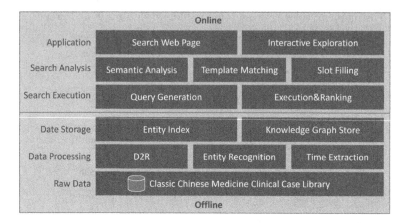

Fig. 2. The architecture of the temporal semantic search system.

3.2 Temporal Semantic Search

Temporal semantic search means that search sentences should contain temporal intentions. For traditional search system, the temporal information can only be retrieved as text. However, in the field of TCM, the temporal information of the search sentence contains complex diagnostic logic, which cannot be retrieved as text. For example, the intention of one sentence "*headache recurred within a month*" is to find a case similar to the symptom "*headache recurred within a month*". Due to the recurrence of diseases, patients need to seek medical treatment multiple times, which will result in multiple medical records. In addition, it is difficult to record a complete symptom change process in one medical record due to the doctor's replacement or the patient's unclear description. Therefore, it is necessary to combine multiple medical records to match the search intention, and the traditional search methods may not obtain an accurate answer because it can only match a single record.

As we store the knowledge graph in the graph database, we need to convert the search sentence into a graph-matching query, which can be represented by a property graph containing variables. Based on the temporal knowledge graph, we construct a series of search templates to convert the temporal intentions into knowledge graph queries.

Example 3. *We convert the search sentence "headache recurred within a month" to a graph-matching query, which can be represented by a property graph as shown in Fig. 3. The symbols $?x, ?y, ?z, ?t_1, ?t_2$ represent the variables in the query. The medical records $?y$ and $?z$ in the query describe the different conditions of the symptom through relationships* **symptom-better** *and* **symptom-worsened**. *In order to match the time requirement "within a month", we can add a* **Filter** *operation $(?t_2 - ?t_1 \leq 1\#\textbf{Month})$ to the query.*

Table 4. Experiment results of the three methods.

Method	Top-1 precision			Top-5 precision		
	TQ	NTQ	AVG	TQ	NTQ	AVG
tf-idf	0.12	0.81	0.465	0.23	0.86	0.545
tf-idf + entity linking	0.15	0.87	0.51	0.29	0.88	0.585
Our method	**0.76**	**0.89**	**0.825**	**0.79**	**0.92**	**0.855**

3.3   Experiments and Results

To verify our model, we crawled lots of hot questions from the TCM forum website, and then randomly selected 100 temporal-independent questions (NTQ) and 100 temporal-related questions (TQ), and finally used these 200 questions as a test set. We implemented two classic semantic search algorithms. One is uses tf-idf for text retrieval, and the other combines tf-idf with entity linking for comprehensive sorting. The top-1 and top-5 precision of the search results were manually evaluated. We invited five TCM doctors to independently evaluate the search results and then calculated the average of the precision. Since we were unable to know all the relevant results, we did not evaluate the recall.

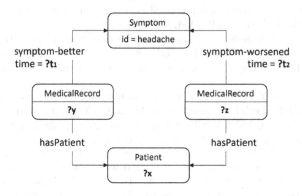

Fig. 3. The property graph for the search sentence "*headache up and down in a month*".

The preliminary results are listed in Table 4. Overall, our system can obtain the best results than other methods, and its average precision of top-1 and top-5 has reached **0.825** and **0.855**. Relatively, other methods are poor to temporal-related questions because they ignore temporal intentions in search sentences. Benefited from our defined temporal knowledge graph and reasoning rules, our system can provide a better experience of the search service.

4   Conclusion and Future Work

In this paper, we proposed a new model tailored for TCM based on temporal knowledge graph and implemented a temporal semantic search system based on it, in which reasoning rules were defined to complete the temporal intention of search sentences. The preliminary result indicated that our system could obtain better results than existing methods in terms of precision.

In the future, we try to extract temporal information from other medical text so as to complete more clinical knowledge for TCM knowledge graph, and optimize our system to reduce the burdens further.

References

1. Wang, Q., Mao, Z., Wang, B., Guo, L.: Knowledge graph embedding: a survey of approaches and applications. IEEE Trans. Knowl. Data Eng. **29**(12), 2724–2743 (2017)
2. Feng, Y., Wu, Z., Zhou, X., Zhou, Z., Fan, W.: Knowledge discovery in traditional Chinese medicine: state of the art and perspectives. Artif. Intell. Med. **38**(3), 219–236 (2006)
3. Zhou, X., Peng, Y., Liu, B.: Text mining for traditional Chinese medical knowledge discovery: a survey. J. Biomed. Inform. **43**(4), 650–660 (2010)
4. Gu, P.: Causal knowledge modeling for traditional Chinese medicine using OWL 2. In: Proceedings of the 9th International Semantic Web Conference, ISWC (2016)
5. Yu, T., et al.: Knowledge graph for TCM health preservation: design, construction, and applications. Artif. Intell. Med. **77**, 48–52 (2017)
6. Weng, H., et al.: A framework for automated knowledge graph construction towards traditional Chinese medicine. In: Siuly, S., et al. (eds.) HIS 2017. LNCS, vol. 10594, pp. 170–181. Springer, Cham (2017). https://doi.org/10.1007/978-3-319-69182-4_18
7. Wang, X., Zhang, Y., Wang, X., Chen, J.: A knowledge graph enhanced topic modeling approach for herb recommendation. In: Li, G., Yang, J., Gama, J., Natwichai, J., Tong, Y. (eds.) DASFAA 2019. LNCS, vol. 11446, pp. 709–724. Springer, Cham (2019). https://doi.org/10.1007/978-3-030-18576-3_42
8. Liu, X., et al.: PatientEG dataset: bringing event graph model with temporal relations to electronic medical records. CoRR arXiv:1812.09905 (2018)
9. Gutierrez, C., Hurtado, C., Vaisman, A.: Temporal RDF. In: Gómez-Pérez, A., Euzenat, J. (eds.) ESWC 2005. LNCS, vol. 3532, pp. 93–107. Springer, Heidelberg (2005). https://doi.org/10.1007/11431053_7
10. Udrea, O., Recupero, D.R., Subrahmanian, V.S.: Annotated RDF. ACM Trans. Comput. Logic (TOCL) **11**(2), 10 (2010)
11. Van Hage, W.R., Malaisé, V., Segers, R., Hollink, L., Schreiber, G.: Design and use of the Simple Event Model (SEM). Web Semant. Sci. Serv. Agents World Wide Web **9**(2), 128–136 (2011)
12. Michel, F., Montagnat, J., Zucker, C.F.: A survey of RDB to RDF translation approaches and tools. Research report, ISRN I3S/RR 2013-04-FR (2014)
13. Gottschalk, S., Demidova, E.: EventKG: a multilingual event-centric temporal knowledge graph. In: Gangemi, A., et al. (eds.) ESWC 2018. LNCS, vol. 10843, pp. 272–287. Springer, Cham (2018). https://doi.org/10.1007/978-3-319-93417-4_18
14. Gottschalk, S., Demidova, E.: EventKG-the hub of event knowledge on the web-and biographical timeline generation. Semant. Web **10**, 1–32 (2019)

Testing of Various Approaches for Semiautomatic Parish Records Word Standardization

Jaroslav Rozman$^{(\boxtimes)}$ (iD), David Hříbek, and František Zbořil

Brno University of Technology, Brno, Czech Republic
{rozmanj,zborilf}@fit.vutbr.cz, xhribe02@stud.fit.vutbr.cz

Abstract. This paper deals with the clustering of words from parish records. Clustering is essential for downstream standardization. In the past, mostly in the 17th and beginning of 18th century, the names did not have a standard form, thus for further work, it is essential to create clusters of words that have the same meaning. Besides names, the parish records are in the various languages - Czech, German, Latin, so if we want to have relations between people, occupations, or causes of death in one language, we need to standardize it.

The first step of standardization is pre-processing, then we compare words, and the last step is classification into clusters. The most crucial step here is a comparison of words. We have tested various approaches like Levenshtein distance and its modifications, Q-grams, Jaro-Winkler, and phonetic codings like Soundex and Double-Metaphone. All those methods have been with types of words that can appear in parish records -first and last names, occupation, village, and relationship between people. From these tests, we have chosen the most suitable ways for the clustering of different types of words.

Keywords: Words clustering · Parish records · Levenshtein distance · Soundex · Double Metaphone

1 Introduction

In this text, we deal with record matching. This technique is used in the world od databases when it is good to identify the same element stored in the database more times. For example, when somebody has ordered several times something in the same e-shop, then he or she is probably stored in a database at different places. Another example is when one commodity, for example a smartphone, is stored at different databases with slightly different descriptions [1].

In the past few years have been written several papers dealing with this methodology, and proposed several new approaches. Another developing area is

This work was supported by TACR No. TL01000130, by BUT project FIT-S-17-4014 and the IT4IXS: IT4Innovations Excellence in Science project (LQ1602).

© Springer Nature Singapore Pte Ltd. 2020
X. Wang et al. (Eds.): JIST 2019, CCIS 1157, pp. 21–33, 2020.
https://doi.org/10.1007/978-981-15-3412-6_3

population reconstruction [2–4]. Here our goal is to reconstruct the population of village/city, area, or even of the whole country. In this task, we use records about persons and their parents/children to reconstruct whole families. The problem here is that there exist only a small number of data that are suitable for this task. These data are handwritten in various books like parish records, censuses, or land records. But what we need is their transcription into some database. And here we see the problem because such transcription is an enormous amount of work that needs lots of people and many years of work. But despite that, some such databases already exist. Some of them are some transcribed parish records of some areas, but usually, they are censuses. An excellent overview of papers describing the reconstruction of populations is in [5].

In our project, we work on community web and database suitable for transcription of not only parish records but also for censuses and other registers. We chose to transliterate all words because it ensures that data in our database is most similar to the original data in the books. But then, there rises a problem. In the past, the writtings had not a consistent form of writing, and also the records language varied often. That makes searching in such a database almost impossible. A user would have to search for all variants of words that is quite a time exhausting. Moreover, she or he does not know them. This means that we need to make some word clustering and to put together words with the same meaning. For example names Jan - Johann - Joannes - Hans are the same. Or jeho žena - uxor ejus - dessen eheweib all means "his wife". Similarly Wawržinec - Vavřinec - Vavřín - Vávra - Wawra all means "Laurentius". Similarly, this can be for occupations, villages, or causes of death.

In our crowdsourcing platform DEMoS (Database of Early Modern Sources) we decided to use semi-automatic word standardization. Here the words are automatically segmented into clusters, and the standardized word form is assigned based on the most common word in a cluster. After that, the user can change the standardized variant or even choose some words in a cluster as standardized in one word and other in other words.

The standardization enables easier searching in the database, and also uses the standardized words for searching for identical persons during population reconstruction [12, 13].

The rest of the paper is organized as follows: the second section describes the pre-processing of data. In the third section, the word comparison is described and Classification is described in fourth section. Fifth and sixth section deals with Implementation and Testing.

2   Pre-processing

The first step in clustering is data preprocessing. The goal is to filter out data that does not contribute to clustering.

Modifications can be considered to be general, and those can be used for all types of data - converting all characters to lowercase or omit repeating characters. We can also convert similar characters like "i" and "y" or "v" and "w".

In our specific task we also omit question marks. They are used when during transcription there is not possible to read some character or when we are not sure in reading of some word. Another example is writing of full word instead of short version, e. g. "Joan. (Joannes)".

Another type of modification can be used for only some specific types of words. E.g. removing of prepositions in the beginning of string with village name - in "von Strzemeniczko" we omit "von". Another example is in "cum sua conjuge" which means "with his wife", where important part is only "conjuge".

3   Word Comparison

There are two big areas for word comparison. First is edit distance, where we compare characters of written string. Most known method is Levenshtein distance or Jaro-Winkler distance. Second is phonetic encoding. Here the written word is transferred into code that corresponds to the way the word sounds when pronounced. A great book about data matching and related problems is [7].

3.1   Edit Distance

The most known algorithm for edit distance is Levenshtein distance [8], it is defined as lowest number of character insertion, deletion or substitution that changes first string into second string. However this method is not suitable for testing names, because it does not take into account where strings are different, in the beginning or in the end.

The similarity between two strings is computed as:

$$sim_{levenshtein}(s_1, s_2) = 1.0 - \frac{dist_{levenshtein}(s_1, s_2)}{max(|s_1|, |s_2|)}, \tag{1}$$

where $dist_{levenshtein}$ is Levenshtein distance, $|s_1|$ and $|s_2|$ are lengths of strings s_1 and s_2.

Extension of Levenshtein distance is Damerau-Levenshtein [9] that adds fourth operation, swapping of two adjacent characters because it is common mistake during transcription.

Q-gram (also known as n-gram) [7] is a method where an input string is divided into substrings with length q. Similarity of two strings is computed as

$$sim_{Q-gram} = \frac{c}{min(c_1, c_2)}, \tag{2}$$

where c is number of common q-gram substrings, c_1 and c_2 are numbers of q-gram substring created from string s_1 and s_2.

Methods that are specifically designed for testing names are Jaro or Jaro-Winkler [10] . They are combining edit distance with approach from Q-gram distance. The difference between Jaro and Jaro-Winkler is that latter puts more importance in differences in the beginning of the strings than differences in the middle or in the end.

The last method we have tested is Longest Common Substring [6]. The main idea of this algorithm is to find and remove the longest substrings that are common in both strings.

3.2   Phonetic Coding

The goal of phonetic coding is to transfer string into code that corresponds to the way of its pronunciation. After performing the phonetic coding the distance between resulting codes can be computed by edit distance algorithms. The most known algorithms for phonetic coding are Soundex, Metaphone or Double-Metaphone [7,11].

In Soundex, the code consists of initial letter, the same as in the string followed by several-digit number code. The process of this code creation uses a transformation table. If the length of code is smaller than some desired length, there are added zeros on the right side. If the length is bigger, then the overlapping part is truncated.

Double-Metaphone is language-independent method. Thus it removes biggest disadvantage of previous algorithm, which is dependance on particular language, usually English. Another advantage here is that it uses up to two phonetic codes for every string. This is done by application of several different phonetic rules. The number of rules is applied for input string, and it is modified into resulting code that does not consist of digits.

NYSIIS (New York State Identification and Intelligence System) [7] transforms input string not into numbers but only into characters and is truncated into 6 characters. This algorithm is the second most popular algorithm after Soundex.

Phonetic coding itself does not compare two strings, so after phonetic coding is performed, it is neccessary to use edit distance method to compute distances from resulting codes.

4   Classification

During classification we compared edit distance from previous step with preset thresholds t_{up} and t_{low}. Based on that we get *Match*, *PotentialMatch* or *Non − Match*.

$$dist[r_i, r_j] \geq t_{up} \Rightarrow [r_i, r_j] \rightarrow Match,$$
$$t_{low} < dist[r_i, r_j] < t_{up} \Rightarrow [r_i, r_j] \rightarrow PotentialMatch,$$
$$dist[r_i, r_j] \leq t_{low} \Rightarrow [r_i, r_j] \rightarrow Non − Match$$

We have used only one threshold so we have classified only into two classes, *Match* and *Non − Match*.

Transitive Closure

Every word can be classified as match with more other words. In such case we get series of words that are matches. There can be situation, that two pairs of words (s_1, s_2) and (s_2, s_3) were classified as matches, but pair (s_1, s_3) as non-match. This can be solved as transitive closure and pair (s_1, s_3) can also be classified as match.

5 Implementation

This work is part of the crowdsourcing project which goal is to create database and GUI where volunteers will transcribe records from parish books and also put standardized variants for clustered words. The standardization is done automatically where the standardised word is automatically chosen as the word that is most common in the cluster. Because true standard word can be different, there is possibility for every word to change its standard word manually. There are two ways, where we can change or enter standardised word. One way is to change standard word for all identical words at once (see Fig. 1). Sometime it is neccessary for two identical words to have two different standard words (e.g. Paulina can sometime be Paulina and sometime Apolena), there is possibility after entering new record set standard word for every word in it.

General scheme of DEMoS web is on Fig. 2 and more detailed scheme of application for word clustering is on Fig. 3 the web is created in PHP (Nette Framework), data are stored in MySQL database and program for classification is written in Python 3. We have used `NumPy` library for matrices, `fuzzy` for NYSIIS, `pyphonetics` for Soundex and `metaphone` for Double-Metaphone. For edit distances we have used `textdistance`. The computations are very time demanding and because it can be easily parallelized, we have used `multiprocessing` for parallelization.

Slovo	Pohlaví	Standardizováno	Autor	Doporučené		Vlastní varianta	Potvrdit
Kateřiny	ž	Kateřina	7 DavidH	Kateřina (1)	↕		Potvrdit
Kateřiny	ž	Catharina	7 počítač	Kateřina (1)	↕		Potvrdit
Kateryna	ž	Kateřina	7 DavidH	Kateřina (1)	↕		Potvrdit
Katerzena	ž	Catharina	7 počítač	Kateřina (4)	↕	Katka	Potvrdit
Katerzina	ž	Kateřina	7 DavidH	Kateřina (1)	↕		Potvrdit
Katerziny	ž	Kateřina	7 DavidH	Kateřina (1)	↕		Potvrdit
Katerzyna	ž	Kateřina	7 DavidH	Kateřina (1)	↕		Potvrdit
Katerzyny	ž	Kateřina	7 DavidH	Kateřina (1)	↕		Potvrdit
Katerži	ž	Catharina	7 počítač	Kateřina (4)	↕		Potvrdit
Kateržina	ž	Kateřina	7 DavidH	Kateřina (1)	↕		Potvrdit

Fig. 1. Example of part of web page for batch standardization of names.

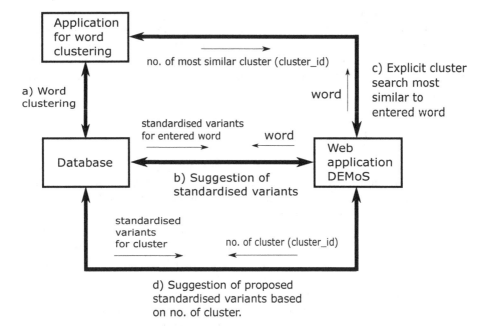

Fig. 2. General scheme of DEMoS, its database, word clustering and relations between them.

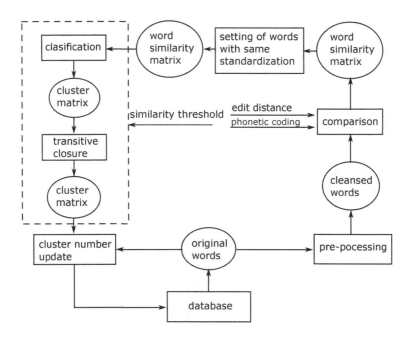

Fig. 3. Detailed scheme of application for word custering.

Parallelization
Comparison of word pairs is most time consuming part of the program. In this part the similarity of two words for every pair is computed and stored into array. For about 3100 words it took about 24 min. Big advantage is that we can use paralelism, because the computation of similarity is independent on other words. Required time is then reduced to 4 min.

6   Testing

We have done testing on the set of data from real parish records from between 17th and 19th century. The parish records are written in czech, latin and german language. There were five types of words - first names, last names, occupations, villages and relations between people. For those records we have created ground truth, which means we know which word belongs to which cluster. For every type we have created various combinations of threshold, phonetic coding, edit distance and transitive closure. We have used Damerau-Levenshtein, Q-gram, Jaro-Winkler and Longest Common Substring for computing of edit distance. The basic Levenshtein method was not used, because its results were similar to extended method. From phonetic coding we have tested Soundex, Double-Metaphone and NYSIIS. We have also tested variant without phonetic coding. For every type of word we have tested all combination of parameters with twenty various thresholds and with and without transitive closure. Therefore we had 4*4*20*2 = 640 tests for every word type.

For measuring of quality of used algorithm we have used precision, recall and computed F-measure. Precision is computed as

$$precision = \frac{TP}{TP + FP}, \tag{3}$$

recall is

$$recall = \frac{TP}{TP + FN}, \tag{4}$$

where TP means true positive, FP means false positive and FN is false negative. F-measure is

$$F - measure = 2 * \frac{precision * recall}{precision + recall} \tag{5}$$

On the Fig. 4 we can see outcome of testing all combinations of edit distance and phonetic coding. On all figures JW means Jaro-Winkler, LCS Longest Common Substring, DL Damerau-Levenshtein, Q is Q-Gram, DM Double-Metaphone, S Soundex and N is NYSIIS. First four examples are only edit distance without any phonetic coding. In Fig. 4 are results of testing with transitive closure, on Fig. 5 are results without transitive closure. We show only this example of results without transitive closure, because its graphs had similar behaviour and the results were worse than with transitive closure.

On all graphs (Figs. 4, 5, 6, 7, 8 and 9) we can see similar behaviour of tested algorithm. There are three clusters of graph series. Four with the peaks most left (this means for best F-measure score was neccessary to set lower threshold) are for the case where Q-gram was used. Its results are always the worst. Most right (highest threshold) are results where Jaro-Winkler distance was used. In the middle is mix of Longest Common Substring and Damerau-Levenshtein. This behaviour can be seen in all graphs. The difference between testing with transitive closure and without it is that without the maximum occurs for lower threshold, but it smaller, that with transitive closure. Only case where the best F-measure was same with or without transitive closure was for relations between persons.

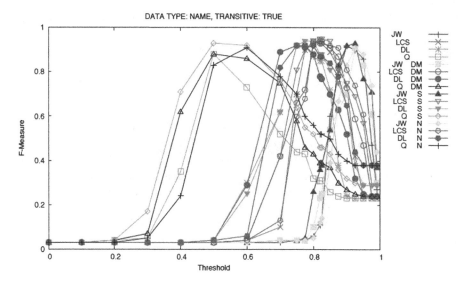

Fig. 4. Graph of first names with transitive closure. Parameters for best results are on bottom right. In this case best results were for combination of Longest Common Substring and Soundex with threshold 0.82. F-measure in this case was 0.95.

In the Table 1 we can see overview of parameters and its F-Measures. We can see that for edit distance algorithm best results are for Longest Common Substring and Jaro-Winkler. They are in combination with three phonetic coding algorithms. For names and surnames best results were for Soundex algorithm, Damerau-Levenshtein has best results for occupations and NYSIIS for villages and relationship. All thresholds are quite high, they are between 0.82 to 0.9. For all word types is better to use transitive closure. Value of F-Measure is between 0.93 and 0.96, except value for surnames, where it is only 0.85. Possible reason behind this small value can be in biggest number of testing words, that was almost 2500, while others were less than 1000 (except for first names that is was 1570).

In the Table 2 we can se F-Measure results for different word types with parameters from Table 1. The words are splitted according to sex and language

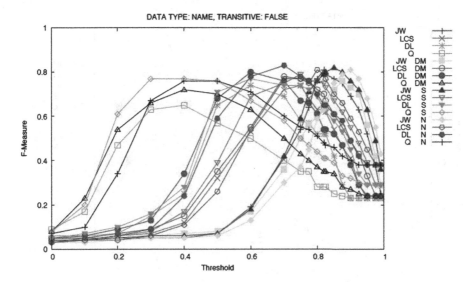

Fig. 5. Graph of first names without transitive closure. We can see that graphs are wider and lower. Highest F-measure here is 0.83 for threshold 0.7 and Damerau-Levenshtein and NYSIIS.

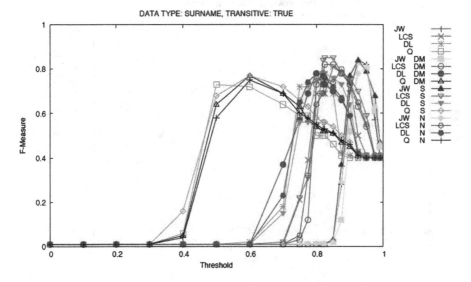

Fig. 6. Graph of surnames. Highest F-measure is 0.85 for threshold 0.825 and Longest Common Substring and Soundex.

and resulting F-Measure is computed. For Sex the values correspond to values in Table 1. For Language the differences in particular languages for different word types are much bigger. It is about 0.1.

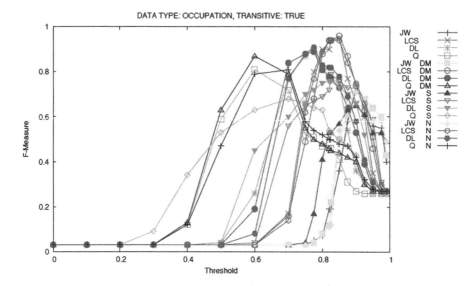

Fig. 7. Graph of occupations. Here highest F-Measure is 0.96 for threshold 0.85 Longest Common Substring and Double Metaphone.

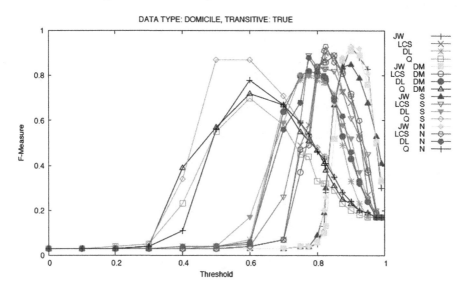

Fig. 8. Graph of villages. This is the only example, where best results were achieved by more algorithm. Highest F-measure is 0.93 and it was achieved with Jaro-Winkler and threshold 0.9, Jaro-Winkler and NYSIIS with threshold 0.9 and Longest Common Substring and NYSIIS and threshold 0.825. The difference is in time of computation, for JW and JW+N it is about 3 s, while for LCS+N it is 26 s.

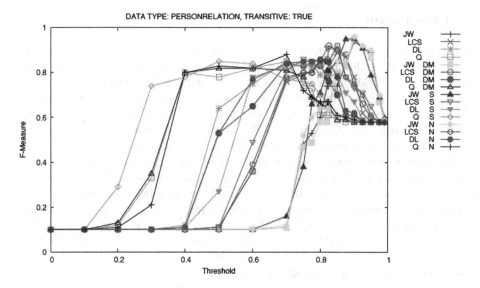

Fig. 9. Graph of relations between persons. Highst F-measure is 0.96 for threshold 0.9 and Jaro-Winkler and NYSIIS.

Table 1. Overview of best values for F-Measure and its parameters.

Word type	Edit distance	Phonetic coding	Transitive		
			Threshold	Closure	F-Measure
Names	LCS	S	0.82	Yes	0.95
Surnames	LCS	S	0.825	Yes	0.85
Occupation	LCS	DM	0.85	Yes	0.96
Villages	JW	N	0.9	Yes	0.93
Relationships	JW	N	0.9	Yes	0.96

Table 2. Values of F-Measures for different Word Types with parameters from Table 1.

Word type	Sex			Language			
				Old			Modern
	Males	Females	Unknown	Czech	German	Latin	Czech
Names	0.94	0.94	0.94	0.92	0.92	0.97	0.97
Surnames	0.86	0.82	0.82	0.89	0.89	0.87	0.93
Occupation				1.0	0.95	0.98	0.96
Villages				0.97	0.98	0.86	1.0
Relationship				1.0	0.89	0.96	0.99

7 Conclusion

In this paper we have described testing of combination of various edit distance and phonetic algorithms for clustering of different word types. This testing was part of project DEMoS whose goal is to create database for transcribing parish books records. Time range of these records is between 17th and 20th century which means one word is written in many ways and it is neccessary to create clusters of words to enable searching. Words that are clustered are first and last names, villages, occupations and relationships between people.

We have tested various combinations of edit distances and phonetic algorithms. The resulting F-measure was between 0.93 and 0.96 with exception for surnames, where it was only 0.85. Best results from edit distance algorithms gave Longest Common Substring and Jaro-Winkler. They were two times in combination with Soundex and NYSIIS and once with Double-Metaphone. We have also tested clustering for various languages that were used in parish books, results here more or less corresponds with overall results, but we would need more testing data, mainly for old czech words.

Our future work will be adding also causes of death and increasing number of tested data, where we want to know if it has meaning to re-computed parameters of algorithms as we will have more data from more transcribed parish records.

References

1. Gottapu, R.D., Dagli, C., Ali, B.: Entity resolution using convolutional neural network. Procedia Comput. Sci. **95**, 153–158 (2016)
2. Dintelman, S., Maness, T.: Reconstituting the population of a small European town using probabilistic record linking: a case study. In: Family History Technology Workshop, BYU (2009)
3. Milani, G., Masciullo, C., et al.: Computer-based genealogy reconstruction in founder populations. J. Biomed. Inf. **44**, 997–1003 (2011)
4. Traglia, M., et al.: Heritability and demographic analyses in the large isolated population of Val Borbera suggest advantages in mapping complex traits genes. PLoS ONE **4**, e7554 (2009)
5. Bloothooft, G., et al.: Population Reconstruction. Springer, Cham (2015). https://doi.org/10.1007/978-3-319-19884-2. ISBN 978-3-319-198833-5
6. Gusfield, D.: Algorithms on Strings, Trees and Sequences: Computer Science and Computational Biology. Cambridge University Press, Cambridge (1997). ISBN 0-521-58519-8
7. Christen, P.: Data Matching: Concepts and Techniques for Record Linkage. Entity Resolution and Duplicate Detection. Springer, Heidelberg (2012). https://doi.org/10.1007/978-3-642-31164-2. ISBN 978-3-642-31163-5
8. Levenshtein, V.I.: Binary codes capable of correcting deletions, insertions, and reversals. Sov. Phys. Dokl. **10**(8), 707–710 (1966)
9. Damerau, F.J.: A technique for computer detection and correction of spelling errors. Commun. ACM **7**(3), 171–176 (1964)
10. Winkler, W.E.: String comparator metrics and enhanced decision rules in the Fellegi-Sunter model of record linkage. In: Proceedings of the Section on Survey Research Methods, pp. 354–359. American Statistical Association (1990)

11. Zobel, J., Dart, P.: Phonetic string matching: lessons from information retrieval. In: Proceedings of the 19th Annual International ACM SIGIR Conference on Research and Development in Information Retrieval, SIGIR 1996, pp. 166–172. ACM, New York (1996). ISBN 0-89791-792-8
12. Zboril, F., Rozman, J., Kocí, R.: Algorithmic creation of genealogical models. In: Abraham, A., Cherukuri, A.K., Melin, P., Gandhi, N. (eds.) ISDA 2018 2018. AISC, vol. 941, pp. 650–658. Springer, Cham (2020). https://doi.org/10.1007/978-3-030-16660-1_63. ISBN 978-3-030-16659-5
13. Rozman, J., Zboril, F.: Persons linking in baptism records. In: Workshop PAOS2018 and PASSCR2018 of JIST2018 Conference, pp. 43–54, Awaji (2018). ISSN 1613–0073

Concept Similarity Under the Agent's Preferences for the Description Logic $\mathcal{ALEH}$

Teeradaj Racharak[1]([✉]), Watanee Jearanaiwongkul[2], and Chutiporn Anutariya[2]

[1] School of Information Science,
Japan Advanced Institute of Science and Technology, Ishikawa, Japan
r.teeradaj@gmail.com
[2] Asian Institute of Technology, Pathum Thani, Thailand
watanee.j@gmail.com,chutiporn@ait.ac.th

Abstract. Computing the degree of concept similarity is an essential problem in description logic ontologies as it has contributions in various applications. However, many computational approaches to concept similarity do not take into account the logical relationships defined in an ontology. Moreover, they cannot be personalized to subjective factors (*i.e.* the agent's preferences). This work introduces a computational approach to concept similarity for the description logic $\mathcal{ALEH}$. Our approach computes the degree of similarity between two concept descriptions structurally under the agent's preferences. Hence, the derived degree is analyzed based on the logical definitions defined in an ontology. We also illustrate its applicability in rice disease detection, in which a farmer queries for relevant disease based on an agricultural observation.

Keywords: Concept similarity · Description Logic $\mathcal{ALEH}$ · Preference profile · Ontological reasoning · Semantic analysis

1 Introduction

Concept similarity refers to the perception of human beings about which similarity degree a pair of concepts is. This kind of perception has contributions in various domains. For instance, it was employed in bio-medical ontology-based applications for discovering functional similarities of gene such as [1] and it can be employed in analogical reasoning such as [11]. Computational approaches to concept similarity can be defined in several means and might come up with a limitation in applicable description logic (DL) languages such as [10] for DL $\mathcal{FL}_0$, [8,9] for DL $\mathcal{ELH}$, and [12] for DL $\mathcal{ALEH}$. In this paper, we show that computational approaches to concept similarity can be derived from the idea of structural matching under the agent's preferences in DL $\mathcal{ALEH}$. Example 1 illustrates an application of similarity computation in rice disease detection domain.

© Springer Nature Singapore Pte Ltd. 2020
X. Wang et al. (Eds.): JIST 2019, CCIS 1157, pp. 34–42, 2020.
https://doi.org/10.1007/978-981-15-3412-6_4

Example 1. Farmer A would like to know what rice diseases have abnormal characteristics similar to his observation. Assume that the farmer sees 'yellow spots on leaf' and uses the following rice disease ontology (revised from [7]):

RiceBacterialBlightDisease ⊑ ∃abnormalityGroup.(BlightOnLeaf ⊓ ∃hasColor.Yellow),
RiceBlastFungalDiease ⊑ ∃abnormalityGroup.(SpotOnLeaf ⊓ ∃hasColor.Brown),
SpotOnLeaf ⊑ ∃hasSymptom.Spot ⊓ ∃hasSymptomAt.Leaf,
BlightOnLeaf ⊑ ∃hasSymptom.Blight ⊓ ∃hasSymptomAt.Leaf

Let the observation of farmer A be represented in description logic concept *i.e.* ObservationA ≡ ∃abnormalityGroup.(SpotOnLeaf ⊓ ∃hasColor.Yellow). Regarding this representation, it is reasonable to say that his observation is similar to either RiceBlastFungalDiease or RiceBacterialBlightDisease equally because a number of common properties shared in each pair are identical.

Moreover, as studied in [6], the subjectivities which are 'relevant' to an application task can contribute to the decision. For instance, when finding relevant diseases, symptom characteristics may play more significant role than color appearance. Hence, ObservationA might be more similar to RiceBlastFungalDiease than RiceBacterialBlightDisease. Thus, we develop a computational approach to $\mathcal{ALEH}$ concept similarity under subjectivities in this work (*cf.* Sect. 3).

2   Preliminaries: Description Logic $\mathcal{ALEH}$

In Description Logics (DLs) [3], *concept descriptions* (shortly, concepts) are inductively defined by the help of a set of constructors, a set of *atomic concepts* $\mathcal{N}_C$ and *atomic roles* $\mathcal{N}_R$. For DL $\mathcal{ALEH}$, concepts C, D are formally defined as: $C, D ::= \top \mid \bot \mid A \mid \neg A \mid C \sqcap D \mid \exists r.C \mid \forall r.C$, where $A \in \mathcal{N}_C$, $r \in \mathcal{N}_R$, $\neg$ denotes the atomic negation, $\top$ denotes the *top* concept, and $\bot$ denotes the *bottom* concept.

A terminology or TBox $\mathcal{T}$ is a finite set of the form $C \sqsubseteq D$ (concept inclusion), $C \equiv D$ (concept equality), and $r \sqsubseteq s$ (role hierarchy). A TBox is called *unfoldable* if it contains at most one concept definition for each concept name in $\mathcal{N}_C$ and does not contain cyclic dependencies. When TBox $\mathcal{T}$ is unfoldable, any $A \sqsubseteq C$ can be transformed into a semantically equivalent one by applying the rule $A \sqsubseteq C \Rightarrow A \equiv X \sqcap C$ where X is a fresh atomic concept. We also call atomic concepts occurring on the left-hand side of statements in $\mathcal{T}$ the *name symbols* (denoted by $\mathcal{N}_\mathcal{T}$) and call other atomic concepts (that occurs only on the right-hand side of statements in $\mathcal{T}$) the *base symbols* (denoted by $\mathcal{B}_\mathcal{T}$).

Let $\mathcal{B}_\mathcal{T}^{\mathsf{node}} := \{A, \neg A \mid A \in \mathcal{B}_\mathcal{T}\} \cup \{\bot\}$. Then, any $\mathcal{ALEH}$ concept description C can be fully expanded to the form: $\sqcap_{i=1}^{l} L_i \sqcap \sqcap_{j=1}^{m} \exists r_j.D_j \sqcap \sqcap_{k=1}^{n} \forall s_k.E_k$, where $L_i \in \mathcal{B}_\mathcal{T}^{\mathsf{node}}$, $r_j, s_k \in \mathcal{N}_R$, and D_j, E_k be $\mathcal{ALEH}$ concept descriptions in the same format as C. We denote the sets $\{L_1, \ldots, L_l\}$, $\{\exists r_1.D_1, \ldots, \exists r_m.D_m\}$, and $\{\forall s_1.E_1, \ldots, \forall s_n.E_n\}$ by $\mathcal{P}_C$, $\mathcal{E}_C$, and $\mathcal{A}_C$, respectively. Moreover, the set of all super-role of r and the set of all sub-roles of r are denoted by $\mathcal{R}^{\exists r}$ and $\mathcal{R}^{\forall r}$, respectively. That is, $\mathcal{R}^{\exists r} := \{s \in \mathcal{N}_R \mid r = s \text{ or } r_i \sqsubseteq r_{i+1} \in \mathcal{T} \text{ where } 1 \leq i \leq n, r_1 = r, r_n = s\}$ and

$\mathcal{R}^{\forall r} := \{t \in \mathcal{N}_R \mid r{=}t \text{ or } r_i \sqsubseteq r_{i+1} \in \mathcal{T} \text{ where } 1{\leq}i{\leq}n, r_1{=}t, r_n{=}r\}$. Here, we restrict that concepts must be normalized after the expansion (*cf.* [2,12] for the normalization rules). Informally, any $\mathcal{ALEH}$ concept C can be recursively translated into the corresponding $\mathcal{ALEH}$ description tree $\mathcal{G}_C := (V, E, v_0, l, \rho)$ where V is a set of nodes, $E \subseteq V \times V$ is a set of edges, $v_0 \in V$ is the root, $l : V \to 2^{\mathcal{B}_T^{\text{node}}}$ is a node labelling function, and $\rho : E \to 2^{\mathcal{N}_R}$ is an edge labelling function. Then, the root v_0 of the description tree $\mathcal{T}_C$ has $\mathcal{P}_C$ as its label, has m outgoing $\exists$-edges labeled with $\mathcal{R}^{\exists r_j}$ to a vertex v_j for $1 \leq j \leq m$, and has n outgoing $\forall$-edges labeled with $\mathcal{R}^{\forall s_k}$ to a vertex v_k for $1 \leq k \leq n$. After that, a subtree with the root v_j (or v_k) is defined recursively in the same way as C.

3   Similarity Computation Under the Agent's Preferences Between $\mathcal{ALEH}$ Concept Descriptions

In this work, we assume that a TBox is unfoldable; hence, concepts can be 'fully expanded' (*cf.* [3] for *unfolding*) and it can be completely disregarded from decision procedures. Then, a computational approach to $\mathcal{ALEH}$ concept similarity can be exploited from calculating the degree of structural matching between two corresponding description trees. Specifically, two concept descriptions are said to be *maximally similar* to each other if their corresponding description trees are perfectly matched. However, when this is not the case, the level of similarity can vary depending on the subjective factors (*e.g.* the agent's preferences).

To accommodate the subjectivities into concept similarity, [9] originally introduced several forms of the agent's preferences over $\mathcal{ELH}$ concept descriptions called *preference profile*. Since $\mathcal{ALEH}$ offers to use value restrictions and the atomic negation for modeling a TBox, preference profile developed in [9] must be extended for $\mathcal{ALEH}$. We formally extend this notion in the following.

3.1   Preference Profile for $\mathcal{ALEH}$ Concepts

Definition 1. *Let $\mathcal{B}_T$ and $\mathcal{N}_R$ be a set of base symbols and a set of atomic roles, respectively. Then, a* primitive concept importance *is a partial function* $\mathfrak{i}^{\mathfrak{c}} : \mathcal{B}_T \to [0, 2]$. *Also, a* role importance *is a partial function* $\mathfrak{i}^{\mathfrak{r}} : \mathcal{N}_R \to [0, 2]$.

For any $A \in \mathcal{B}_T$, $\mathfrak{i}^{\mathfrak{c}}(A) := 1$ captures an expression of normal importance for A, $\mathfrak{i}^{\mathfrak{c}}(A) > 1$ (and $\mathfrak{i}^{\mathfrak{c}}(A) < 1$) indicates that A has higher (and lower, respectively) importance, and $\mathfrak{i}^{\mathfrak{c}}(A) := 0$ indicates that A is of no importance to the agent. The similar fashion is also applied to $\mathfrak{i}^{\mathfrak{r}}$. Apart from this, function $\mathfrak{i}^{\mathfrak{c}}$ is also inductively extended to deal with the atomic negation of any base symbol in an appropriate way: $\mathfrak{i}^{\mathfrak{c}}(\neg A) := \mathfrak{i}^{\mathfrak{c}}(A)$.

Definition 2. *Let $\mathcal{B}_T$ and $\mathcal{N}_R$ be a set of base symbols and a set of atomic roles, respectively. For any $A, B \in \mathcal{B}_T$, a* primitive concept similarity *is a partial function* $\mathfrak{s}^{\mathfrak{c}} : \mathcal{B}_T \times \mathcal{B}_T \to [0, 1]$ *such that $\mathfrak{s}^{\mathfrak{c}}(A, B) = \mathfrak{s}^{\mathfrak{c}}(B, A)$ and $\mathfrak{s}^{\mathfrak{c}}(A, A) := 1$. Also, for any $r, s \in \mathcal{N}_R$, a* primitive role similarity *is a partial function* $\mathfrak{s}^{\mathfrak{r}} : \mathcal{N}_R \times \mathcal{N}_R \to [0, 1]$ *such that $\mathfrak{s}^{\mathfrak{r}}(r, s) = \mathfrak{s}^{\mathfrak{r}}(s, r)$ and $\mathfrak{s}^{\mathfrak{r}}(r, r) := 1$.*

For any $A, B \in \mathcal{B}_T$, $\mathfrak{s}^c(A, B) := 1$ indicates the maximal similarity between A and B. Furthermore, $\mathfrak{s}^c(A, B) := 0$ indicates having no relation between A and B. The similar fashion is also applied to $\mathfrak{s}^r$. Since $\mathcal{ALEH}$ concept descriptions may contain atomic negations, function $\mathfrak{s}^c$ is also inductively extended appropriately: $\mathfrak{s}^c(\neg A, B) := 1 - \mathfrak{s}^c(A, B)$.

Definition 3. *Let $\mathcal{N}_R$ be a set of atomic roles. Then, a* role discount factor *is a partial function* $\mathfrak{d} : \mathcal{N}_R \to [0, 1]$.

For any $r \in \mathcal{N}_R$, $\mathfrak{d}(r) := 1$ captures an expression of maximal importance on a role (beyond a corresponding nested concept description) and $\mathfrak{d}(r) := 0$ captures an expression of maximal importance on a nested concept description. Note that ones can use $\mathfrak{d}$ to handle some special designs of ontologies (*cf.* Example 2).

Definition 4. *A* preference profile *(denoted by π) is a 5-tuple* $\langle i^c, i^r, \mathfrak{s}^c, \mathfrak{s}^r, \mathfrak{d} \rangle$ *where* i^c, i^r, $\mathfrak{s}^c$, $\mathfrak{s}^r$, $\mathfrak{d}$ *are as defined above.*

3.2   Structural Concept Similarity Under Preference Profile

We need to wrap up each preference function in term of 'total' functions in order to avoid computing null values. First, an *importance* function $\hat{i}$ is introduced based on the primitive concept importance and the role importance:

$$\hat{i}(x) := \begin{cases} i^c(x) & \text{if } i^c \text{ is defined on } x \\ i^r(x) & \text{if } i^r \text{ is defined on } x \\ 1 & \text{otherwise;} \end{cases} \tag{1}$$

Second, a *similarity* function $\hat{\mathfrak{s}}$ is also introduced based on the primitive concept similarity and the primitive role similarity:

$$\hat{\mathfrak{s}}(x, y) := \begin{cases} 1 & \text{if } x = y \\ \mathfrak{s}^c(x, y) & \text{if } \mathfrak{s}^c \text{ is defined on } (x, y) \\ \mathfrak{s}^r(x, y) & \text{if } \mathfrak{s}^r \text{ is defined on } (x, y) \\ 0 & \text{otherwise;} \end{cases} \tag{2}$$

Third, a *discount factor* function $\hat{\mathfrak{d}}$ is also introduced based on the role discount factor. For that, we let a number represent the default contribution degree of edge matching. For instance, 0.4 in Eq. 3 indicates that a matched edge x contribute 0.4 importance. Note that this is a user-defined number.

$$\hat{\mathfrak{d}}(x) := \begin{cases} \mathfrak{d}(x) & \text{if } \mathfrak{d} \text{ is defined on } x \\ 0.4 & \text{otherwise.} \end{cases} \tag{3}$$

Definition 5. *Let* $\mathbf{G}^{\mathcal{ALEH}}$ *be the set of all* $\mathcal{ALEH}$ *description trees and* π *be a preference profile. The* homomorphism degree under preference profile hd^{π} : $\mathbf{G}^{\mathcal{ALEH}} \times \mathbf{G}^{\mathcal{ALEH}} \to [0,1]$ *is defined as follows:*[1]

$$\mathrm{hd}^{\pi}(\mathcal{G}_D, \mathcal{G}_C) := (1 - \mu^e - \mu^a) \cdot \mathrm{p\text{-}hd}^{\pi}(\mathcal{P}_D, \mathcal{P}_C) + \\ \mu^e \cdot \mathrm{e\text{-}set\text{-}hd}^{\pi}(\mathcal{E}_D, \mathcal{E}_C) + \mu^a \cdot \mathrm{a\text{-}set\text{-}hd}^{\pi}(\mathcal{A}_D, \mathcal{A}_C) \tag{4}$$

where

$$\mu^e(\mathcal{P}_D, \mathcal{E}_D, \mathcal{A}_D) := \begin{cases} 0 & \text{if } \sum\limits_{A \in \mathcal{P}_D} \hat{\mathrm{i}}(A) + \sum\limits_{\exists r.X \in \mathcal{E}_D} \hat{\mathrm{i}}(r) + \sum\limits_{\forall r.X \in \mathcal{A}_D} \hat{\mathrm{i}}(r) = 0 \quad (5) \\[2em] \dfrac{\sum\limits_{\exists r.X \in \mathcal{E}_D} \hat{\mathrm{i}}(r)}{\sum\limits_{A \in \mathcal{P}_D} \hat{\mathrm{i}}(A) + \sum\limits_{\exists r.X \in \mathcal{E}_D} \hat{\mathrm{i}}(r) + \sum\limits_{\forall r.X \in \mathcal{A}_D} \hat{\mathrm{i}}(r)} & \text{otherwise;} \end{cases}$$

$$\mu^a(\mathcal{P}_D, \mathcal{E}_D, \mathcal{A}_D) := \begin{cases} 0 & \text{if } \sum\limits_{A \in \mathcal{P}_D} \hat{\mathrm{i}}(A) + \sum\limits_{\exists r.X \in \mathcal{E}_D} \hat{\mathrm{i}}(r) + \sum\limits_{\forall r.X \in \mathcal{A}_D} \hat{\mathrm{i}}(r) = 0 \quad (6) \\[2em] \dfrac{\sum\limits_{\forall r.X \in \mathcal{A}_D} \hat{\mathrm{i}}(r)}{\sum\limits_{A \in \mathcal{P}_D} \hat{\mathrm{i}}(A) + \sum\limits_{\exists r.X \in \mathcal{E}_D} \hat{\mathrm{i}}(r) + \sum\limits_{\forall r.X \in \mathcal{A}_D} \hat{\mathrm{i}}(r)} & \text{otherwise;} \end{cases}$$

$$\mathrm{p\text{-}hd}^{\pi}(\mathcal{P}_D, \mathcal{P}_C) := \begin{cases} 1 & \text{if } \sum\limits_{A \in \mathcal{P}_D} \hat{\mathrm{i}}(A) = 0 \text{ or } \mathcal{P}_C = \{\bot\} \\[1em] 0 & \text{if } \sum\limits_{A \in \mathcal{P}_D} \hat{\mathrm{i}}(A) \neq 0 \text{ and} \\ & \quad \sum\limits_{B \in \mathcal{P}_C} \hat{\mathrm{i}}(B) = 0 \quad (7) \\[1.5em] \dfrac{\sum\limits_{A \in \mathcal{P}_D} \hat{\mathrm{i}}(A) \cdot \max\limits_{B \in \mathcal{P}_C} \{\hat{\mathrm{s}}(A,B)\}}{\sum\limits_{A \in \mathcal{P}_D} \hat{\mathrm{i}}(A)} & \text{otherwise;} \end{cases}$$

---

[1] For the sake of cleanliness, we simply write μ^e and μ^a for $\mu^e(\mathcal{P}_D, \mathcal{E}_D, \mathcal{A}_D)$ and $\mu^a(\mathcal{P}_D, \mathcal{E}_D, \mathcal{A}_D)$, respectively, in Eq. 4.

$$\text{e-set-hd}^{\pi}(\mathcal{E}_D, \mathcal{E}_C) := \begin{cases} 1 & \text{if } \sum_{\exists r.X \in \mathcal{E}_D} \hat{\text{i}}(r) = 0 \\ 0 & \text{if } \sum_{\exists r.X \in \mathcal{E}_D} \hat{\text{i}}(r) \neq 0 \text{ and} \\ & \sum_{\exists s.Y \in \mathcal{E}_C} \hat{\text{i}}(s) = 0 \\ \dfrac{\sum_{\exists r.X \in \mathcal{E}_D} \hat{\text{i}}(r) \cdot \max_{\epsilon_j \in \mathcal{E}_C} \{\text{e-hd}^{\pi}(\exists r.X, \epsilon_j)\}}{\sum_{\exists r.X \in \mathcal{E}_D} \hat{\text{i}}(r)} & \text{otherwise;} \end{cases}$$

$$(8)$$

where ϵ_j is an existential restriction; and

$$\text{e-hd}^{\pi}(\exists r.X, \exists s.Y) := \text{e-}\gamma^{\pi}(r, s) \cdot \left(\hat{\partial}(r) + (1 - \hat{\partial}(r)) \cdot \text{hd}^{\pi}(\mathcal{G}_X, \mathcal{G}_Y)\right) \qquad (9)$$

where

$$\text{e-}\gamma^{\pi}(r, s) := \begin{cases} 1 & \text{if } \sum_{r' \in \mathcal{R}^{\exists r}} \hat{\text{i}}(r') = 0 \\ \dfrac{\sum_{r' \in \mathcal{R}^{\exists r}} \hat{\text{i}}(r') \cdot \max_{s' \in \mathcal{R}^{\exists s}} \{\hat{\text{s}}(r', s')\}}{\sum_{r' \in \mathcal{R}^{\exists r}} \hat{\text{i}}(r')} & \text{otherwise;} \end{cases} \qquad (10)$$

$$\text{a-set-hd}^{\pi}(\mathcal{A}_D, \mathcal{A}_C) := \begin{cases} 1 & \text{if } \sum_{\forall r.X \in \mathcal{A}_D} \hat{\text{i}}(r) = 0 \\ 0 & \text{if } \sum_{\forall r.X \in \mathcal{A}_D} \hat{\text{i}}(r) \neq 0 \text{ and} \\ & \sum_{\forall s.Y \in \mathcal{A}_C} \hat{\text{i}}(s) = 0 \\ \dfrac{\sum_{\forall r.X \in \mathcal{A}_D} \hat{\text{i}}(r) \cdot \max_{\alpha_j \in \mathcal{A}_C} \{\text{a-hd}^{\pi}(\forall r.X, \alpha_j)\}}{\sum_{\forall r.X \in \mathcal{A}_D} \hat{\text{i}}(r)} & \text{otherwise;} \end{cases}$$

$$(11)$$

where α_j is a value restriction; and

$$\text{a-hd}^{\pi}(\forall r.X, \forall s.Y) := \begin{cases} \text{a-}\gamma^{\pi}(r, s) & \text{if } \mathcal{P}_Y = \{\bot\} \\ \text{a-}\gamma^{\pi}(r, s) \cdot \left(\hat{\partial}(r) + (1 - \hat{\partial}(r)) \cdot \text{hd}^{\pi}(\mathcal{G}_X, \mathcal{G}_Y)\right) & \text{otherwise;} \end{cases}$$

$$(12)$$

where

$$\text{a-}\gamma^{\pi}(r, s) := \begin{cases} 1 & \text{if } \sum_{r' \in \mathcal{R}^{\forall r}} \hat{\text{i}}(r') = 0 \\ \dfrac{\sum_{r' \in \mathcal{R}^{\forall r}} \hat{\text{i}}(r') \cdot \max_{s' \in \mathcal{R}^{\forall s}} \{\hat{\text{s}}(r', s')\}}{\sum_{r' \in \mathcal{R}^{\forall r}} \hat{\text{i}}(r')} & \text{otherwise.} \end{cases} \qquad (13)$$

Starting from the roots of two description trees $\mathcal{G}_D, \mathcal{G}_C$, Eq. 4 calculates the degree of node matching, the degree of $\exists$-edge matching, and the degree of $\forall$-edge matching among two trees under preference profile π. To compute the degree of node matching under preference profile π, Eq. 7 takes into account the importance of different node labels appropriately according to the user-defined importance function and similarity function. Similarly, Eqs. 8 and 11 calculate the degree of $\exists$-edge matching and the degree of $\forall$-edge matching, respectively, based on the user-defined importance function and similarity function (*cf.* Eqs. 10 and 13). Once the degree of node matching and two different kinds of edge matching are calculated, the procedure further proceeds to their sub-structures. This is defined recursively as $\mathsf{hd}^\pi(\mathcal{G}_X, \mathcal{G}_Y)$ in Eqs. 9 and 12.

Example 2. (Continuation of Example 1) Assume that a symptom is more significant than other concepts; also, it is acceptable to say that brown and yellow are similar. Thus, he can initialize his preference profile as follows:[2] $\mathfrak{i}^{\mathfrak{c}}(\mathsf{S}) := 1.6$, $\mathfrak{i}^{\mathfrak{r}}(\mathsf{hS}) := 1.6$, and $\mathfrak{s}^{\mathfrak{c}}(\mathsf{Bro}, \mathsf{Yel}) := 0.6$. Since aG was designed to group a set of related existential information [7], farmer A should also define $\mathfrak{d}(\mathsf{aG}) := 0$ in his preference profile. We exemplify the usage of Definition 5 as follows:

$$\mathsf{hd}^\pi(\mathcal{G}_{\mathsf{OA}}, \mathcal{G}_{\mathsf{RBFD}}) := (1 - \mu^e - \mu^a) \cdot \mathsf{p\text{-}hd}^\pi(\mathcal{P}_{\mathsf{OA}}, \mathcal{P}_{\mathsf{RBFD}}) +$$
$$\mu^e \cdot \mathsf{e\text{-}set\text{-}hd}^\pi(\mathcal{E}_{\mathsf{OA}}, \mathcal{E}_{\mathsf{RBFD}}) + \mu^a \cdot \mathsf{a\text{-}set\text{-}hd}^\pi(\mathcal{A}_{\mathsf{OA}}, \mathcal{A}_{\mathsf{RBFD}})$$
$$:= \left(1 - \left(\frac{1}{0 + 1 + 0}\right) + 0\right) \cdot \mathsf{p\text{-}hd}^\pi(\mathcal{P}_{\mathsf{OA}}, \mathcal{P}_{\mathsf{RBFD}}) +$$
$$1 \cdot \mathsf{e\text{-}set\text{-}hd}^\pi(\mathcal{E}_{\mathsf{OA}}, \mathcal{E}_{\mathsf{RBFD}}) + 0 \cdot \mathsf{a\text{-}set\text{-}hd}^\pi(\mathcal{A}_{\mathsf{OA}}, \mathcal{A}_{\mathsf{RFBD}})$$
$$:= \frac{1}{4.6} + \frac{3.6}{4.6} \cdot \left(\frac{1.6 \cdot 1 + 1 \cdot 1 + 1 \cdot 0.76}{1.6 + 1 + 1}\right) \approx 0.95$$

Analogously, we have $\mathsf{hd}^\pi(\mathcal{G}_{\mathsf{RBFD}}, \mathcal{G}_{\mathsf{OA}}) \approx 0.47$, $\mathsf{hd}^\pi(\mathcal{G}_{\mathsf{OA}}, \mathcal{G}_{\mathsf{RBBD}}) \approx 0.57$, and $\mathsf{hd}^\pi(\mathcal{G}_{\mathsf{RBBD}}, \mathcal{G}_{\mathsf{OA}}) \approx 0.29$.

Definition 6. *Let C, D be two $\mathcal{ALEH}$ concept descriptions and $\mathcal{G}_C, \mathcal{G}_D$ be the corresponding $\mathcal{ALEH}$ description trees, and π be a preference profile. Then, the $\mathcal{ALEH}$ concept similarity under preference profile π between C and D (denoted by $\mathsf{sim}^\pi(C, D)$) is defined as follows:*

$$\mathsf{sim}^\pi(C, D) := \frac{\mathsf{hd}^\pi(\mathcal{G}_C, \mathcal{G}_D) + \mathsf{hd}^\pi(\mathcal{G}_D, \mathcal{G}_C)}{2} \tag{14}$$

Semantically, $\mathsf{sim}^\pi(C, D) = 1$ indicates that "concepts C and D are maximally similar to each other under the preference profile π" whereas $\mathsf{sim}^\pi(C, D) = 0$ indicates that "concepts C and D have no relationship to each other under the preference profile π". For instance, it yields that $\mathsf{sim}^\pi(\mathsf{OA}, \mathsf{RBFD}) \approx 0.71$ and $\mathsf{sim}^\pi(\mathsf{OA}, \mathsf{RBBD}) \approx 0.43$ by Definition 6. These values indicate that OA is more similar to RBFD than RBBD under the given preference profile π.

4   Related Work and Conclusion

Various methods have been proposed to compute the similarity score between concepts. Initially, the approaches to this problem are classified into: the path-finding (*e.g.* [5]) and the edit-distance (*e.g.* [4]). However, those approaches omit

---

[2] Obvious abbreviations may be used for succinctness *e.g.* S stands for Spot.

to consider the logical relationships defined in an ontology. Hence, modern techniques (called *semantic similarity*) which consider either the structure or the interpretation of concepts were developed. Rather, they are restricted to particular DLs (*cf.* existing work given in Sect. 1 and the related work in [9]). In this work, we propose an approach to semantic similarity for the DL $\mathcal{ALEH}$, in which not only objective factors but also the subjective ones are considered. The similarity degree between two concepts is calculated based on the average of two directions of structural matching between two corresponding description trees.

Since our method calculates the degree of concept similarity based on the structure of concept descriptions, it is a natural step to investigate its relationship to the standard concept equivalence reasoning service. Apart from this theoretical investigation, we aim at analyzing its desirable properties (as introduced in [9]). Other possible directions are to investigate how an explanation for similarity of concepts can be automatically generated from the similarity calculation; and, to improve the method for dealing with more expressive DLs.

References

1. Ashburner, M., et al.: Gene ontology: tool for the unification of biology. Nat. Genet. **25**(1), 25–29 (2000). https://doi.org/10.1038/75556
2. Baader, F., Küsters, R.: Nonstandard inferences in description logics: the story so far. In: Gabbay, D., Goncharov, S., Zakharyaschev, M. (eds.) Mathematical Problems from Applied Logic I, International Mathematical Series, vol. 4, pp. 1–75. Springer, New York (2006). https://doi.org/10.1007/0-387-31072-X_1
3. Baader, F., Calvanese, D., McGuinness, D.L., Nardi, D., Patel-Schneider, P.F.: The Description Logic Handbook: Theory, Implementation and Applications, 2nd edn. Cambridge University Press, New York (2010)
4. Bille, P.: A survey on tree edit distance and related problems. Theor. Comput. Sci. **337**(1–3), 217–239 (2005)
5. Ge, J., Qiu, Y.: Concept similarity matching based on semantic distance. In: Proceedings of the 4th International Conference on Semantics, Knowledge and Grid. pp. 380–383, December 2008. https://doi.org/10.1109/SKG.2008.24
6. Hesse, M.B.: Models and Analogies in Science (1965)
7. Jearanaiwongkul, W., Anutariya, C., Andres, F.: An ontology-based approach to plant disease identification system (accepted). New Generation Computing (2019)
8. Lehmann, K., Turhan, A.Y.: A framework for semantic-based similarity measures for $\mathcal{ELH}$ -concepts. In: del Cerro, L.F., Herzig, A., Mengin, J. (eds.) Logics in Artificial Intelligence, pp. 307–319. Springer, Berlin (2012). https://doi.org/10.1007/978-3-642-33353-8_24
9. Racharak, T., Suntisrivaraporn, B., Tojo, S.: Personalizing a concept similarity measure in the description logic $\mathcal{ELH}$ with preference profile. Comput. Inform. **37**(3), 581–613 (2018)
10. Racharak, T., Tojo, S.: Concept similarity under the agent's preferences for the description logic $\mathcal{FL}_0$ with unfoldable TBox. In: Proceedings of the 10th International Conference on Agents and Artificial Intelligence, ICAART 2018, Funchal, Madeira, Portugal, 16–18 January 2018, vol. 2, pp. 201–210 (2018). https://doi.org/10.5220/0006653402010210

11. Racharak, T., Tojo, S., Hung, N.D., Boonkwan, P.: Combining answer set programming with description logics for analogical reasoning under an agent's preferences. In: Benferhat, S., Tabia, K., Ali, M. (eds.) IEA/AIE 2017. LNCS (LNAI), vol. 10351, pp. 306–316. Springer, Cham (2017). https://doi.org/10.1007/978-3-319-60045-1_33

12. Suntisrivaraporn., B., Tongphu., S.: A structural subsumption based similarity measure for the description logic $\mathcal{ALEH}$. In: Proceedings of the 8th International Conference on Agents and Artificial Intelligence -ICAART, vol. 2, pp. 204–212. INSTICC, SciTePress (2016). https://doi.org/10.5220/0005819302040212

Data Quality for Deep Learning of Judgment Documents: An Empirical Study

Jiawei Liu[1,2], Dong Wang[2], Zhenzhen Wang[2,3(✉)], and Zhenyu Chen[1,2]

[1] State Key Laboratory for Novel Software Technology, Nanjing University, Nanjing, China
[2] Software Testing Engineering Laboratory of Jiangsu Province, Nanjing, China
[3] School of Software, Jinling Institute of Technology, Nanjing, China
wangzhenzhen@jit.edu.cn

Abstract. The revolution in hardware technology has made it possible to obtain high-definition data through highly sophisticated algorithms. Deep learning has emerged and is widely used in various fields, and the judicial area is no exception. As the carrier of the litigation activities, the judgment documents record the process and results of the people's courts, and their quality directly affects the fairness and credibility of the law. To be able to measure the quality of judgment documents, the interpretability of judgment documents has been an indispensable dimension. Unfortunately, due to the various uncontrollable factors during the process, such as data transmission and storage, The data set for training usually has a poor quality. Besides, due to the severe imbalance of the distribution of case data, data augmentation is essential to generate data for low-frequency cases. Based on the existing data set and the application scenarios, we explore data quality issues in four areas. Then we systematically investigate them to figure out their impact on the data set. After that, we compare the four dimensions to find out which one has the most considerable damage to the data set.

Keywords: Judgment document · Deep learning · Quality measurement · Natural language processing

1 Introduction

Since data becomes an essential resource for all organizations, data quality has been critical for managers and operational process to determine relevant performance issues [1]. Compared to structured data, unstructured data (text, voice, video, and images, etc.) does not have a data model that can be used directly by computers [2]. Since reality is usually represented by a message that contains real-world features, such as landscape photography or abstract environments expressed in novels and poems, quality issues are also different in representing information, such as images and unstructured text [3].

© Springer Nature Singapore Pte Ltd. 2020
X. Wang et al. (Eds.): JIST 2019, CCIS 1157, pp. 43–50, 2020.
https://doi.org/10.1007/978-981-15-3412-6_5

Image quality has been generally understood as a subjective impression of the object world. The dimensions of the evaluation of image quality include fidelity (the degree of matching with the original image), usefulness (the degree of applicability to a particular task) and naturalness (the degree of matching of the content itself) [4]. While text data differs from image data in quality, it has different characteristics, such as average sentence length or the number of misspellings and abbreviations. These text features have an impact on the quality of text mining results [5]. There are eight dimensions for the quality metrics of text data, including accuracy, completeness, accessibility, consistency, simplicity, interpretability, credibility, and usability [2]. It can be seen that the image data and text data quality evaluation methods have considerable differences. The main reason for these differences is that although both have significant subjective speculations, the image data pay more attention to the accurate reflection of the objective world, while the text data focuses on the logic of the data content. Obviously, interpretability measures the extent to which the data reflects the philosophy of the text and leads in all dimensions [6,7].

Data and model have always been playing essential roles in the field of deep learning. People have invested a lot in the study of training models, and have neglected the research of the training set itself [8]. It is well known that the quality of the data set plays a decisive role in the final training results. For example, it is not possible to train a high-quality model with very high accuracy on a badly damaged data set. As a result, what is the dimension that measures the quality of the data set has always been a problem that needs to be resolved. Solving such issues not only helps people understand the quality of the data set but also balance the cost and accuracy of training when developing deep learning applications. In addition, it may contribute to the study of antagonistic instances and data augmentation.

This paper is about how to measure the quality of the training data of the judgment documents and uses a reasonable neural network model to test. The data set we use has a significant impact on building deep learning architecture. In order to improve the robustness of the deep learning model by enhancing the data quality of the data set, we conducted an in-depth empirical study of the quality of the deep learning, mainly using control variate method to compare the experimental results. We experimented on several existing networks and tried to use several different data sets. According to the real problems and the needs of data amplification, this paper focuses on the impact of training data set in four aspects:

(1) Incomplete data set: This problem is usually inevitable in data transmission and storage.
(2) Data set size: This problem is common in the handling of low-frequency cases.
(3) Label quality: When labeling large data sets, in order to pursue efficiency, it will inevitably reduce the quality requirement.
(4) Data set contamination: In addition to objective reasons, the problem of sound pollution caused by human factors is not to be underestimated.

2   Related Work

In the sequence labeling task (Chinese word segmentation, part-of-speech tag, named entity recognition, etc.), the current mainstream deep learning framework is BiLSTM with CRF. BiLSTM combines the two groups of learning directions (one in sentence order and one sentence in reverse order). The LSTM layer can theoretically realize that the current word contains historical information and future information, which is more conducive to labeling the current word [9]. Scholars in natural language processing have proposed a layer of CRF followed by BiLSTM for learning the optimal tag sequence over the entire sequence [10].

The model calculates the optimal labeling sequence by the following formula, the A matrix is the label transition probability, the $\mathbf{y}$ is a sequence of predictions$(y_1, y_2, \ldots, y_n)$ and the P matrix is the prediction result of BiLSTM [11].

$$s(\mathbf{X}, \mathbf{y}) = \sum_{i=0}^{n} A_{y_i, y_{i+1}} + \sum_{i=1}^{n} P_{i, y_i}$$

When the model is trained, the log loss function is optimized for each sequence y, and the value of matrix A is adjusted. A softmax over all possible tag sequences yields a probability for the sequence y:

$$p(\mathbf{y}|\mathbf{X}) = \frac{e^{s(\mathbf{X}, \mathbf{y})}}{\sum_{\tilde{\mathbf{y}} \in Y_{\mathbf{x}}} e^{s(\mathbf{X}, \tilde{\mathbf{y}})}}$$

During the training, the log-probability of the correct tag sequence is also maximized as:

$$\log(p(\mathbf{y}|\mathbf{X})) = s(\mathbf{X}, \mathbf{y}) - \log\left(\sum_{\tilde{\mathbf{y}} \in Y_{\mathbf{x}}} e^{s(\mathbf{X}, \tilde{\mathbf{y}})}\right) = s(\mathbf{X}, \mathbf{y}) - \underset{\tilde{\mathbf{y}} \in Y_{\mathbf{x}}}{\text{logadd}} s(\mathbf{X}, \tilde{\mathbf{y}})$$

When the model training is completed and the predictions are ready, the optimal path can be found according to the following formula (Y_x represents all possible sequence sets, and y^* represents the sequence in the set that maximizes the Score function):

$$\mathbf{y}^* = \underset{\tilde{\mathbf{y}} \in Y_{\mathbf{x}}}{\text{argmax}} s(\mathbf{X}, \tilde{\mathbf{y}})$$

For a participle task, the label of the current word is only associated with the first few words. When BiLSTM learns a long sentence, it may discard some critical information because of the model capacity problem. Therefore, we consider adding a CNN layer to the model to extract the local features of the current word.

The goal of the experiment was to observe the impact of four dimensions of the quality of the data set. In addition to the accuracy and loss in the training process, three other quality indicators will be introduced to better describe the impact on the model in different situations [12].

$$Precision = \frac{correct\ pieces\ of\ the\ extracted}{pieces\ of\ the\ extracted} \tag{1}$$

$$Recall = \frac{pieces\ of\ the\ extracted}{pieces\ of\ the\ sample} \tag{2}$$

$$F - Measure = \frac{Precision * Recall * 2}{(Precision + Recall)} \tag{3}$$

Precision and recall are two metrics that are widely used in the field of information retrieval and statistical classification to assess the quality of results. The precision is the ratio of the number of related documents retrieved to the total number of documents retrieved, and the extent of the retrieval system is measured. The recall refers to the ratio of the number of related documents retrieved and the number of related documents in the document library. The range of these two metrics is between 0 and 1. The closer the value is to 1, the higher the precision or recall [13]. The F-Measure is an evaluation index that combines the two indicators for synthesis and reflects the overall indicators. Precision and recall indicators sometimes have contradictory situations, so we need to consider them comprehensively. The most common method is the F-Measure, which combines the results of precision and recall. When F-Measure is higher, it can be proved that the test method is more effective [14].

3   Experiment

The followings are the research questions of our paper, and the models we used are for text segmentation.

RQ1: What does the incompletion of data set do to the accuracy of a model?

RQ2: Whether and how the size of a data set will change the accuracy of a model? Is it accepted?

RQ3: When the data set is deformed, what will happen? Why?

RQ4: Will the order of the document affects the accuracy of a model?

3.1   Experiment Setup

The data set used in these experiments is the judgment documents of the civil case trial, and the controlled experiments are based on the above four research questions.

For the first research experiment, we first use the *tell*() and *truncate*() to get the incomplete of data set. After that, we measure the final performance with the loss and accuracy.

For the second research experiment, we modify the size of the training set by randomly deleting a specific percentage of text files in the training set. Compared with the baseline experiment in the metrics mentioned above, we can describe the experiment results.

In the third experiment, in order to obtain the data of the error label, we append the error data such as "training data" at the end of the text using the *append*() method. The number of error labels added depends on the length of the text.

In the fourth experiment, we slightly modify the word order of the sentences in the text statement. First, split a complete text data into an array of sentences according to the *split*() method. Then use the *shuffle*() function to reorder the array and get a random sort result and rewrite it back to the file. Next, we can measure the impact of out-of-order data by precision, recall and F-Measure.

3.2   Experiment Results

In the case of using a completely correct training set, the evaluation results of the above indicators are shown in the first 2 columns in Table 1.

Table 1. The precision, recall and F-Measure.

Indicator	Original set	Disordered set in RQ4
Precision	0.919644	0.925966
Recall	0.906250	0.924153
F-Measure	0.912898	0.925059

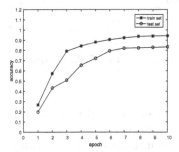

Fig. 1. Accuracy of dataset.

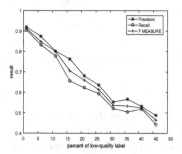

Fig. 2. Loss of dataset.

The Figs. 1 and 2 illustrate the accuracy and the loss during the training process of the baseline experiment, which are also used as a reference for the following experiments.

4   Results and Remarks

RQ1. As is shown in Fig. 3, it is not difficult to find that as the missing part of the document continues to increase, the quality of the final model is generally getting worse. Although the data indicators are continually fluctuating, they are still in the acceptable range, and the ideal training results can yet be obtained. However, when the missing part is further enlarged, the quality of the model will begin to change by a large margin.

Taking the impact of the wrong label factor into consideration, it is not difficult to find that the incompleteness of the text content has a certain probability of generating a wrong label of data. Once a correctly labeled test case is internally deleted, it will be mislabeled, which could reduce the quality of the model significantly.

RQ2. In this section, the changes in precision, recall and F-Measure are shown in Fig. 4. Although the quality of the training model is reduced, when the number of files is only half of the reference set, the quality of the model still has a satisfactory result, which reveals a significant fact that if the quality of the documents can be ensured, we can still get ideal model in the areas of low-frequency cases. This is good news for researchers in low-frequency cases because it breaks their fears that the data set is not big enough.

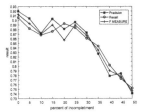 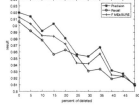 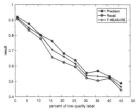

Fig. 3. Incomplete dataset.   **Fig. 4.** Dataset size.   **Fig. 5.** Label quality.

RQ3. Through continuous experimentation, we get the results shown in Fig. 5. Compared with the above two experiments, this experiment obviously demonstrates that the label quality reflects data quality intuitively. As the wrong word segmentation data enters the training set, the quality of the model begins to decline dramatically. However, it is interesting that the declining is slower initially. Compared with the slight uptrend in Fig. 3, we can find that a small number of error labels can enhance the robustness of the model, and finally optimize the model. As the minor errors caused by staff, this can bring benefits within a specific limit. Once beyond the border, the impact of low-quality labels on the quality of the model is devastating, since text data is a kind of extraordinary unstructured data. Correct word segmentation is an essential basis for obtaining high-quality models.

RQ4. Interestingly, it can be seen from Fig. 6 and Table 1 that after the word order transformation of the judgment documents, the change in accuracy during the training process is almost the same as the original data set, especially after the 7th epoch. To further observe the training details, we increased the epoch from 10 to 100 and focused on the data from the 70th epoch. As shown in Fig. 7, the accuracy of the two experiments, although continually fluctuating, the actual values are within a similar range.

Since this article only examines the impact on CWS, even if the current text is combined with the context, satisfying results can be obtained in the case of out-of-order. The reason for this problem is whether the CWS is not sensitive to the word order or the limitations of the network model have not to be further worked yet.

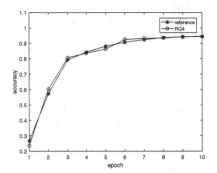
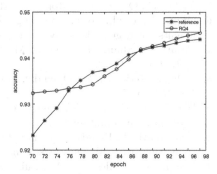

Fig. 6. Data contamination in 10 epoch.   **Fig. 7.** Data contamination in more details.

5   Conclusion and Future Work

In this paper, we study the four dimensions that affect the quality of the data set in detail and give the experimental results of the civil law case as the source of the training set under different experimental conditions. We have found that low quality is allowed or even necessary within a certain range. However, it is significant to control this specific scope strictly, otherwise, it will have serious consequences. In addition, for low-frequency cases, slightly smaller data samples can also perform well. If you want to pursue better performance, you can consider data augmentation by disrupting the text order, because through experiments, we find that under certain conditions, disordered data does not affect the word segmentation performance. Some modifications to the text itself may vary from data set to data set. In the next study, we will focus on word order and data set quality, explore the deep relationship between them and give more reliable data augmentation ideas.

Acknowledgment. The work is supported in part by the National Key Research and Development Program of China (2016YFC0800805) and the National Natural Science Foundation of China (61832009, 61932012).

References

1. Sidi, F., Panahy, P.H.S., Affendey, L.S., Jabar, M.A., Ibrahim, H., Mustapha, A.: Data quality: a survey of data quality dimensions. In: 2012 International Conference on Information Retrieval & Knowledge Management, pp. 300–304. IEEE (2012)
2. Kiefer, C.: Assessing the quality of unstructured data: an initial overview. In: LWDA, pp. 62–73 (2016)
3. Firmani, D., Mecella, M., Scannapieco, M., Batini, C.: On the meaningfulness of "big data quality". Data Sci. Eng. 1(1), 6–20 (2016)
4. Batini, C., Scannapieco, M., et al.: Data and Information Quality. Springer, Cham (2016). https://doi.org/10.1007/978-3-319-24106-7
5. Kiefer, C.: Quality indicators for text data. BTW 2019-Workshopband (2019)
6. Gupta, A., et al.: Toward building a legal knowledge-base of Chinese judicial documents for large-scale analytics. Legal knowledge and information systems (2017)
7. Casati, F., Shan, M.C., Sayal, M.: Investigating business processes. US Patent 7,610,211, 27 Oct 2009
8. Sadiq, S., Indulska, M.: Open data: quality over quantity. Int. J. Inf. Manag. 37(3), 150–154 (2017)
9. Wu, Y., et al.: Google's neural machine translation system: bridging the gap between human and machine translation. Computation and Language (2016)
10. Cuayahuitl, H., Renals, S., Lemon, O., Shimodaira, H.: Human-computer dialogue simulation using hidden Markov models, pp. 290–295 (2005)
11. Lample, G., Ballesteros, M., Subramanian, S., Kawakami, K., Dyer, C.: Neural architectures for named entity recognition. In: North American Chapter of the Association for Computational Linguistics, pp. 260–270 (2016)
12. Simon, L., Webster, R., Rabin, J.: Revisiting precision and recall definition for generative model evaluation. Learning (2019)
13. Wasikowski, M., Chen, X.W.: Combating the small sample class imbalance problem using feature selection. IEEE Trans. Knowl. Data Eng. 22(10), 1388–1400 (2010)
14. Batini, C., Palmonari, M., Viscusi, G.: The many faces of information and their impact on information quality. In: AISB/IACAP World Congress 2012-Information Quality, pp. 212–228 (2012)

Aligning Sentences Between Comparable Texts of Different Styles

Xiwen Chen[✉], Mengxue Zhang, and Kenny Qili Zhu

Advanced Data and Programming Technology Lab, Computer Science Department,
Shanghai Jiao Tong University, 800 Dong Chuan Road, Shanghai, China
{victoria-x,lovealice}@sjtu.edu.cn, kzhu@cs.sjtu.edu.cn
https://adapt.seiee.sjtu.edu.cn/

Abstract. Monolingual parallel corpus is crucial for training and evaluating text rewriting or paraphrasing models. Aligning parallel sentences between two large body of texts is a key step toward automatic construction of such parallel corpora. We propose a greedy alignment algorithm that makes use of strong unsupervised similarity measures. The algorithm aligns sentences with state-of-the-art accuracy while being more robust on corpora with special linguistic features. Using this alignment algorithm, we automatically constructed a large English parallel corpus from various translated works of classic literature.

Keywords: Monolingual parallel corpora · Sentence alignment · Unsupervised algorithms

1 Introduction

In natural language processing, there are many supervised learning models that require the existence of parallel corpus for training. However, manual annotation, which is used in constructing many reliable parallel corpora, is inefficient and time-consuming. Cross-lingual sentence alignment has been extensively studied for machine translation, but the construction of monolingual parallel corpus is also gaining its interest. For cross-lingual alignment, different words are relatively discriminative in data distribution, while in monolingual alignment, the "style" of a word might be much more subtle to distinguish. Monolingual parallel corpora can be used to learn text rewriting rules, which is involved in sentence simplification, natural language style transfer, and document summarization [5]. It can also be used to learn the relation between monolingual texts such as semantic relatedness and similarity.

The monolingual sentence alignment model takes two comparable monolingual texts as an input, and outputs a x-to-y alignment of these two corpora, where the sequential combination of x sentences from the first corpus is aligned with y sentences from the second corpus, and both combinations are "similar" in content. For instance, the following sentences, although different in their expressions, can be properly aligned to each other in terms of content.

X. Wang et al. (Eds.): JIST 2019, CCIS 1157, pp. 51–64, 2020.
https://doi.org/10.1007/978-981-15-3412-6_6

Alyosha got up, walked over to the door, and reported that no one was listening to them.

Alyosha went, opened the door a little, and reported that no one was eavesdropping.

In previous research, mainly one-to-one and n-to-one matching schemes are studied. When only one-to-one sentence mapping is assumed, the similarity scores for each pair of sentences can be precomputed [8], which largely simplifies the problem. However, this condition does not hold for literature corpora, since one sentence might be rephrased as different number of sentences in another expression. In the work of Hwang et al. [5], many-to-one mappings are taken into consideration to align simple and standard Wikipedia, which is a safe assumption because a sentence in standard Wikipedia is very likely to be broken into several short sentences in simple Wikipedia. But this is not the case for general comparable texts. Our x-to-y sentence mapping assumption is more challenging but practical.

The challenge of our problem is two-fold. First, similarity measure of sentences, which is crucial in alignment decision, is difficult to design for different corpora with different semantic features. Second, in each aligned pair, the number of successive sentences on each side is not known in advance but has to be discovered during the sequential alignment process. Moreover, some measurements that show higher accuracy in similarity evaluation work relatively slow when aligning large corpora. Therefore, the similarity measure for every possible pair and every possible sentence length cannot be assumed to be known, and thus the problem cannot be resolved as a simple matching problem. The second challenge is more significant in our x-to-y matching scheme. These challenges are not present in previous problems, but are inevitable in our case because the monolingual documents differ in "style" in general and not as specific as "simple/complex".

The contributions of this work are the following.

1. We extend the monolingual alignment problem to the x-to-y matching solution of two documents in different styles, and devise an unsupervised alignment scheme that produces high-quality matching pairs. The styles of documents are not limited to simple/complex language (Sect. 3).
2. We experiment similarity measures based on Word2Vec model [10], Universal Sentence Encoder [1] and InferSent model [2]. We evaluate the performance of these measures and compare with baseline models for paraphrase detection, and verify that our unsupervised methods have comparable performances with state-of-art (supervised and unsupervised) methods (Sect. 5).
3. Using a greedy algorithm and a filter mechanism for sequence alignment, we compare the performances of our model with baseline sentence alignment models on literature works with different linguistic characteristics. The results show that the filter mechanism can significantly improve the quantity of aligned sentences while preserving a reasonable quality (Sects. 3 and 5).

4. We construct a monolingual parallel corpus from various literature translations. This corpus can be used to learn general text rewriting models, and specifically, the "style" of a text (Sect. 6).

2 Related Work

With several exceptions, the sentence similarity measure task is fulfilled in two general approaches: (a) sentence embeddings or word embeddings are first obtained and similarity score is calculated based on mathematical measure on vector distance, such as normalized Euclidean distance, cosine distance and earth mover's distance, or (b) similarity score is learned by semantic features or distributional statistics.

In explorations of word-level similarities, word vectors mostly relied on pretrained word vectors such as GloVe [13] and fasttext [7] pretrained word vectors. Then word-level similarity and multiple word alignment rules are applied to obtain sentence-level similarities. By directly obtaining sentence vectors, other studies focused more on the forms of distance measure for sentence vectors to better capture the real semantic distance [8].

Based on word embeddings, Zhu et al. constructed a parallel corpus for text simplification using cosine similarity between TF-IDF vectors of sentences [15]. Later studies considered more sentence semantic features including sentence ordering [3] and word-level similarity [5]. Kajiwara et al. used four word-level alignment methods for similarity measure, and constructed a monolingual parallel corpus for text simplification using similarity matrix and a given threshold [8]. Hatzlvassiloglou et al. evaluated the incorporation of multiple linguistic features and the combinations of them in text similarity measure [4].

In sentence alignment task, Zamani et al. modeled the sequential alignment process using integer programming, arguing that a weak similarity measure is compensated by an optimal sequential alignment algorithm [14]. Hwang et al. compared a greedy alignment pattern with an ordered alignment algorithm by dynamic programming, and proved the practical priority of the former [5].

3 Methodology

An overview of the model architecture is shown in Fig. 1. Under the assumption that the two documents have comparable order in sentences, the model aligns the two texts as follows.

1. Given a similarity measure f_1, the similarity measurement model computes the scores for all possible one-to-one pairs within a certain distance. This distance is defined as MAX_DISTANCE, and is the maximum relative distance (given by the index of a sentence in the document) between two single sentences that are considered at this stage.

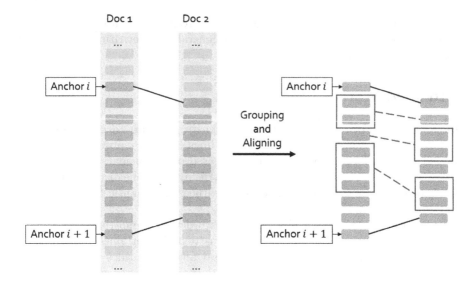

Fig. 1. Model overview.

2. Pairs whose similarity scores are above a given threshold t are supposed to be the "anchors" and are appended to an anchor list. The anchors divide the original document into parts that are relatively shorter and easier for later alignment.
3. For each part between two pairs of anchors, a local alignment algorithm is performed using a certain similarity measure, where we need to group the sentences and then align the groups.
4. Finally, an optional filtering process is performed. This is due to the observation that, including only one kind of similarity measure might result in unreasonable alignment or too strict alignment rules. To capture the semantic features in different perspectives, an additional similarity measure can be used to perform a filtering stage for sentences that are not successfully aligned at previous stages. At this stage, we only consider one-to-one alignment.

In sum, the model consists of basic similarity measurements and a local sequential alignment in each part separated by successive anchors. The effect of the final filtering stage will also be explored in this work.

3.1   Similarity Measure

The first subtask is to give a similarity score for each pair of sentences in order to further align them. In practice, the scoring requires a clustering strategy, since one-to-one sentence mapping is not necessarily required in the sequential alignment task. At this stage, we restrict ourselves to first evaluating the performance of different similarity measures. Namely, given two sentences $(w_1^{(a)}, w_2^{(a)}, \ldots, w_{l_a}^{(a)})$ and $(w_1^{(b)}, w_2^{(b)}, \ldots, w_{l_b}^{(b)})$, where each word in the sequence is a fixed dimensional vector $w_i^{(a)}, w_j^{(b)} \in \mathbb{R}^d$. Then each pair of the sentences a, b are mapped to a score $r \in [0, 1]$ representing their sentence similarity. The compared models are evaluated based on their accuracies of paraphrase detection task, with corpora including MSRC, SICK, and Shakespeare scripts.

The general approach for unsupervised similarity measure is composed of a (hopefully strong) sentence representation model and a simple distance measure.

- **Gensim Word2Vec (WDV).** The Gensim implementation of Word2Vec model uses CBOW and Skip-gram models [10]. In our implementation, the word vectors are trained on the two documents to be aligned, rather than using pretrained word vectors given by independent large corpus. This is under the consideration that, since our sentence alignment task is performed on stylized sentences, a corpus-specific Word2Vec model better fits in our scheme.

  After obtaining word embeddings, the sentence embedding is the average of the sum of word vectors in a sentence. Then the final similarity is the average of word similarities according to a max alignment. Each word in sentence 1 is aligned to the most similar word in sentence 2, while each word in sentence 2 is aligned to the most similar word in sentence 1. Then the scores for the alignments in both directions are added and normalized by sentence length.

- **Universal Sentence Encoder (UNV).** Universal Sentence Encoder proposed by Cer et al. [1] is designed to encode sentences into embedding vectors that specifically target transfer learning. This model is found to be useful in the filtering stage in this study.

- **InferSent Model (INF).** InferSent model first proposed as a Facebook research project of learning universal representations of sentences [2]. In our study, we explore both GloVe and FastText pretrained word vectors proposed in their model [7, 13].

Using sentence embeddings, cosine and arccos measures are used to calculate the final similarity score, defined as follows.

$$sim_{\cos} = \cos(v_1, v_2),$$
$$sim_{\arccos} = 1 - \frac{\arccos(\cos(v_1, v_2))}{\pi}.$$

Particularly, it is shown from the results that cosine distance measure is superior to the arccos measure.

These unsupervised methods are compared with the state-of-art supervised methods in paraphrase detection task, in order to evaluate the ability of the similarity measures used in the alignment. These methods include:

- Siamese Recurrent Neural Networks (MaLSTM) [11].
- TF-KLD: a discriminative improvement to distributional sentence similarity proposed by Ji et al. [6].

3.2 Sequential Alignment

In our scheme of constructing parallel corpus from comparable documents, we need to consider (a) the documents being aligned are potentially large, and (b) there exist sentences that are aligned with two or more sentences from the other document, and there also exist sentences that are not aligned at all.

These two scenarios lead to challenges in designing the sequential alignment algorithm, since the grouping of the sentences are not known in advance, the similarity score for each pair of groups is not pre-calculated. Furthermore, exhaustive enumeration of all possible groupings is intractable. Therefore, we make the following assumptions.

1. The number of sentences in each group does not exceed a maximum window size MAX_WINDOW_SIZE for each part enclosed by any two successive anchors of the document. Moreover, to handle the situation of shorter parts, the maximum number of sentences is proportional to a factor, defined as SIZE_PER_TEN. The scaled limit

$$w_{max} = \texttt{SIZE\_PER\_TEN} \times \texttt{len}(part)/10$$

   is then compared with MAX_WINDOW_SIZE, and the minimum of them is the maximum number of sentences in a group.
2. Two aligned groups cannot appear farther than a limit MAX_DISTANCE. The assumption is that the aligned groups in the two documents do not locate far from each other, considering relative distance for the whole document. Suppose the index of a sentence in *doc1* is i, then the relative corresponding index in *doc2* is defined by $j = i \cdot \dfrac{l_2}{l_1}$, where $l_k, k = 1, 2$ denotes the document length, and the sentences in *doc2* out of the range $[j - \texttt{MAX\_LENGTH}, j + \texttt{MAX\_LENGTH}]$ will not be considered.

Based on these assumptions, we use a greedy alignment scheme. Between each successive pairs of anchors, the similarity scores for all possible pairs are calculated and sorted in decreasing order. In each pairing, the most similar pair is popped from the candidate list, and the remaining groups that include any sentence in the selected pair is deleted from the candidate list. The pairing stops until the similarity score for the most similar pair is below a predefined threshold, or the candidate list becomes empty. The greedy alignment process is illustrated in Algorithm 1.

Algorithm 1. Greedy Alignment.

Input: A sorted array (based on similarity score sim) of sentence group pairs
$Arr = [[g_1, g_2, sim], \ldots]$
Output: An collection of paired sentence groups
1 $A \leftarrow \emptyset$;
2 **while** $Arr[0].sim > threshold$ **do**
3 | $p \leftarrow Arr.pop(0)$;
4 | Add p into A; **foreach** $sentence\ s\ in\ p.g_1$ **do**
5 | | remove p' from Arr if $p'.g_1$ contains s;
6 | **end**
7 | **foreach** $sentence\ s\ in\ p.g_2$ **do**
8 | | remove p' from Arr if $p'.g_2$ contains s;
9 | **end**
10 **end**
11 **return** A;

---

4   Experimental Setup

We design two experiments, one for evaluating different similarity measures, and the other one for the sentence alignment. The datasets and metrics used are introduced below.

4.1   Similarity Measure

The similarity measure is evaluated based on a paraphrase detection task performed on Microsoft Research Paraphrase Corpus (MSRC), SICK, and Modern/Original Version of Shakespeare scripts. For unsupervised similarity measure, the three sentence embedding schemes with multiple embedding dimensions for word embeddings are combined with the two distance measures, and together with a set of thresholds, are used to label sentences with a similarity score above threshold as paraphrases. We also used BLEU [12] and ROUGE [9], as baseline models in this task.

4.2   Sentence Alignment

The datasets on sentence alignment are a part of the final documents that are aligned, including *Anna Karenina, The Story of Stone* and *The Brothers Karamazov*. Related data for each corpus is shown in Table 1.

Table 1. Size of datasets (number of words).

Corpus	Translation 1	Translation 2
Anna Karenina	21,398	20,973
The Story of Stone	46,034	56,256
The Brothers Karamazov	24,133	20,288

The evaluation of sentence alignment is based on the following considerations.

1. *Efficiency.* The time a model takes to align sentences should be reasonable with respect to the number of sentences in the raw documents.
2. *Percentage of aligned sentences.* Although the main focus of this research is to construct a corpus with high quality, the percentage of aligned sentences should also be considered. Namely, we want to assess how many sentences should be aligned are actually aligned by the model.
3. *Quality.* Since it is hard to assess whether all sentences are properly aligned or not, we sample a fraction of aligned sentences and decide whether each pair should be aligned manually. The quality of the alignment is evaluated as the percentage of the pairs that are "properly aligned" with respect to the number of total aligned pairs. The level of properness for a aligned pair is defined as follows, based on Huang's criteria [5].
   - **Good**:
     (a) completely the same;
     (b) possibly some word substitutions and structural modifications;
     (c) describe the same object, environment, or situation using different but the same type of adjectives, nouns, sentiments, etc.;
     (d) convey the same type of sentiments in short conversations.
   - **Good Partial**:
     (a) one sentence is good aligned with respect to a part of the other sentence;
     (b) the sentence contains some additional clauses or phrases that have information which is not contained within the other sentence;
   - **Partial**:
     (a) a part of a sentence is good aligned with respect to a part of the other sentence;
     (b) both sentences contain some additional clauses or phrases that have information which is not contained within the other;
   - **Bad**: the sentences discuss unrelated contents.

From above, the first three categories are considered as "properly aligned". The definition is relatively loose for stylized expressions. It happens that in an aligned sentence pair, one contains additional expressions than the other. But the main content of the pair should be consistent.

For the following discussion, the "percentage" represents the portion of sentences that are aligned in the raw documents, and the "quality" represents the portion of aligned pairs that are proper.

5   Results

Experimental results for similarity measure and sentence alignment are presented in the next two sections. It is shown that the unsupervised similarity measure is comparable with supervised similarity measures, and that we have a relatively strong similarity scoring system for sentence alignment. Then we verify that our sentence alignment model is superior to the baseline model in terms of robustness and quality.

5.1   Similarity Measure

The result for MSRC with different thresholds is shown in Fig. 2. From the figure we can observe that the highest accuracy is reached by "WDV + MAX + COS" at threshold around 0.7, with the second highest accuracy reached by the "UNV + COS" combination.

One observation is that the cosine measurement is superior to the arccos measurement, which is the case also for SICK and Shakespeare (SHPR). This might be an indication that cosine measure is a more reasonable measure for spatial distance in the vector space of sentence embeddings.

For each experimented similarity measurement method, the best dimension for word embedding and the best threshold is used for the final comparison. The dimension is fixed as 100. The results for both supervised and unsupervised methods are shown in Table 2. (INF-F and INF-G are InferSent models using GloVe and fasttext pretrained word vectors, respectively).

From the results, we can conclude that the similarity measurement ability on both standard paraphrase corpus and literature corpus is competent compared with state-of-art similarity models, and especially, supervised models. In the sentence alignment task, the ability to measure sentence similarity and the

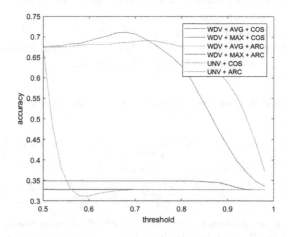

Fig. 2. Accuracies for MSRC with different threshold t.

Table 2. Paraphrase detection accuracies.

Method	Corpus		
	Accuracy (%)		
	MSRC	SICK	SHPR
WDV + AVG + COS	32.8	36.6	52.5
WDV + MAX + COS	71.1	68.1	72.0
WDV + AVG + ARC	32.9	36.7	53.9
WDV + MAX + ARC	34.9	39.4	54.7
UNV + COS	67.9	**74.2**	77.6
UNV + ARC	67.2	63.5	50.0
INF-F + COS	**72.2**	72.5	**78.6**
INF-F + ARC	67.2	63.5	50.6
INF-G + COS	70.4	73.0	73.9
INF-G + ARC	67.2	63.4	50.8
MaLSTM	56.9	78.3	71.6
TF-KLD	70.8	74.5	86.1
BLEU	69.9	65.9	71.0
ROUGE	71.3	67.8	71.8

efficiency of this evaluation should both be considered, since the documents to be aligned might be so large that the sentence encoding model costs a lot of computing resources.

5.2   Sentence Alignment

Table 3 shows how filter mechanism affects the alignment quantity and quality[1]. The results verify that our filter scheme does largely improve the overall performances of alignment models. Specifically, "BLEU + UNV" and "WDV + UNV" combinations outperform other models in both quality and quantity, these two combinations will be used for end-to-end comparison.

Table 3. Quantitative results (*Notre Dame de Paris*).

Result	Model									
	BLEU	INF	WDV	UNV	BLEU + UNV	BLEU + INF	WDV + UNV	WDV + INF	INF + UNV	UNV + INF
Time	1.9 min	8.4 min	4.5 min	1.7 h	10.8 min	9.8 min	19.4 min	8.1 min	24.8 min	3.6 h
Percentage [%]	73.7	70.9	73.7	42.2	87.1	85.0	85.6	85.2	17.7	53.6
Quality [%]	100	98	98	91	100	100	98	97	100	99

---

[1] The model names are abbreviated as "model + filter" schemes. For instance, "BLEU + UNV" means BLEU model for the first three stages of alignment, and Universal Sentence Encoder model for the last stage of filtering.

We perform our alignment model on other three pairs of documents, *Anna Karenina*, *The Story of Stone*, and *The Brothers Karamazov*. The results are shown in Table 4.

Table 4. Quantitative results ([1] *Notre Dame de Paris*, [2] *The Story of Stone*) G: Good, GP: Good Partial, P: Partial, B: Bad.

Model	Result						
	Time	Percentage [%]	G [%]	GP [%]	P [%]	B [%]	Quality [%]
Anna Karenina							
This work	0.78 h	**68.7**	90	5	3	2	**98**
Bleualign	23.44 s	37.2	53	19	5	23	77
The Story of Stone							
This work	8.2 h	19.2	35	29	16	20	**80**
Bleualign	51.56 s	25.5	10	11	19	60	40
The Brothers Karamazov							
This work	1.1 h	**53.2**	67	24	7	2	**98**
Bleualign	24.33 s	33.0	32	38	9	21	79

Although the baseline model, Bleualign performs the fastest among the compared schemes, it does not guarantee the quality of aligned sentences. Moreover, since it highly relies on word alignment, it fails in aligning comparable documents that are not so much alike at the first glance, such as *The Story of Stone*. The following shows a sample pair which is misaligned by the Bleualign model, but is properly aligned by our method.

Sentence: *His second child was a daughter, born strangely enough on the first day of the year.*
Bleualign: *The first qin emperor,*
Our model: *The second child she bore him was a little girl, rather remarkable because she was born on new year day.*

As a qualitative analysis on model misbehaviors, we take a few representative sentences from the results that are not properly aligned by different models in the experiment, as is in Table 5.

One can notice that word-based alignment schemes, such as BLEU, WDV, and the Bleualign model, is not competent in handling short sentences, while sentence-based alignment schemes fail in cases of longer sentences. This can serve as an argument for using similarity measurements from both perspectives, as a compensation for each other. Furthermore, word-level similarity measures

Table 5. Sample misaligned sentences.

Model	Misaligned Sentence (False Positive [FP] or False Negative [FN])
Bleualign [FP]	*baoyu clapped his hands in approval* *you're getting quite a temper lately, master bao*
BLEU [FN]	*xiang-yan and bao-chai were present that day, it was true; but the absence of...to burst into tears* *seeing xiangyun and baochai there but not...wanted to take off some clothes*
INF [FP]	*the priest whom the girls had noticed...was indeed archdeacon claude frollo.* (31 words) *but she has three things...hands by squeezing her waist* (79 words)
WDV [FP]	*what's at stake here are the women* *are there women or are there not?*
UNV [FP]	*the mob repeated with a frenzied cheer* *and among the monsters thus...in front of a candle* (48 words)

can serve as better anchors in the first stage of our model, and sentence-level similarity measures serve well as filters in the second stage, since sentence level encoders normally takes longer time to embed sentences in every single run.

6   Constructing a Monolingual Parallel Corpus

We then proceed to construct a monolingual parallel corpus using the sentence alignment model. The corpus mainly comes from different versions of translation of 10 literature works. A complete list of information about the aligned works is shown Table 6.

To evaluate the quality of the alignment, a sample batch of sentences are selected and manually decided on whether the alignment is reasonable based on the criteria described above. The quality of the parallel corpus is represented by the percentage of "true positive" with respect to the total number of aligned pairs. Our work achieves reasonable alignment efficiency and generates high quality sentences for text rewriting rules.

In order to guarantee the quality of the corpus, the percentage of aligned sentences with respect to the original length is not necessarily maximized. Besides, some aligned pairs contain sentences that are exactly identical. We did not discard them, since in order to learn monolingual text rewriting rules, the mappings of some expressions to themselves is also included in the style parameter. However, for training or evaluating semantic similarity models, those sentences might be ignored.

Table 6. Aligned corpora.

Corpus	Information				
	Author	Translator	Length	Aligned (%)	Quality (%)
Notre Dame de Paris	Victor Hugo	Alban Krailsheimer	10272	86.3	99.4
		I. F. Hapgood	10179	87.0	
Les Miserables	Victor Hugo	Julie Rose	34145	76.4	99.0
		I. F. Hapgood	34328	76.0	
The Story of Stone	Cao Xueqin	Yang Xianyi	46034	9.7	94.0
		David Hawkes	56256	8.6	
The Brothers Karamazov	F. Dostoevsky	A. R. MacAndrew	24133	58.6	95.3
		Richard Pevear	20288	68.1	
Crime and Punishment	F. Dostoevsky	Michael R. Katz	14503	70.6	93.9
		Richard Pevear	12938	76.2	
The Magic Mountain	Thomas Mann	John E. Woods	14464	83.8	97.6
		H. T. Lowe-Porter	14231	83.8	
The Illiad	Homer	Ian C. Johnston	7744	68.1	72.5
		Robert Fagles	7237	58.5	
Don Quixote	Cervantes Saavedra	John Rutherford	11902	48.5	84.4
		John Ormsby	9056	58.3	
Anna Karenina	Leo Tolstoy	Pevear and Volokhonsky	21398	74.6	99.3
		Rosamund Bartlett	20971	74.5	
Madame Bovary	Gustave Flaubert	Eleanor Marx-Aveling	6670	73.9	97.6
		Margaret Mauldon	6837	72.8	

7   Discussion and Conclusion

From our results we can conclude that performances of models based on word-level similarity, such as BLEU and Word2Vec model, are in general better than those based on sentence-level similarity, such as InferSent and Universal Sentence Encoder. When aligning different versions of a literature work, word-level similarity is sufficient to identify paraphrases based on common or similar words, while a second filtering further enhance the performance as a compensation for sentence semantics. Therefore, for aligning new documents, BLEU + UNV or Word2Vec + UNV might be the first things to try because they mostly rely on word-level similarities.

In sum, we made a comprehensive analysis of similarity measures, and demonstrated the competence of unsupervised methods, which are then used for sentence alignment. We experimented multiple alignment schemes and compared the quality and efficiency with currently popular alignment model. We then constructed a parallel corpus from different versions of literature works. This corpus can serve as a high-quality learning source or an evaluation set for text rewriting rules, especially for text style transfer.

References

1. Cer, D., et al.: Universal sentence encoder. arXiv preprint arXiv:1803.11175 (2018)

2. Conneau, A., Kiela, D., Schwenk, H., Barrault, L., Bordes, A.: Supervised learning of universal sentence representations from natural language inference data. arXiv preprint arXiv:1705.02364 (2017)

3. Coster, W., Kauchak, D.: Learning to simplify sentences using Wikipedia. In: Proceedings of the Workshop on Monolingual Text-to-Text Generation, pp. 1–9. Association for Computational Linguistics (2011)

4. Hatzlvassiloglou, V., Klavans, J.L., Eskin, E.: Detecting text similarity over short passages: exploring linguistic feature combinations via machine learning. In: 1999 Joint SIGDAT Conference on Empirical Methods in Natural Language Processing and Very Large Corpora (1999)

5. Hwang, W., Hajishirzi, H., Ostendorf, M., Wu, W.: Aligning sentences from standard Wikipedia to simple Wikipedia. In: Proceedings of the 2015 Conference of the North American Chapter of the Association for Computational Linguistics: Human Language Technologies, pp. 211–217 (2015)

6. Ji, Y., Eisenstein, J.: Discriminative improvements to distributional sentence similarity. In: Proceedings of the 2013 Conference on Empirical Methods in Natural Language Processing, pp. 891–896 (2013)

7. Joulin, A., Grave, E., Bojanowski, P., Mikolov, T.: Bag of tricks for efficient text classification. In: Proceedings of the 15th Conference of the European Chapter of the Association for Computational Linguistics: Volume 2, Short Papers, pp. 427–431. Association for Computational Linguistics (April 2017)

8. Kajiwara, T., Komachi, M.: Building a monolingual parallel corpus for text simplification using sentence similarity based on alignment between word embeddings. In: Proceedings of COLING 2016, The 26th International Conference on Computational Linguistics: Technical Papers, pp. 1147–1158 (2016)

9. Lin, C.Y.: ROUGE: a package for automatic evaluation of summaries. Text Summarization Branches Out (2004)

10. Mikolov, T., Sutskever, I., Chen, K., Corrado, G.S., Dean, J.: Distributed representations of words and phrases and their compositionality. In: Advances in Neural Information Processing Systems, pp. 3111–3119 (2013)

11. Mueller, J., Thyagarajan, A.: Siamese recurrent architectures for learning sentence similarity. In: Thirtieth AAAI Conference on Artificial Intelligence (2016)

12. Papineni, K., Roukos, S., Ward, T., Zhu, W.J.: BLEU: a method for automatic evaluation of machine translation. In: Proceedings of the 40th Annual Meeting on Association for Computational Linguistics, pp. 311–318. Association for Computational Linguistics (2002)

13. Pennington, J., Socher, R., Manning, C.: Glove: global vectors for word representation. In: Proceedings of the 2014 Conference on Empirical Methods in Natural Language Processing (EMNLP), pp. 1532–1543 (2014)

14. Zamani, H., Faili, H., Shakery, A.: Sentence alignment using local and global information. Comput. Speech Lang. **39**, 88–107 (2016)

15. Zhu, Z., Bernhard, D., Gurevych, I.: A monolingual tree-based translation model for sentence simplification. In: Proceedings of the 23rd International Conference on Computational Linguistics, pp. 1353–1361. Association for Computational Linguistics (2010)

An In-depth Analysis of Graph Neural Networks for Semi-supervised Learning

Yuyan Chen, Sen Hu, and Lei Zou$^{(\boxtimes)}$

Peking University, Beijing, China
{yuyanchen,husen,zoulei}@pku.edu.cn

Abstract. Graph Neural Networks have experienced a rapid development in the last few years and become powerful tools for many machine learning tasks in graph domain. Graph Convolution Network is a breakthrough and become a strong baseline for node classification task. To this end, we perform a thorough experiment for several prominent GCN-related models, including GAT, AGNN, Co-Training GCN and Stochastic GCN. We found that different models take their advantages in different scenarios, depending on training set size, graph structure and datasets. Through our in-depth analysis of attention mechanism, dataset splits and the preprocessing for knowledge graphs, we report some interesting findings. And we look into GCNs for knowledge graphs carefully, then propose a new scheme for data processing, which achieves a better performance compared to traditional methods.

Keywords: GCN · Attention mechanism · Knowledge graph

1 Introduction

Graph neural networks (GNNs) are deep learning methods targeting on graph domain, first introduced in [5] and [10]. The main idea of GNNs is to make use of graph topology structure as well as nodes' (and edges') features. More specifically, GNNs update a node's hidden state using its neighbors', edges' and its own hidden states in last layer [16], which can be denoted as follow:

$$\mathbf{h}_v^{(t+1)} = f(\mathbf{h}_v^{(t)}, \mathbf{h}_{ne[v]}^{(t)}, \mathbf{h}_{co[v]}^{(t)}) \tag{1}$$

where $\mathbf{h}_v^{(t)}$ denotes the hidden state vector of node v at the time step t, $\mathbf{h}_{ne[v]}^{(t)}$ denotes the representation of v's neighbors, and $\mathbf{h}_{co[v]}^{(t)}$ stands for the representation of its edges.

Many variants of GNNs were proposed in recent years and have achieved state-of-the-art performance. Roughly speaking, these models vary in terms of tasks, propagation step or training step. Graph analysis involves various tasks, including node classification, link prediction, graph classification, and clustering, etc. Node classification on graphs consisting of node information and undirected edges is one of the most classic problems, which is our main interest

X. Wang et al. (Eds.): JIST 2019, CCIS 1157, pp. 65–77, 2020.
https://doi.org/10.1007/978-981-15-3412-6_7

in this paper. On the propagation step, various aggregators can be adopted, which makes the main difference, such as convolutional aggregator [6,7], attention aggregator [12,13] and gate updater [9]. And for training methods, variants mainly include neighborhood sampling [6], receptive field control [4] and boosting [8]. We choose some representative models from aforementioned works to examine their performance.

Prominent models include graph attention networks (GATs) [13], Attention-based Graph Neural Networks (AGNNs) [12], Stochastic GCN [4], Co-Training GCN and Self-Training GCN [8]. Among these models, GATs and AGNNs introduce attention mechanism in different ways; Stochastic GCN proposes a stochastic approximation algorithm, speeding up GCN by a large margin; Co-Training GCN and Self-Training GCN manage to enlarge the training set with limited labeled data.

Our motivation of performing an evaluation is based on following reasons. First, not all these models evaluate on the same datasets. For instance, the NELL dataset is only evaluated in GCN and Stochastic GCN, and other models' performance on this dataset is unclear. Second, the experiment settings are different, e.g., Co-Training series methods report test accuracy under different label rate. Although all these models report experiment results, it's hard to determine their relative performance characteristics. Third, it is beneficial to further analyze some key components of these models, such as the attention mechanism and the preprocessing scheme used for knowledge graphs.

The main contributions of this paper can be summarized as follows:

- We run thorough experiments for several prominent GCN-related models, and find that their performance varies in different situations. GAT outperforms GCN in most cases, Co-Training Series methods might be useful in weak supervised settings, and Stochastic GCN achieves similar accuracy as GCN with much training time reduced.
- We analyze the attention mechanism deeply, including the difference between GAT and AGNN and how they work respectively. De facto, we find that the improvement of GAT may come mostly from its multi-head mechanism rather than the attention itself.
- We look into the correlation between test accuracy and data splits, finding that accuracy is related to the rate of *consistent nodes* in training set. And we run an extra experiment to prove this statistical finding, which may be able to guide a better data labeling for application.
- We introduce FB15K for multi-label node classification task, which allows us to do further experiments about the preprocessing scheme of knowledge graphs. We prove that current solution of running GCN on knowledge graphs has severe shortcomings, leading to relatively poor performance. Furthermore, we propose a new scheme of running GCN on knowledge graphs and achieve a better result.

The remainder of this paper is organized as follows. Section 2 reviews the background and preliminaries about graph neural networks. Section 3 describes the models we test in details. Section 4 shows our experiment results and take a deep analysis and Sect. 5 gives summarization and conclusion.

2   Preliminaries

Many real-world data are inherently graphs, such as social networks, chemical structures, protein structures and so on. Besides, due to the great expressive abilities, people use graph to denote various information, e.g., knowledge graph is a multi-relational graph composed of entities (nodes) and relations (edges).

Given a graph $\mathcal{G} = (\mathcal{V}, \mathcal{E})$, $\mathcal{V}$ is the set of nodes with $|\mathcal{V}| = n$ and $\mathcal{E}$ is the set of edges. Each node can have zero, one or multiple labels. We use $\mathcal{N}_i$ to indicate the set of node i's neighbors, and let $\tilde{\mathcal{N}}_i := \mathcal{N}_i \cup \{i\}$. $\mathbf{X}_i$ and Y_i denote the feature vector and label set of node i respectively. Y_L denotes the labels of a subset $L \subset V$ which are revealed to us. By putting nodes' features together, we get the feature matrix $\mathbf{X} = [\mathbf{X}_1, \mathbf{X}_2, ..., \mathbf{X}_n]$. Adjacency matrix $\mathbf{A} \in \mathbb{N}^{n \times n}$ is used to describe the graph. A non-zero value a_{ij} implies there is an edge from node i to node j. For unweighted graph, the matrix is binary. Otherwise, the value indicates the edge weight. Diagonal matrix $\mathbf{D} = \text{diag}(d_1, d_2, ..., d_n)$ is the degree matrix of $\mathbf{A}$ where $d_i = \sum_j a_{ij}$.

In a graph neural network, $\mathbf{W}$ is the weight matrix need to be trained by the network. And we use $\mathbf{O}$ to denote the final output matrix of the network, as $\mathbf{o_i}$ refers to the output of node i.

We have summarize some variants of GNNs in the last section. Among various models, we choose GCN, GAT, AGNN, Co-Training GCN and Stochastic GCN to run experiments. We will describe these models in detail in next section.

3   Models

3.1   GCN

The propagation of GCN can be generally formulated as follow:

$$\mathbf{H}^{(t+1)} = \sigma(\mathbf{P}\mathbf{H}^{(t)}\mathbf{W}^{(t)}), \quad \text{with} \quad \mathbf{P} = \tilde{\mathbf{D}}^{-\frac{1}{2}}\tilde{\mathbf{A}}\tilde{\mathbf{D}}^{-\frac{1}{2}} \tag{2}$$

where $\tilde{\mathbf{A}} = \mathbf{A} + \mathbf{I}_n$, $\tilde{\mathbf{D}}_{i,i} = \sum_j \tilde{\mathbf{A}}_{i,j}$ and σ is the activation function. More specifically, a two-layer GCN for multi-class classification would have the form

$$\mathbf{O} = \text{softmax}(\mathbf{P}\text{ReLU}(\mathbf{PXW}^{(0)})\mathbf{W}^{(1)}) \tag{3}$$

3.2   GAT

GAT is composed of several graph attention layers. A graph attention layer first applies a weight matrix to every node, completing a dimension transformation for nodes' hidden states, then a shared attention mechanism is used to compute attention coefficients between every two connected nodes. Afterwards, there follows a LeakyReLU function for nonlinearity and a softmax function for normalization. Additionally, multi-head attention is employed to keep the learning process steady, i.e., train K independent attention then concatenate or averaging output vectors. A two-layer GAT used in our experiment settings can be denoted as follows:

$$\alpha_{ij}^{(l)} = \text{softmax}_j(\text{LeakyReLU}([\mathbf{h}_i^{(l)}\mathbf{W}||\mathbf{h}_j^{(l)}\mathbf{W}]\mathbf{a}^{(l)})) \tag{4}$$

$$\mathbf{h}_i^{(1)} = \overset{K}{\underset{k=1}{||}} \text{ELU}(\sum_{j\in\tilde{\mathcal{N}}_i} \alpha_{ij}^k \mathbf{x}_j \mathbf{W}^{(0)}) \tag{5}$$

$$\mathbf{o}_i = \text{softmax}(\frac{1}{K}\sum_{k=1}^{K}\sum_{j\in\tilde{\mathcal{N}}_i} \alpha_{ij}^k \mathbf{h}_j^{(1)}\mathbf{W}^{(1)}) \tag{6}$$

where l indicates that current layer is l-th layer in the network, $\mathbf{h}_i^{(l)} \in \mathbb{R}^{d^{(l)}}$ is the $d^{(l)}$-dimensional hidden state of node i, $\mathbf{a}^{(l)} \in \mathbb{R}^{2d^{(l)}\times 1}$ is trained by the network.

3.3   AGNN

AGNN starts with a word-embedding layer, followed by several attention-guided propagation layers, at last an output layer. At the word-embedding layer, a dimension transformation is operated, simply a fully connected layer with ReLU activation:

$$\mathbf{H}^{(1)} = \text{ReLU}(\mathbf{X}\mathbf{W}^{(0)}) \tag{7}$$

At each attention-guided propagation layer, only a single parameter β need to be trained to calculate attention coefficients.

$$\alpha_{ij}^{(l)} = \text{softmax}_j(\beta^{(l)}\cos(\mathbf{h}_i^{(l)}, \mathbf{h}_j^{(l)})) \tag{8}$$

$$\mathbf{h}_i^{(l+1)} = \sum_{j\in\tilde{\mathcal{N}}_i} \alpha_{ij}^{(l)}\mathbf{h}_j^{(l)} \tag{9}$$

The output layer is similar to the word-embedding layer:

$$\mathbf{O} = \text{softmax}(\mathbf{H}^{(l+1)}\mathbf{W}^{(1)}) \tag{10}$$

3.4   Co-Training GCN and Self-Training GCN

Co-Training GCN and Self-Training GCN are actually pre-train techniques useful in weakly supervised settings. Co-Training GCN uses a random walk model to enlarge training set, while Self-Training uses a GCN instead.

Firstly, we need to determine how many labeled nodes are needed. The authors suggested to calculate η by $\bar{d}^\tau \times \eta \approx n$, with $\bar{d}$ be the average degree and τ be the number of layers of GCN, so η is expected to be the number of labels needed for a GCN to propagate them to cover the whole graph. Then a random walk model or a GCN model is run, and the most confident nodes for each class are added to the training set.

Co-Training GCN and Self-Training GCN can be combined. By adding the most confident nodes from Co-Training as well as those from Self-Training to the training set, we get "Union" method. We can also add common nodes from Co-Training and Self-Training, so the extended training set should be more accurate, and this is called "Intersection" method.

3.5 Stochastic GCN

The main contribution of Stochastic GCN is that it proposes an approximation for GCN iteration, which can save much computation, and theoretically converge to a local optimum of GCN. The neighbor sampling (NS) model was proposed by [6]. NS randomly chooses $D^{(l)}$ neighbors for each node at layer l, then the convolution become:

$$\mathbf{H}^{(l+1)} = \sigma((\hat{\mathbf{P}}^{(l)}\mathbf{H}^{(l)}\mathbf{W}^{(l)}) \tag{11}$$

where $\hat{\mathbf{P}}^{(l)}$ is the propagation matrix with a neighborhood sampling, in detail:

$$\hat{\mathbf{P}}^{(l)}_{ij} = \begin{cases} \frac{|\tilde{\mathcal{N}}_i|}{D^{(l)}}\mathbf{P}_{ij} & \text{if } j \in \hat{\mathcal{N}}(i) \\ 0 & \text{otherwise} \end{cases} \tag{12}$$

where $\hat{\mathcal{N}}(i)$ is a subset of $\tilde{\mathcal{N}}_i$, which is drawn randomly at each iteration. And $D^{(l)}$ is the neighbor sampling size set manually, so we have $\left|\hat{\mathcal{N}}(i)\right| = D^{(l)}$.

A control variate is added to the NS estimator to reduce its variance. A single layer of this control variate (CV) based model can be denoted as follow:

$$\mathbf{H}^{(l+1)} = \sigma((\hat{\mathbf{P}}^{(l)}(\mathbf{H}^{(l)} - \bar{\mathbf{H}}^{(l)}) + \mathbf{P}\bar{\mathbf{H}}^{(l)})\mathbf{W}^{(l)}) \tag{13}$$

where $\bar{\mathbf{H}}^{(l)}$ is the historical activations need to be maintained additionally.

There are two sources of randomness in such a model, one comes from neighbor sampling, which is estimated via CV, the other comes from random dropout of features. To deal with dropout, another estimator—control variate for dropout (CVD)—was proposed. Let $\text{dropout}_p(\mathbf{X}) = \mathbf{M} \circ \mathbf{X}$ be the dropout operation and E_M be the expectation over dropout masks, with $\mathbf{M}$ following a Bernoulli distribution and $\circ$ being element-wise product. Then CVD stores $\mu^{(l)} := E_M[\mathbf{H}^{(l)}]$ instead of $\mathbf{H}^{(l)}$, so as to get historical mean activation $\bar{\mu}^{(l)}$. The CVD model can be denoted with following form:

$$\mathbf{H}^{(l+1)} = \sigma(((\frac{1}{D^{(l)}}\mathbf{D})^{-\frac{1}{2}}\hat{\mathbf{P}}^{(l)}(\mathbf{H}^{(l)} - \mu^{(l)}) + \hat{\mathbf{P}}^{(l)}(\mu^{(l)} - \bar{\mu}^{(l)}) + \mathbf{P}\bar{\mu}^{(l)})\mathbf{W}^{(l)}) \tag{14}$$

4 Evaluations

4.1 Dataset

We use four datasets to test these models. Cora, Citeseer and Pubmed are citation networks from [7], and NELL is a knowledge graph from [4]. The NELL dataset used in [4] is slightly different from that given by [7] in terms of data split and nodes features.[1] In citation networks, nodes are documents with bag-of-words or TF-IDF features, and edges are citation relations treated as undirected in our experiments. NELL is a knowledge graph composed of triples. As GCN doesn't have the ability to deal with edge information, each relation is split into two nodes, converting triple (s, p, o) to (s, p_1) and (o, p_2) [15]. After the splitting, we get a heterogeneous bipartite graph. More statistical information about datasets are summarized in Table 1. As GAT stores different transition matrix in each layer, it requires memory proportional to the quadratic of number of nodes. So it is difficult to run the original NELL dataset. To solve this problem, we extract a subgraph of NELL composed of 11,460 nodes, called NELL-10K. And it achieves similar accuracy in GCN, with training time reducing more than 90%. We use NELL-10K for experiments.

Table 1. Dataset statistics.

Dataset	Type	Nodes	Edges	Classes	Features
Cora	Citation network	2,708	5,429	7	Bag-of-words
Citeseer	Citation network	3,327	4,732	6	Bag-of-words
Pubmed	Citation network	19,717	44,338	3	TF-IDF
NELL	Knowledge graph	65,755	266,144	105	One-hot encoding
NELL-10K	Knowledge graph	11,460	49,780	105	One-hot encoding

4.2   Setup

For each model to be tested, we follow the setup and hyper-parameters in original literature unless otherwise mentioned. Firstly, we test the classification accuracy based on the given data split, which contains 20 labeled data per class, and 500 nodes for validation, 1000 nodes for test. Then we alter the training set size and report corresponding results.

4.3   Results

Accuracy on Fixed Data Splits. We run tests on fixed data splits from [7] on all models. NELL dataset is not fully tested in original experiments. While some models may not be designed for NELL, we run the experiment and report the results anyway. As Co-Training series approaches follow GCN's architecture, we just use the same hyper-parameters. We did a grid search for GAT and AGNN, and the best performance presents with a 3-layer GAT, each layer consisting of 8 attention heads computing 32 features, and a 3-layer AGNN with hidden layer size of 32 units. We perform 10 runs and report the mean classification accuracy and standard deviation in percent, see Table 2.

---

[1] The NELL data we used can be found in https://github.com/thu-ml/stochastic_gcn/releases/download/0.1/nell.tar.gz.

Table 2. Classification accuracy in percent on given data split.

	Cora	Citeseer	Pubmed	NELL-10K
GCN	81.5 ± 0.71	70.8 ± 0.89	79.0 ± 0.28	65.8 ± 1.48
GAT	83.8 ± 0.64	72.2 ± 0.40	77.7 ± 0.70	68.8 ± 1.76
AGNN	81.9 ± 0.34	70.4 ± 0.41	78.8 ± 0.62	68.5 ± 1.31
Co-Training	81.2 ± 0.51	69.2 ± 0.61	77.7 ± 0.24	51.3 ± 0.27
Self-Training	80.9 ± 0.65	70.5 ± 0.81	78.6 ± 0.40	62.6 ± 1.54
Union	81.8 ± 0.61	69.2 ± 0.47	78.8 ± 0.39	60.2 ± 1.21
Intersection	78.1 ± 0.58	72.1 ± 0.46	77.7 ± 0.62	65.5 ± 1.47
Stochastic - exact	81.4 ± 0.78	70.8 ± 0.67	78.3 ± 0.40	64.8 ± 1.14
Stochastic - NS	75.7 ± 1.59	68.0 ± 1.46	74.6 ± 1.53	54.7 ± 1.42
Stochastic - CV	81.0 ± 0.85	69.9 ± 0.82	77.6 ± 0.79	64.6 ± 1.03
Stochastic - CVD	80.5 ± 0.40	70.7 ± 0.94	78.9 ± 0.66	64.8 ± 1.25

Table 3. Training time of Stochastic models (seconds).

	Cora	Citeseer	Pubmed	NELL-10K
Stochastic - exact	4.52	4.12	6.46	2.51
Stochastic - NS	1.69	1.39	1.32	1.75
Stochastic - CV	3.02	2.51	2.08	2.89
Stochastic - CVD	2.90	2.66	2.68	3.15

GAT shows better performance on Cora, Citeseer and NELL-10K with a gap larger than the standard deviation compared to GCN. Intersection proves to be useful on Citeseer. And AGNN achieve similar performance as GAT on NELL-10K. While in other cases, no models outperform GCN significantly.

Table 4. Accuracy under different training set size on Cora.

	2	4	10	20	50
GCN	54.9 ± 8.59	63.0 ± 5.16	74.4 ± 1.63	79.9 ± 1.42	83.6 ± 0.73
Co-Training	58.6 ± 6.61	65.1 ± 6.33	72.7 ± 3.35	79.1 ± 1.71	83.1 ± 1.09
Self-Training	61.1 ± 7.06	68.7 ± 3.33	76.1 ± 1.38	79.9 ± 1.19	82.7 ± 1.05
LP	57.0 ± 8.18	60.4 ± 5.25	62.7 ± 3.56	67.8 ± 1.90	72.6 ± 1.79
Union	60.9 ± 6.40	68.5 ± 3.91	76.2 ± 1.68	80.5 ± 1.23	83.3 ± 1.04
Intersection	60.1 ± 6.69	68.9 ± 2.97	73.7 ± 1.53	79.2 ± 1.37	82.7 ± 0.77
GAT	63.4 ± 8.32	72.1 ± 3.12	77.4 ± 1.88	81.8 ± 1.31	85.1 ± 1.05
AGNN	54.3 ± 6.93	65.1 ± 3.83	75.5 ± 2.01	79.6 ± 1.67	83.8 ± 0.97

Table 5. Accuracy under different training set size on Citeseer.

	2	4	10	20	50	100
GCN	44.1 ± 5.97	53.7 ± 4.28	65.2 ± 1.93	67.7 ± 1.84	71.6 ± 1.24	72.8 ± 0.85
Co-Training	40.4 ± 7.23	51.0 ± 6.72	59.8 ± 3.86	64.0 ± 2.52	68.6 ± 1.59	70.3 ± 0.82
Self-Training	50.4 ± 5.39	59.3 ± 4.44	66.0 ± 1.11	67.8 ± 1.22	70.7 ± 1.43	71.4 ± 0.84
LP	36.7 ± 6.06	38.8 ± 4.62	43.0 ± 2.16	44.5 ± 2.79	49.5 ± 2.49	54.1 ± 1.78
Union	49.0 ± 5.05	55.6 ± 5.04	63.4 ± 2.15	65.7 ± 1.95	69.4 ± 1.53	70.6 ± 0.74
Intersection	49.0 ± 7.38	60.5 ± 7.69	68.2 ± 1.17	69.8 ± 1.43	71.4 ± 1.48	72.0 ± 6.53
GAT	49.7 ± 6.57	59.1 ± 4.11	67.2 ± 1.98	69.3 ± 1.63	72.4 ± 1.17	74.1 ± 1.17
AGNN	50.0 ± 6.37	58.3 ± 3.64	66.6 ± 1.34	69.5 ± 1.28	73.8 ± 1.45	74.3 ± 0.93

Table 6. Accuracy under different training set size on Pubmed.

	2	4	10	20	50	100
GCN	63.3 ± 7.78	67.9 ± 4.99	75.4 ± 1.79	78.8 ± 1.87	82.2 ± 1.83	84.3 ± 0.87
Co-Training	62.9 ± 8.87	67.4 ± 6.18	75.2 ± 5.79	77.6 ± 3.07	81.7 ± 1.27	83.8 ± 1.12
Self-Training	66.7 ± 9.14	69.4 ± 5.10	75.7 ± 2.11	77.6 ± 2.49	81.5 ± 1.33	82.7 ± 0.78
LP	62.5 ± 10.37	65.3 ± 7.70	68.0 ± 4.32	68.5 ± 2.20	69.3 ± 2.65	70.5 ± 1.14
Union	65.8 ± 8.80	68.9 ± 5.29	77.1 ± 2.09	78.9 ± 2.04	82.4 ± 0.95	84.0 ± 0.90
Intersection	66.0 ± 8.47	69.1 ± 4.20	74.4 ± 2.79	77.0 ± 2.45	70.5 ± 1.63	83.0 ± 0.70
GAT	66.7 ± 7.51	69.2 ± 4.01	75.0 ± 2.05	78.0 ± 1.99	81.4 ± 1.40	83.5 ± 0.73
AGNN	63.4 ± 8.85	67.9 ± 4.66	74.4 ± 2.66	77.4 ± 1.32	80.1 ± 1.77	81.8 ± 1.49

Stochastic GCN implements several models, where the exact model is equivalent to GCN and NS, CV, CVD are approximations of GCN. Their training time is summarized in Table 3. CV and CVD model achieve similar accuracy as GCN, while reducing training time by a large margin.

Accuracy Under Different Training Set Size. [8] claims that Co-Training and Self-Training approaches can improve GCN with very few labels, so we alter training set size, and run GCN, Co-Training, Self-Training, GAT and AGNN to check their performance. We set the training set as 2, 4, 10, 20, 50 nodes per class on Cora, and 2, 4, 10, 20, 50, 100 on Citeseer and Pubmed. Validation is only used in GAT for early stopping. We do 10 random splits and share them among all models. Other parameters for models remain unchanged. Results are reported in Tables 4, 5 and 6.

On all three datasets, Co-Training series approaches perform better than GCN only when labeled nodes are few. When there are sufficient nodes (20 nodes per class seem to be enough), Co-Training and Self-Training do not take their advantages. Co-Training relies heavily on the quality of graph structure, as we can see that when LP method performs poorly, e.g., in Citeseer where the graph is composed of several components, Co-Training leads to worse performance.

Surprisingly, GAT outperforms GCN by a large margin with few labeled nodes. We will do more analysis about GAT and AGNN in next subsection.

4.4   Analysis

Attention Mechanism. GAT and AGNN both introduce attention mechanism, but in different ways. GAT refers to self-attention, concatenating two hidden states and product a layer-shared vector to get coefficients, while AGNN computes the cosine similarity between nodes' states, assuming that more information should be passed between similar nodes than different ones.

We calculate inter-class relevance score by accumulating propagation coefficients between classes, i.e, the total amount of message passed between classes, then comparing it to a constant attention mechanism where $\alpha_{ij} = \frac{1}{|N(i)|}$.

$$Message(c_2 \rightarrow c_1) = \frac{1}{|S_{c_1,c_2}|} \sum_{(i,j) \in S_{c_1,c_2}} \alpha_{ij} \tag{15}$$

$$Relevance_{Model}(c_2 \rightarrow c_1) = \frac{Message_{Model}(c_2 \rightarrow c_1) - Message_{constant}(c_2 \rightarrow c_1)}{Message_{constant}(c_2 \rightarrow c_1)} \tag{16}$$

where $S_{c_1,c_2} = \{(i,j)|(i,j) \in \mathcal{E} \wedge Y_i = c_1 \wedge Y_j = c_2\}$.

Due to limited space, we only present the attention matrix of Cora in Fig. 1.

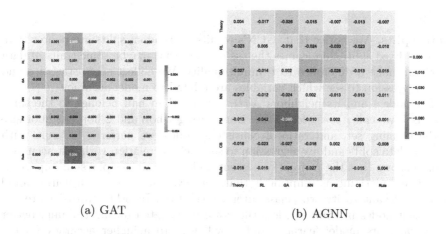

(a) GAT   (b) AGNN

Fig. 1. Inter-class relevance for GAT and AGNN on Cora dataset.

The diagonal entries for AGNN are all positive, indicating that AGNN puts more weight on the message passed between the same class, while GAT does not show such tendencies. Actually, the attention coefficients calculated by GAT are very similar to constant attention. When we remove the multi-head attention in GAT, the test results do not outperform GCN. Since the propagation doesn't have much variance, the improvement of GAT may come mostly from its multi-head mechanism rather than the attention.

[8] proves that the graph convolution is a special form of Laplacian smoothing. So as the number of graph convolution layers goes up, the features of vertices within a component tends to converge to same values, which makes nodes of different types indistinguishable. GCN achieves the best performance with two convolutional layers and suffers from converging features as well as overfitting when adopting a deeper model. Attention mechanism, on the other hand, makes deeper models possible. By putting different weights to edges, more useful message and less noise are passed across the graph. AGNN only trains one parameter on each propagation layer, so the over-fitting problem caused by too many parameters is avoided to some extent. As shown in Table 7, GCN's performance drops rapidly with deeper models, GAT shows a slow decrease and AGNN basically keeps steady.

Table 7. Various layers GCN, GAT and AGNN performance on Citeseer.

	GCN	GAT	AGNN
2-layer	70.8 ± 0.89	72.2 ± 0.48	70.6 ± 0.34
3-layer	64.6 ± 3.56	71.4 ± 0.97	70.1 ± 0.44
4-layer	50.0 ± 11.06	68.0 ± 1.99	70.4 ± 0.41

Data Splits. We notice that, GCN's results on random splits are poorer than those on fixed split. Here comes the assumption that maybe some traits of data split can make a difference to training quality. We collect some statistics and run a regression to see which variables are related to model accuracy.

For node i and its neighbors $\mathcal{N}(i)$, if more than half belongs to the same class as i, we call i *consistent node*. Considering 1-hop and 2-hop neighbor size of the training set, and ratio of consistent nodes, we perform 100 runs with random data splits and use regression to see their correlation with test accuracy. Table 8 shows that the ratio of consistent nodes in train set plays an important role. The underlying assumption is that, an inconsistent node's features would be less relevant to its true class after convolution. In other words, more the consistent nodes in train set, less the noise propagated during training, better the parameters model learned, and it will lead to a higher accuracy on the test set.

Next, we remove all edges connecting two nodes belonging to different types, and feed this adjacency in training. Then for testing, we feed the original adjacency matrix. This method is called M1. Results in Table 9 show a significant increase. Such results in turn support out previous assumption, that decrease noise helps training the model. This can be a useful guideline for data labeling in real-world application. Meanwhile, it also suggests possible improvement if we are able to reduce noise or somehow let model learn such information.

Table 8. Regression results between accuracy and some variables.

	1-hop size		2-hop size		rate_0		rate_1		rate_2	
	t	p	t	p	t	p	t	p	t	p
Cora	.67	.503	.57	.567	**2.13**	**.036**	.061	.546	.41	.681
Citeseer	−1.18	.239	.15	.881	**2.82**	**.006**	1.70	.092	.37	.712
Pubmed	.50	.619	−.49	.627	**4.02**	**.000**	.91	.367	−.37	.714

[1] 1-hop size and 2-hop size refer to the number of nodes in 1-hop and 2-hop of train nodes respectively, rate_0 refers to the rate of consistent nodes in train set, rate_1 and rate_2 stand for the rate of consistent nodes in 1-hop and 2-hop neighbors of train nodes.

[2] Statistic t comes from a linear regression t-test. Greater the absolute value of t, less the p value, more relevant is the dependent variable to the independent variable. A p value less than significance level (usually chosen as 0.05) indicates significant correlation between two variables.

Table 9. Results of feeding noiseless adjacency during training.

	Cora	Citeseer	Pubmed
GCN	79.9 ± 1.42	67.7 ± 1.84	78.8 ± 1.87
M1	$\textbf{81.5} \pm \textbf{1.29}$	$\textbf{70.3} \pm \textbf{1.67}$	$\textbf{79.7} \pm \textbf{2.63}$

4.5 Knowledge Graph

The preprocessing scheme used for knowledge graph—splitting (s, p, o) to (s, p_1) and (o, p_2)—was widely used. A significant shortcoming of such procedure is that it removes the link between s and o. Examples are demonstrated in Fig. 2.

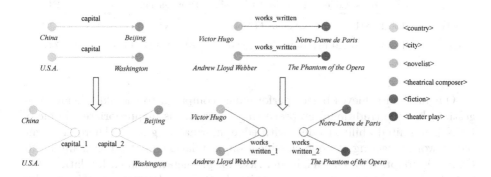

Fig. 2. Examples of the preprocessing scheme for knowledge graph.

By a 2-layer GCN, *China* and *U.S.A*, *Beijing* and *Washington* convolve each other's features. There underlies the assumption that entities on the same end of one relation tend to have the same type. So it is helpful for classifying nodes of type <country> as they always present on the left end of relation "capital", and type <city> on the right end. However, sometimes this scheme will confuse entities of different types. Given the triples (*Victor Hugo*, works_written, *Notre-Dame de Paris*) and (*Andrew Lloyd Webber*, works_written, *The Phantom of the Opera*), if we know that *Notre-Dame de Paris* is a fiction and *The Phantom of the Opera* is a theater play, it's not difficult to classify *Victor Hugo* to a novelist and *Andrew Lloyd Webber* to a theatrical composer. But in the split graph, *Victor Hugo* and *Andrew Lloyd Webber* would become indistinguishable.

We propose a new method of fitting knowledge graph to GCN: the relation linked to an entity is used as features (relations of s and o are treated differently), then GCN is operated in original graph regardless of edges' information. To better preserve features of current nodes, we replace $\mathbf{P} = \tilde{\mathbf{D}}^{-\frac{1}{2}}\tilde{\mathbf{A}}\tilde{\mathbf{D}}^{-\frac{1}{2}}$ by $\mathbf{P} = \rho(\mathbf{D}^{-\frac{1}{2}}\mathbf{A}\mathbf{D}^{-\frac{1}{2}}) + (1-\rho)\mathbf{I}_n$, where $\rho \in (0,1)$ is an additional trainable variable.

We here introduce FB15K [2]—a database extracted from a large-scale KG, FreeBase [1]—for further experiments on multi-label classification. Following [14], we extracted all type information of entities in FB15K from Freebase, then sort by frequencies. Top 50 types, except for the first one "common/topic" almost all entities have, are selected for classification.

FB15K contains 14,951 entities and 1,345 relations. So our method will assign 2,690-dimensional features to entities. We did a slight change to the preprocessing scheme in [15], that is, if there are multiple edges between an entity node and a relation node, we maintain the frequency in adjacency matrix instead of setting them to 1. We select 144 labeled nodes as training set, ensuring that positive examples for each class occur no less than 10 times. Some statistics and test results are summarized in Table 10.

Table 10. Data statistics and F1 score on FB15K with two solutions.

	Nodes	Edges	Features (dimension)	Propagation	F1
Scheme in [15]	17,641	308,006	One-hot (17,641)	$\tilde{\mathbf{D}}^{-\frac{1}{2}}\tilde{\mathbf{A}}\tilde{\mathbf{D}}^{-\frac{1}{2}}$	73.1
Our method	14,951	260,184	Relations (2,690)	$\rho(\mathbf{D}^{-\frac{1}{2}}\mathbf{A}\mathbf{D}^{-\frac{1}{2}}) + (1-\rho)\mathbf{I}_n$	**74.1**

Our method achieves better performance compared to the old scheme, suggesting that the traditional preprocessing procedure is inappropriate. De facto, GCN has limited ability to deal with edge-informative graphs. There are some recent work targeting at node classification on relational data. For example, R-GCN [11] adopts different weight matrices for propagation on each relation, and RGAT [3] introduces attention mechanism to R-GCN. However, in a knowledge graph with thousands of relations, such huge amounts of parameters may be hard to train. GNNs for knowledge graphs remains a challenge.

5   Conclusion

In this paper, we present a comparison of several prominent models for node classification, including GCN, GAT, AGNN, Co-Training GCN and Stochastic GCN. Generally speaking, GAT performs best while its improvement may come mostly from the multi-head mechanism rather than the attention mechanism. Co-Training series methods are useful with very few labeled nodes. We found test accuracy is significantly related to the rate of consistent nodes in the training set, which means if we can remove as much noise as we can for training, it may help improve the model. The preprocessing scheme used for knowledge graph involves message loss, then we propose a new scheme and achieve better performance. Still, new GNN models designed for knowledge graph are needed.

References

1. Bollacker, K., Evans, C., Paritosh, P., Sturge, T., Taylor, J.: Freebase: a collaboratively created graph database for structuring human knowledge. In: SIGMOD, pp. 1247–1250. ACM (2008)
2. Bordes, A., Usunier, N., Garcia-Duran, A., Weston, J., Yakhnenko, O.: Translating embeddings for modeling multi-relational data. In: NIPS, pp. 2787–2795 (2013)
3. Busbridge, D., Sherburn, D., Cavallo, P., Hammerla, N.Y.: Relational graph attention networks. arXiv preprint arXiv:1904.05811 (2019)
4. Chen, J., Zhu, J., Song, L.: Stochastic training of graph convolutional networks with variance reduction. In: ICML, pp. 941–949 (2018)
5. Gori, M., Monfardini, G., Scarselli, F.: A new model for learning in graph domains. In: IJCNN, vol. 2, pp. 729–734. IEEE (2005)
6. Hamilton, W., Ying, Z., Leskovec, J.: Inductive representation learning on large graphs. In: NIPS, pp. 1024–1034 (2017)
7. Kipf, T.N., Welling, M.: Semi-supervised classification with graph convolutional networks. In: ICLR (2017)
8. Li, Q., Han, Z., Wu, X.M.: Deeper insights into graph convolutional networks for semi-supervised learning. In: AAAI (2018)
9. Li, Y., Tarlow, D., Brockschmidt, M., Zemel, R.: Gated graph sequence neural networks. arXiv preprint arXiv:1511.05493 (2015)
10. Scarselli, F., Gori, M., Tsoi, A.C., Hagenbuchner, M., Monfardini, G.: The graph neural network model. IEEE Trans. Neural Netw. 20(1), 61–80 (2009)
11. Schlichtkrull, M., Kipf, T.N., Bloem, P., van den Berg, R., Titov, I., Welling, M.: Modeling relational data with graph convolutional networks. In: Gangemi, A., et al. (eds.) ESWC 2018. LNCS, vol. 10843, pp. 593–607. Springer, Cham (2018). https://doi.org/10.1007/978-3-319-93417-4_38
12. Thekumparampil, K.K., Wang, C., Oh, S., Li, L.J.: Attention-based graph neural network for semi-supervised learning. arXiv preprint arXiv:1803.03735 (2018)
13. Velikovi, P., Cucurull, G., Casanova, A., Romero, A., Lió, P., Bengio, Y.: Graph attention networks. In: ICLR (2018)
14. Xie, R., Liu, Z., Jia, J., Luan, H., Sun, M.: Representation learning of knowledge graphs with entity descriptions. In: AAAI (2016)
15. Yang, Z., Cohen, W., Salakhudinov, R.: Revisiting semi-supervised learning with graph embeddings. In: International Conference on Machine Learning, pp. 40–48 (2016)
16. Zhou, J., Cui, G., Zhang, Z., Yang, C., Liu, Z., Sun, M.: Graph neural networks: a review of methods and applications. arXiv preprint arXiv:1812.08434 (2018)

XTransE: Explainable Knowledge Graph Embedding for Link Prediction with Lifestyles in e-Commerce

Wen Zhang[1,2], Shumin Deng[1,2], Han Wang[1,2], Qiang Chen[3], Wei Zhang[3], and Huajun Chen[1,2(✉)]

[1] College of Computer Science and Technology, Zhejiang University,
Hangzhou, China
{wenzhang2015,231sm,wanghanwh,huajunsir}@zju.edu.cn
[2] Alibaba-Zhejiang University Joint Institute of Frontier Technologies,
Hangzhou, China
[3] Alibaba Group, Hangzhou, China
{lapu.cq,lantu.zw}@alibaba-inc.com

Abstract. In e-Commerce, we are interested in deals by lifestyle which will improve the diversity of items shown to users. A lifestyle, an important motivation for consumption, is a person's pattern of living in the world as expressed in activities, interests, and opinions. In this paper, we focus on the key task for deals by lifestyle, establishing linkage between items and lifestyles. We build an item-lifestyle knowledge graph to fully utilize the information about them and formulate it as a knowledge graph link prediction task. A lot of knowledge graph embedding methods are proposed to accomplish relational learning in academia. Although these methods got impressive results on benchmark datasets, they can't provide insights and explanations for their prediction which limit their usage in industry. In this scenario, we concern about not only linking prediction results, but also explanations for predicted results and human-understandable rules, because explanations help us deal with uncertainty from algorithms and rules can be easily transferred to other platforms. Our proposal includes an explainable knowledge graph embedding method (XTransE), an explanation generator and a rule collector, which outperforms traditional classifier models and original embedding method during prediction, and successfully generates explanations and collects meaningful rules.

Keywords: e-Commerce knowledge graph · Lifestyle · Relational learning · Explanation · Rules

1 Introduction

E-Commerce marketplaces such as Amazon and Alibaba have billions of items where millions of users trade online every day. Therefore, helping users reach

X. Wang et al. (Eds.): JIST 2019, CCIS 1157, pp. 78–87, 2020.
https://doi.org/10.1007/978-981-15-3412-6_8

desired items is a crucial task. For e-Commerce platforms, search queries from users are valuable information to understand their shopping motivations. In most cases, these platforms return items that exactly match the query, as shown in the left side of Fig. 1. Obviously, such result lucks diversity.

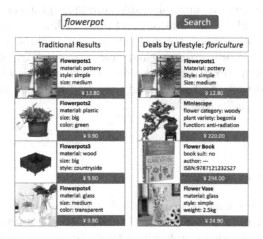

Fig. 1. An application example of deals by lifestyle.

To tackle this problem, we introduce deals by lifestyle. A lifestyle is users's pattern of living in the world, expressed in activities, interests, and opinions. It portrays the "whole user" interacting with his or her environment. Marketers are always trying to search for relationships between their products and lifestyle groups [8]. Deals by lifestyle make it possible to show all kinds of items related to users' lifestyles inferred from their queries.

An example of deals by lifestyle is shown in Fig. 1. It shows that when a user searches 'flowerpot', not only flowerpots but also miniascapes, flower books and flower vases will be returned because they are all related to a lifestyle called 'floriculture'.

Given items and lifestyles, the key task for deals by lifestyle is to establish linkage between them, called *item-lifestyle link prediction*, and we solve this problem in the context of knowledge graph. A knowledge graph store facts as triples, (*head entity, relation, tail entity*), abbreviated as (h, r, t). Each triple expresses that head entity h and tail entity t has relation r, for example (*JIST2019, isHeldIn, Hangzhou*).

Link prediction aims to learn latent relationship between entities. Among all relational learning methods, knowledge graph embedding (KGE) methods aiming at learning latent representation for entities and relations in continues vector space has proven to be efficient and effective. KGEs accomplish predictions via calculation between entities and relations embeddings, which is efficient and easy. While predictions from most KGEs lack transparency, causing difficulties to incorporate expert's knowledge and judgement on these results.

In item-lifestyle link prediction, explanations are necessary because we need to filter wrong predictions from algorithms, and explanations will help us quickly find them via checking consistency between explanations and corresponding predictions. Rules are also necessary because we want to transfer deals by lifestyle to other platforms without re-collecting training data and re-training.

In this paper, we propose an explainable knowledge graph embedding method XTransE, based on which explanations and rules for link prediction can be generated by a explanation generator and rule collector. Through experiments on real e-Commerce data, we prove that our new proposal XTransE is better than various baselines and can generate meaningful explanations and rule for item-lifestyle link prediction. And surprisingly, we find that our explanations also contribute to data quality checking.

2   Method

2.1   Problem Formulation

We formulate it as a knowledge graph link prediction (KGLP) task in order to utilize complex links between items and lifestyles. For this task, we build an item-lifestyle knowledge graph where triples represent properties of items, such as *(IPhoneXS-01, color, Black)*, and relation *belongTo* represents the linkage between items and lifestyles, for example, *(SwimmingTrunks-01, belongTo, Swimming)*. With item-lifestyle knowledge graph, item-lifestyle link prediction is defined as a special KGLP task as follows: *Given lifestyle-item knowledge graph $\mathcal{K} = \{\mathcal{E}, \mathcal{R}, \mathcal{T}\}$, where $\mathcal{E} = \{\mathcal{L}, \mathcal{I}, \mathcal{V}\}$ is a set of entities union with lifestyle entity set $\mathcal{L}$, item entity set $\mathcal{I}$ and value entity set $\mathcal{V}$. $\mathcal{R}$ is a set of relations including relation belongTo and a set of properties $\mathcal{P}$. $\mathcal{T}$ is a set of triples. The task is to predict the lifestyle entity e_L given an item entity e_I and relation belongTo, formulated as $(e_I, belongTo, ?)$.*

2.2   Our Proposal

Considering desired characteristics explained in Sect. 1, our proposal includes three parts, a **knowledge graph embedding model**, a **prediction explanation generator** and a **rule collector**.

Knowledge Graph Embedding Model. A simple and effective KGE method is TransE [1], which embeds entities and relations as vectors. For a triple (h, r, t), it regards relation r as a translation from the head entity h to the tail entity t, denoting that $\mathbf{h} + \mathbf{r} \approx \mathbf{t}$, in which $\mathbf{h} \in \mathbb{R}^{1 \times d}, \mathbf{r} \in \mathbb{R}^{1 \times d}, \mathbf{t} \in \mathbb{R}^{1 \times d}$ are head entity embedding, relation embedding, and tail entity embedding respectively. d is embedding dimension. Based on TransE's assumption, we propose a novel *explainable knowledge graph embedding method for a specific relation* with an attention mechanism, called **XTransE**.

The input of XTransE are item-lifestyle triples (e_I, r_b, e_L), where $e_I \in \mathcal{I}, e_L \in \mathcal{L}$ and r_b is *belongTo*. The score function for an item-lifestyle triple is defined as

$$f(e_I, r_b, e_L) = \|\mathbf{e}_I + \mathbf{r}_b - \mathbf{e}_L\|_2^2 \tag{1}$$

where $\mathbf{e}_I, \mathbf{r}_b$ and $\mathbf{e}_L$ are embeddings of item e_I, relation *belongTo* and lifestyle e_L. $\| \cdot \|_2^2$ is Euclidean distance. In order to generate explanations, we introduce an attention mechanism on item e_I. Lifestyle's attention on different property-value pairs of an item helps us understand the correlations between them. Thus, $\mathbf{e}_I$ in XTransE is calculated from its triple specific embeddings with different property-values. Triple specific embeddings for e_I with (e_I, r, e) is calculated by:

$$\mathbf{e}_{I(r,e)} = \mathbf{e} - \mathbf{r} \tag{2}$$

$\mathbf{e}_I$ in Eq. (1) is a weighted sum of it's triple specific embeddings:

$$\mathbf{e}_I = \sum_{(e_I, r, e) \in \mathcal{T}} \mathbf{a}_{e_L(r,e)} \mathbf{e}_{I(r,e)} \tag{3}$$

where $\mathbf{a}_{e_L(r,e)}$ is the attention of $\mathbf{e}_{I(r_b, e_L)}$ on $\mathbf{e}_{I(r,e)}$ and is calculated by:

$$\mathbf{a}_{e_I(r,e)} = \frac{e^{\mathbf{e}_{I(r_b, e_L)} \mathbf{e}_{I(r,e)}}}{\sum_{(e_I, r_j, e_j) \in \mathcal{K}, \ r_j \in \mathcal{P}} e^{\mathbf{e}_{I(r_b, e_L)} \mathbf{e}_{I(r_j, e_j)}}} \tag{4}$$

A max margin loss function is devised as the training objective to minimize:

$$L = \sum_{(e_I, r_b, e_L) \in \mathcal{K}} \max(0, \gamma + f(e_I, r_b, e_L) - f(e_I, r_b, e_L')) \tag{5}$$

where (e_I, r_b, e_L') is the negative triple constructed for (e_I, r_b, e_L) via randomly replacing e_L with another $e_L' \in \mathcal{L}$.

Explanation Generator. As in XTransE, attention values reveal the relevance between different property-value pairs and current item-lifestyle prediction.

Thus the main explanations provided in this paper are property-value triples (e_I, p, v), For example, an item $Item_X$ is linked to lifestyle 'Playing Music' because of $(item_X, category, earphone)$.

For a predicted triple (e_I, r_b, e_L), explanation generator ranks all $\mathbf{a}_{e_I(r,e)}$ and selects property-value triples with top k attention values as explanations, depicted in Fig. 1.

Table 1. Example for explanation generator with $k = 2$. The darker the color is, the higher the attention is.

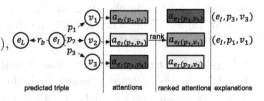

Rule Collector. Generating rules is one of the desired characteristics in our scenario. A rule consists of a head and a body like *head ← body* which could expanded as $a_0 \leftarrow a_1 \wedge a_2 \wedge ... \wedge a_n$ where head contains one atom a_0 and body contains multiple atoms $a_1, a_2, ..., a_n$. An atom a is a triple with head or tail entity as variable(s).

In this paper, we learn rules with $(\underline{e_I}, r_b, e_L)$ as head, where the underlined item entity is a variable, and body containing atoms $(\underline{e_L}, p, v)$, *e.g.*, $(iPhoneXS-01, brand, Apple)$. Thus the rule we intend to learn is denoted as follows:

$$(\underline{e_I}, r_b, e_L) \leftarrow (\underline{e_I}, p_1, v_1), ..., (\underline{e_I}, p_n, v_n)$$

Given k explanations for the triple (e_I, r_b, e_L) from explanation generator, we generate multiple rules with different combinations of explanations as rule body. For example, for a triple with 3 explanations, we will generate $C_3^1 + C_3^2 + C_3^3 = 7$ rules.

3 Experiments and Results

Dataset. The item-lifestyle knowledge graph dataset used in experiment includes 72849 entities, 758 property relation, a *belongTo* relation, and 1875438 triples. We split item-lifestyle triples into training dataset and testing dataset, with ratio around 80% and 20% respectively. Finally there are 39696 triples in training dataset and 10031 in test dataset.

3.1 Prediction

Evaluation Metrics. We adopt two metrics, *Accuracy* and *Mean Rank(MR)*. For each test triple (e_I, r_b, e_L), we replace e_L with each $e_L' \in \mathcal{L}$, and calculate the score of replaced triples according to (1). Then we rank these scores in ascending order and get the rank of triple (e_I, r_b, e_L). With ranks for all test triples, *Accuracy* is the percentage of test triples with rank 1. *MR* is the average rank of all test triples. Generally, a better item-lifestyle link prediction result means a higher *Accuracy* and a lower *MR*.

Baselines. There are two type of baselines in this paper. The one is traditional machine learning classifier model, because item-lifestyle link prediction also could be regarded as lifestyle classification for items. 6 classifier models are chose as shown in Table 2. The other is KGE methods and we choose TransE [1] as a baseline because XTransE is built based on it.

Settings and Results. We initialize all embeddings from the uniform distribution $U[-\frac{6}{\sqrt{d}}, \frac{6}{\sqrt{d}}]$. During training, embedding dimension $d = 100$ and margin $\gamma = 2.0$. We optimize XTransE via Adaptive Moment Estimation (Adam) [7] with learning rate 0.01 for max 20 iterations with early stopping. The prediction results are shown in Table 2.

Result Analysis. Table 2 shows that XTransE achieves the best results on both *Accuracy* and *MR*, with 5.38% and 8.33% improvement compared with the second best results respectively. Compared to TransE, XTransE achieves improvements with 51.03% on Accuracy and 40.86% on MR, showing that general KGE method should be adjusted when applied to specific real-life applications, especially when only one or a few type of relational triples need to be completed.

Table 2. Prediction results. The bold results are the best and the underlined ones are the second best.

Methods	Accuracy	MR
SVM [4]	80.74%	1.29
BNB [12]	81.08%	1.36
KNN [6]	83.91%	1.47
DT [15]	86.47%	1.30
GDBT [2]	86.62%	<u>1.20</u>
RF [9]	<u>86.75%</u>	1.22
TransE [1]	60.53%	1.86
XTranE	**91.42%**	**1.10**

3.2 Explanation Evaluation

We generate explanations for predictions following Sect. 2.2. To evaluate explanations, we randomly sample 500 correctly predicted and 500 wrongly predicted test triples and manually check whether their explanations are consistent to predictions. Explanations showing that it is reasonable to make current prediction are classified as *consistent*. If there is conflict between explanation and prediction, the explanation is *inconsistent*. Explanations which could be classified into consistent and inconsistent ones, we regard them as *uncertain* explanation. Evaluation results are shown in Table 3.

Result Analysis. There are more *consistent explanations*, than inconsistent ones for both correct and wrong predictions, indicating effectiveness of utilizing attention values to generate explanations.

Table 3. Explanation evaluation results.

	Correct	Wrong	All
Consistent	231(46.2%)	143(28.6%)	374(37.4%)
Uncertain	217(43.4%)	293(58.6%)	510(51.0%)
Inconsistent	52(10.4%)	64(12.8%)	116(11.6%)

The percentage of consistent explanations for wrong predictions is 28.6%, revealing that some items belong to multiple lifestyles and they are not really wrongly predicted but caused by data incompletion.

There are 11.6%, the smallest percentage, *inconsistent explanations*, demonstrating that explanations are reliable in general. 10.4% inconsistent explanations for correct predictions reveals there are noisy items-lifestyle links in original data. Therefore some labels are not reliable, and explanations among noisy data are especially necessary.

In *uncertain explanations*, wrong predictions are much more (19.6%) than correct ones, showing that if XTransE fails to catch significant features of items, it is more possible to predict wrongly than correctly. And there are 43.4% uncertain explanations for correct predictions, a quite high percentage, indicating that there are statistical features in data helping model make correct predictions but may not reasonable for human.

Case Study. Explanation examples for different types of predictions are shown in Table 4. For item 1, it is correctly predicted because its categories are music and CD/DVD which are closely related to 'making music'. For item 2, explanations, especially its title containing 'car' and 'crystal', are not related to 'making

Table 4. Explanations for predicted results. *'true'* denotes the triple in the dataset. *'pred'* denotes predicted triples. *'expn'* denotes explanation.

	Correct-Consistent	Correct-Inconsistent	Wrong-Consistent	Wrong-Inconsistent
true	(item 1, scene, making music)	(item 2, scene, making dessert)	(item 3, scene, diving)	(item 4, scene, sketch)
pred	(item 1, scene, making music)	(item 2, scene, making dessert)	(item 3, scene, breaststroke)	(item 4, scene, boxing)
expn 1	(item 1, hasProperty, type)	(item 2, hasProperty, color)	(item 3, titleContains, Speedo)	(item 4, category, sketch)
expn 2	(item 1, titleContains, CD)	(item 2, hasProperty, goodsID)	(item 3, titleContains, sports)	(item 4, titleContains, training)
expn 3	(item 1, category, music)	(item 2, titleContains, brand)	(item 3, hasProperty, color)	(item 4, titleContains, teaching)
expn 4	(item 1, category, CD/DVD)	(item 2, titleContains, car)	(item 3, brand, Speedo)	(item 4, titleContains, sketch)
expn 5	(item 1, hasProperty, region)	(item 2, titleContains, crystal)	(item 3, category, sports)	(item 4, titleContains, drawing)

dessert'. It is easy for us find this prediction is wrong even labeled as correct. For item 3, explanations that its brand is Speedo, an Australian manufacturer and distributor of swimwear and swim-related accessories, clearly indicates that it belongs to lifestyle 'breaststroke'. While this prediction is labeled as wrong because item 3 can belong to 'diving' as well as 'breaststroke'. For item 4, explanations that its title containing 'sketch' and 'drawing', show it should belong to lifestyle 'sketch' rather than 'boxing'. Explanations can help us find this is a truly wrong prediction.

3.3   Rule Evaluation

Aggregating all explanations for both train and test triples, we collect rules following Sect. 2.2. High-quality rules are selected out by two widely used metrics, *head coverage(HC)* and *confidence(conf)* [3]. For a *rule : head ← body*, head coverage and confidence are defined by:

$$HC(rule) = \frac{support(rule)}{\#e_x : head(rule|e_x)}, \quad conf(rule) = \frac{support(rule)}{\#(e_x) : body(rule)}$$

where *support(rule)* is the number of possible combination for entity replacement of the variable in *rule*. $\#e_x : head(rule|e_x)$ is the number of e_x that the triple exists in knowledge after replacing variable in *rule* head with entity e_x. $\#(e_x) : body(rule)$ is the number of replacement for rule body.

We defined high-quality rules that to be selected out are rules with $HC > 0.3$ and $conf > 0.8$. Finally, we learned **252** rules from the explanations.

Case Study. 5 detailed examples are shown in Table 5. In 4 of these examples, atoms related to 'category' are in the rule body, showing that most rules are associated with categories of items. In the last example, the rule is composed of 4 property-value pairs, which is purely caused by data associations while may not make sense for human. However, it is still a high-quality rule.

Table 5. Collected rule examples with different length.

Rule head	Rule body	HC	Conf
(*item X*, scene, making dessert)	(*item X*, category, cookware)	0.33	1.00
(*item X*, scene, making music)	(*item X*, category, news music) ∧ (*item X*, hasProperty, ISBN)	0.32	0.97
(*item X*, scene, boxing)	(*item X*, hasProperty, size) ∧ (*item X*, titleContains, protective clothing)	0.33	0.96
(*item X*, scene, sketch)	(*item X*, hasProperty, brand) ∧ (*item X*, hasProperty, suitable age) ∧ (*item X*, category, painting supplies)	0.40	1.00
(*item X*, scene, outdoor survival)	(*item X*, hasProperty, brand) ∧ (*item X*, hasProperty, color) ∧ (*item X*, hasProperty, tag price) ∧ (*item X*, hasProperty, origin)	0.38	0.81

4 Related Work

The same as types of baselines in this paper, the related work are mainly two parts, one is classifier models and the other is knowledge graph embedding methods.

Classifier Models. For the classifier models, we mainly introduce baselines we choose. SVM (Support Vector Machine) [4] is a supervised learning algorithm, whose basic model is to find the best classification hyperplane, and then maximize category intervals. BNB (Bernoulli Naive Bayes) [12] is a naive bayes classification for multiple Bernoulli distribution data, where each feature is assumed to be a binary variable. For KNN (K-Nearest Neighbor) [6], if the majority of top K similar instances in the feature space belong to a certain category, the instance also belongs to this one. DT (Decision Tree) [15] implements classification by finding the best division feature, and then learning the instance path, based on the known occurrence probability of various situations. GDBT (Gradient Boosting) [2], as one of ensemble learning methods, chooses the direction of gradient descents during iteration to ensure the final result achieve the best. RF (Random Forest) [9] is also an ensemble learning method, which combines multiple weak classifiers into a strong one, and uses DT as a model in bagging.

Knowledge Graph Embedding. Apart from TransE [1] introduced before, there are a lot of knowledge graph embedding methods proposed. TransH [18], TransR [10] and TransD [5] are proposed based on TransE in order to better encode one to many or many to one links. DistMult [19], ComplEx [17] and ANALOGY [11] are proposed based on linear map assumption that $\mathbf{hM_r} \approx \mathbf{t}$. And there are also other methods like NTN [16] and HOLE [13]. These methods all rely on only embeddings for current triples' entities and relation to conduct link prediction, making them completely black-box models and unexplainable. CrossE [21] proposes a way to generate prediction explanations based on embeddings, but it still can't ensure explanations for each prediction, thus not an explainable knowledge graph embedding method. [14,19,20] learn rules from embeddings while without explanations.

5   Conclusion

In this paper, we introduce a real application, deals by lifestyle, in e-Commerce application and propose an explainable knowledge graph embedding method XTransE for item-lifestyle link prediction. XTransE is effective and outperforms many traditional classifier models and TransE. We also generate explanations for prediction results and rules that can be used for item-lifestyle link prediction. In our scenario, prediction results, explanations and rules are three desired characteristics.

There are a few points can be concluded: (1) knowledge graph embedding method is effective for link prediction tasks but should be adapted when applied to real applications which concentrate on prediction of a few relations rather than all of them. (2) Explanations for prediction results are important because (i) the majority of machine learning methods do not achieve 100% accuracy thus will introduce noise into dataset, and explanations for prediction can help human quickly filter wrong predictions, and (ii) datasets in real application are always noisy and explanations for training data are helpful when we are trying to clean the dataset.

For future works, we will continually dig the value of deals by lifestyle and develop more explainable models with the capability of learning rules for real-life applications.

Acknowledgments. This work is funded by NSFC 91846204/61473260, national key research program YS2018YFB140004, and Alibaba CangJingGe (Knowledge Engine) Research Plan.

References

1. Bordes, A., Usunier, N., García-Durán, A., Weston, J., Yakhnenko, O.: Translating embeddings for modeling multi-relational data. In: NIPS, pp. 2787–2795 (2013)
2. Friedman, J.H.: Greedy function approximation: a gradient boosting machine. Ann. Stat. **29**, 1189–1232 (2001)
3. Galárraga, L.A., Teflioudi, C., Hose, K., Suchanek, F.M.: AMIE: association rule mining under incomplete evidence in ontological knowledge bases. In: WWW, pp. 413–422 (2013)
4. Hearst, M.A., Dumais, S.T., Osuna, E., Platt, J., Scholkopf, B.: Support vector machines. IEEE Intell. Syst. Appl. **13**(4), 18–28 (1998)
5. Ji, G., He, S., Xu, L., Liu, K., Zhao, J.: Knowledge graph embedding via dynamic mapping matrix. In: Proceedings of ACL, pp. 687–696 (2015)
6. Keller, J.M., Gray, M.R., Givens, J.A.: A fuzzy k-nearest neighbor algorithm. IEEE Trans. Syst. Man Cybern. **4**, 580–585 (1985)
7. Kingma, D.P., Ba, J.: Adam: a method for stochastic optimization. abs/1412.6980 (2014)
8. Kotler, P.: Marketing Management (2012)
9. Liaw, A., Wiener, M., et al.: Classification and regression by randomforest. R N. **2**(3), 18–22 (2002)
10. Lin, Y., Liu, Z., Sun, M., Liu, Y., Zhu, X.: Learning entity and relation embeddings for knowledge graph completion. In: AAAI, pp. 2181–2187. AAAI Press (2015)

11. Liu, H., Wu, Y., Yang, Y.: Analogical inference for multi-relational embeddings. In: Proceedings ICML, pp. 2168–2178 (2017)
12. Murphy, K.P., et al.: Naive bayes classifiers. Univ. Brit. Columbia **18**, 60 (2006)
13. Nickel, M., Rosasco, L., Poggio, T.A.: Holographic embeddings of knowledge graphs. In: Proceedings of AAAI, pp. 1955–1961 (2016)
14. Omran, P.G., Wang, K., Wang, Z.: Scalable rule learning via learning representation. In: IJCAI, pp. 2149–2155. ijcai.org (2018)
15. Safavian, S.R., Landgrebe, D.: A survey of decision tree classifier methodology. IEEE Trans. Syst. Man Cybern. **21**(3), 660–674 (1991)
16. Socher, R., Chen, D., Manning, C.D., Ng, A.Y.: Reasoning with neural tensor networks for knowledge base completion, pp. 926–934 (2013)
17. Trouillon, T., Welbl, J., Riedel, S., Gaussier, É., Bouchard, G.: Complex embeddings for simple link prediction. In: Proceedings ICML, pp. 2071–2080 (2016)
18. Wang, Z., Zhang, J., Feng, J., Chen, Z.: Knowledge graph embedding by translating on hyperplanes. In: Proceedings of AAAI, pp. 1112–1119 (2014)
19. Yang, B., Yih, W.T., He, X., Gao, J., Deng, L.: Embedding entities and relations for learning and inference in knowledge bases. In: Proceedings of ICLR (2015)
20. Zhang, W., et al.: Iteratively learning embeddings and rules for knowledge graph reasoning. In: WWW, pp. 2366–2377. ACM (2019)
21. Zhang, W., Paudel, B., Zhang, W., Bernstein, A., Chen, H.: Interaction embeddings for prediction and explanation in knowledge graphs. In: WSDM, pp. 96–104. ACM (2019)

Feasibility Study: Rule Generation for Ontology-Based Decision-Making Systems

Juha Hovi$^{(\boxtimes)}$ and Ryutaro Ichise

National Institute of Informatics, Tokyo, Japan
{hovi,ichise}@nii.ac.jp

Abstract. Ontology-based systems can offer enticing benefits for autonomous vehicle applications. One such system is an ontology-based decision-making system. This system takes advantage of highly abstracted semantic knowledge that describes the state of the vehicle as well as the state of its environment. Knowledge on scenario state combined with a set of logical rules is then used to determine correct actions for the vehicle. However, creating a set of rules for this safety-critical application is a challenging problem which must be solved to enable the use of the decision-making system in practical applications. This work explores the feasibility of generating rules for the reasoning system through machine learning. We propose a process for the rule generation and create a set of rules describing vehicle behavior in an uncontrolled four-way intersection.

Keywords: Autonomous driving · Ontology · Decision-making · Data mining · Machine learning

1 Introduction

Autonomous driving and advanced driver assistant systems (ADAS) are currently one of the most topical fields of research relating to vehicles in both academia as well as industry. Popular approaches to decision-making, such as one introduced by Bojarski et al. in 2016 [3], take advantage of neural networks. These systems can be challenging to adapt to practical applications. This is due to autonomous driving applications being highly safety-critical while neural networks are mainly used as black boxes where internal operations of the systems are difficult for humans to understand. As such, verifying the behavior of the vehicle in all possible different scenarios encountered by the vehicle remains a challenge. Ontology-based systems can aid this problem by introducing a process that remains understandable for humans from beginning to end. This adds an option of expert review to complement other verification methods such as rigorous testing through simulations and field tests.

Ontology-based systems operate on semantic knowledge formatted according to a vocabulary declared in an ontology. This introduces a shared baseline vocabulary that can be used by different applications and enables transferring

© Springer Nature Singapore Pte Ltd. 2020
X. Wang et al. (Eds.): JIST 2019, CCIS 1157, pp. 88–99, 2020.
https://doi.org/10.1007/978-981-15-3412-6_9

features of systems more easily to other systems. By combining the knowledge gained through vehicle sensors with existing knowledge as well as logical rules, an ontology-based decision-making system can determine correct actions for each scenario. The logical rules describe the cause and effect relationship between sets of observations and sets of actions. However, creating these rules is not a simple task. Traffic is an extremely complex and varied operating environment where determining the correct action relies on both clearly stated rules as well as more subtle negotiations between actors. Furthermore, traffic cultures around the world have distinct differences between them. While some rules would be straightforward to replicate from law, representing more subtle patterns is crucial for the success of practical applications. As a result, the set of rules required to operate correctly is complex in nature and challenging to create. Due to this, writing the rules by hand is an extremely high effort undertaking while being difficult to maintain or scale.

We propose generating the rules for decision-making through data-driven machine learning. This paper studies the feasibility of this approach in an uncontrolled four-way intersection. The purpose of the study is to evaluate the feasibility of the proposed approach, identify future research directions, and provide a starting point for the overarching goal of generating a set of rules.

The paper is structured as follows. Section 2 discusses the background of this work and the related works it is based on. Section 3 introduces the proposed method of generating rules. Section 4 presents and discusses the setup for experiments and the generated set of rules. Finally, Sect. 5 reflects upon the work done and discusses the implications of the results.

2 Background

This study builds on previous research on subjects such as an ontology designed for usage in autonomous vehicle systems as well as an ontology-based decision-making system.

2.1 ADAS Ontology

Advanced driver assistant system (ADAS) ontology is a set of three core ontologies designed for autonomous driving applications [7]. Specifically, these ontologies are the car ontology, the control ontology, and the map ontology [9]. The main classes within the map and the control ontology are visualized in Fig. 1.

The car ontology contains vocabulary for vehicle characteristics. This includes vehicle sub-types such as truck, bus, bicycle, and a regular car. Additionally, vocabulary for vehicle parts such as sensors is included. Properties of this ontology include a way to tie the vehicle to a location through assigning a lane the vehicle is running on. Finally, the ontology contains a way to assign a planned path to the vehicle.

The control ontology focuses on vehicle control. This includes driving actions such as stopping, proceeding, and turning. Additionally, lane changes and traffic

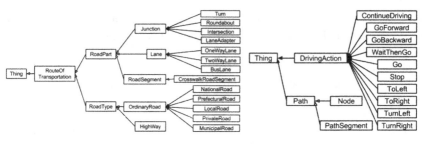

(a) Classes of map ontology.   (b) Classes of control ontology.

Fig. 1. Visualization of the main classes within the map ontology and the control ontology [9].

signals can be represented. Path-following related control is enabled through vocabulary for path segments. The control ontology also includes warnings such as collision warning, speeding warning, and a warning for leaving a lane.

The map ontology is designed to describe a map in a machine-readable format. This is achieved through describing points in the map such as intersections which are connected to lanes. In an intersection, relative positions of lanes are represented through such properties as *turnLeftTo* and *turnRightTo*. The lanes can be then assigned to be on a specific roads which have different types and properties such as speed limits. In addition to road and intersection data, common objects in traffic are also included. These consist of objects such as traffic signs, signals, buildings, and natural formations such as lakes.

2.2   Ontology-Based Decision-Making System

An existing system for decision-making based on semantic knowledge was introduced by Zhao et al. in 2017 [8]. This system takes in pre-processed sensor data in a highly abstract semantic format. It then combines the dynamic sensor data with static data such as map data that has been previously saved in its knowledge base. The dynamic and static data of the vehicle environment is used in conjunction with a set of logical rules to determine correct actions for the vehicle. These rules are expressed in Semantic Web Rule Language (SWRL) [6]. The rules map sets of observations on the states of the ego-vehicle and its environment into actions. As such, the rules are of form $\{X \Rightarrow Y\}$ where X is a conjunction of observations and Y is a conjunction of actions. Thus, the actions included in Y should be taken if the conditions in X are observed.

Due to the ontology-based decision-making system being reliant on the logical rules, one problem with this system is the availability of the ruleset. The previous work of Zhao et al. was a feasibility study and due to its focused scope the ruleset was written by hand. Traffic as an operating environment, however, is extremely varied. As such, writing a suitable set of rules by hand is challenging. Furthermore, maintaining the ruleset and adapting it to different traffic cultures requires additional effort. We propose generating these rules through machine learning.

3   Rule Generation

The rule generation process for this work consisted of two main phases. First, a suitable dataset had to be acquired. Next, the patterns in the data that form the rules were extracted through data mining.

3.1   Dataset Generation

Multiple datasets are readily available for autonomous driving research. However, these datasets typically focus on providing the data in the most general format: raw sensor data. This poses problems for using the data in this work as highly abstract data is required. Some datasets, such as the KITTI dataset [5] are available with additional annotations such as semantic segmentation. While these annotations are the first step towards a suitable data format, a considerable amount of further processing is necessary. As such, the data for this work was generated through simulation where high-level abstract data is more straightforward to acquire. This includes data such as vehicle location. Locating vehicles in sensor data can be done through, for example, detecting vehicles in RGB-camera feed and detecting clusters in LIDAR-data. As the relative locations of the camera and the LIDAR are known, the location of the vehicle in the RGB-image can be matched with the 3D-coordinates of the cluster in LIDAR-data. Thus, a vehicle can be assigned a location relative to the ego-vehicle. In simulations, this data is available with minimal processing required.

Before generating the data, the scope of the dataset was defined. The scope was chosen to be non-exceptional scenarios in an uncontrolled four-way intersection. This scope was defined with restrictions of

- only two and three vehicle scenarios are included
- no rule-breaking vehicle behavior can occur
- all vehicles involved approach the intersection simultaneously
- maximum of one vehicle can approach the intersection from a single direction.

This scope was chosen due to the clear rules stated in traffic laws governing the behavior of the vehicles. As discussed earlier, traffic contains situations where rules are not clear and vehicle behaviour is akin to social interaction and negotiations. These situations are of high importance for real-world applications. For this feasibility study, a scenario with clearly stated rules was chosen. Additionally, the chosen scope allows constructing the vocabulary for the rules to represent real-world traffic rules. This, in turn, allows for verification of results through human review.

3.2 Rule Vocabulary

Extracting rules from the data requires identification and definition of the vocabulary required to describe vehicle behavior. In the chosen scope, the correct behavior is dictated by traffic rules as they act as an agreement between vehicles. This agreement assigns every actor in the scenario their turn to cross the intersection. The case of a vehicle approaching the intersection from all four directions simultaneously is not inspected in this work due to the situation being unclear and difficult for even human drivers. One-vehicle scenarios involving only the ego-vehicle were not inspected due to their trivial nature. As the default action of the vehicle was defined to be proceeding on the planned path, any situations where this is the case did not produce any rules. Thus, exclusion of one-vehicle scenarios where the ego-vehicle can always proceed did not affect the results.

The relevant knowledge items for the vehicle to behave appropriately in a four-way intersection where scenarios unfold in a safe and traffic rule obeying fashion consist of

- relative direction of approach of non-ego-vehicles
- planned intersection exit direction of non-ego-vehicles
- ego-vehicle goal direction
- ego-vehicle action.

where non-ego-vehicle refers to any vehicle involved in the scenario that is not the ego-vehicle. Planned intersection exit direction is determined by the goal of each vehicle: turning left, turning right, or driving straight across the intersection. This list produces the vocabulary shown in Table 1 and is created by the following reasoning.

Approach Direction. In an uncontrolled intersection, the relative position of the vehicles acts as the primary factor when vehicles are assigned right-of-way. Right-of-way refers to the privilege to enter the intersection before another vehicle. This work discusses scenarios in right-side traffic. Thus, the right-of-way is assigned to the vehicle that is on the right of another vehicle. As such, the first identified piece of knowledge that needs to be represented and extracted is the relative position of vehicles from the point-of-view of the ego-vehicle.

Goal Direction. Taking into account the relative location from where a vehicle is approaching the intersection gives the basic crossing order for many situations. However, it leaves out the possibility of more than one vehicle crossing the intersection simultaneously. In order to achieve safe simultaneous intersection crossing, knowledge on the intended goal direction of each vehicle is required. For example, if two vehicles approach the intersection from opposite sides and intend to drive straight through, they can cross simultaneously assuming no other vehicles are present. Additionally, knowing the intended goal direction of each vehicle is required for reasoning the correct action when another vehicle is approaching the intersection from the opposite side of the intersection from

Table 1. The vocabulary for capturing vehicle behavior in an uncontrolled four-way intersection where scenarios unfold safely and actors obey traffic rules. Multiple-valued entries have been split into mutually exclusive boolean truth-valued entries.

Ego-vehicle	
Stop	Giving way to another vehicle
Left	Heading left
Right	Heading right
Straight	Heading straight across
Vehicle approaching from left of ego-vehicle	
Left	Heading left
Right	Heading right
Straight	Heading straight across
Vehicle approaching from opposite of ego-vehicle	
Left	Heading left
Right	Heading right
Straight	Heading straight across
Vehicle approaching from right of ego-vehicle	
Left	Heading left
Right	Heading right
Straight	Heading straight across

ego-vehicle point-of-view. Vehicles driving straight have the right-of-way over vehicles turning and as such the right-of-way is assigned according to intended goal direction.

Actions. The directions for approaching the intersection as well as leaving it are both observations. In order for the vehicle to react appropriately, the observations must be complemented by actions. In this work, it is assumed that tasks such as high-level path planning as well as low-level control are left to other systems. As such, the decision-making system in question is responsible for deciding between two actions: proceeding on the path or stopping to give way to another vehicle. The default action was decided to be the vehicle proceeding on its path. As such, whenever a rule was generated, it had a rule head of exactly *Stop*. Thus, it is required to detect and extract data on the event of ego-vehicle stopping to give way to another vehicle.

Vocabulary in SWRL. The ontology-based decision-making system uses rules expressed in SWRL. In this work, it is assumed that these rules are constructed using the vocabulary present in the ADAS ontology. Thus, while the rules can be generated using a different intermediate format, it must be possible to automatically translate the generated rules into SWRL-format to use them with the

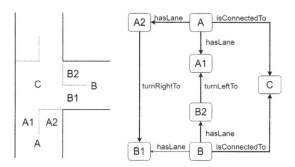

Fig. 2. A map of an intersection expressed as a graph using the vocabulary of ADAS ontology. *A* and *B* are roads. *C* is an intersection. *A1*, *A2*, *B1*, and *B2* are lanes.

decision-making system. As such, the expressive power of the ADAS ontology was inspected to ensure that the vocabulary in Table 1 is representable through it. The *Stop* action of the ego-vehicle is directly declared in the control ontology along with *giveWay*. The ability to express relative directions directly using the ADAS ontology is limited. However, having a previously known map of the area expressed using the map ontology enables describing relative positions of vehicles. This can be done by the following process for which an example map is visualized in Fig. 2 where the set of roads is {A, B}, the set of intersections is {C}, and the set of lanes is {A1, A2, B1, B2}. First, the vehicles are detected and assigned on lanes using the *isRunningOn* property declared in the car ontology. Then, the relation between these lanes can be inspected through *turnLeftTo*, *turnRightTo*, and *goStraightTo* properties that connect them at an intersection. However, as a road typically has separate lanes for different directions of traffic, these lanes must be connected. The property *hasLane* is used for this purpose as it enables checking if lanes are on the same *RoadSegment*. Intended vehicle direction can be expressed through *TurnLeft*, *TurnRight*, and *GoForward* which can be reasoned from the path of the vehicle.

3.3   Rule Extraction

Association rule learning [1] was used to extract patterns from the data. The data was formatted into suitable item-transaction format by defining the knowledge items so that each has a boolean truth value. Any multiple-valued knowledge items were split into multiple parts. This format is illustrated in Table 2 where observations and actions correspond to items while samples correspond to transactions.

The Apriori algorithm [2] was used to find frequent itemsets. A suitable support threshold was defined in order to define the threshold between frequent and non-frequent itemsets. The support s of an itemset X indicates that itemset X is present in s% of transactions in the database [1].

Once the frequent itemsets were found, irrelevant frequent itemsets were identified and pruned based on the requirements set for rule format. The rule

Table 2. Example part of a boolean data table. Columns correspond to observations and actions, rows correspond to a sampled time instants. The illustrated scenario includes the ego-vehicle and one other vehicle. Ego-vehicle is turning left. The other vehicle is approaching the intersection from the opposite side of the intersection and is driving straight across the intersection. Thus, the ego-vehicle is giving way to the other vehicle until that vehicle has exited the intersection.

Sample	Ego: stop	Ego: left	$\cdots$	Opposite: straight	Opposite: right
1	True	True		True	False
2	True	True		True	False
...					
10	False	True		False	False
11	False	True		False	False

body can only contain observations and the rule head can only contain actions. Thus, a rule as a whole must contain at least one observation and at least one action. This combined with the mechanism of rule creation allows pruning. Both the rule body and the rule head are created from a single itemset by dividing it into two parts. As a result, any frequent itemset without both an observation and an action can be safely discarded.

After the itemsets with the potential to form valid rules were selected, a suitable confidence threshold was defined to construct rules. For a rule $X \Rightarrow Y$, confidence c indicates that $c\%$ of transactions in the database that include X also include Y [1]. Thus, confidence depends on the direction of the rule. Again, knowledge on the desired rule format was used to avoid creation of invalid rules. Each itemset only results in one candidate rule where all observations are in the rule body and all actions are in the rule head. If the confidence value of the candidate rule was greater than the set threshold, a rule was formed.

The process of rule learning was augmented with further rule pruning. This pruning was based on a set of pruning principles which exploit prior knowledge on the nature of the data, rule format, as well as properties of conjunctions. These principles state that

- each rule body must include an observation on ego-vehicle state
- each rule body must include an observation on non-ego-vehicle state
- the ruleset must not include redundant rules

where the first two principles rely on the data containing certain elements whenever a rule is necessary as well as the rule format. These two pruning principles were not implemented in the initial rule generation process due to their application specific nature. The third principle relies on conjunction elimination which states that if a conjunction evaluates to true, then any conjunction of a subset of its elements must also evaluate to true. As a result, any long rule can be removed if its body is a superset of a body of a shorter rule when the rules share the same rule head. While the removal of redundant rules is not strictly

Table 3. Examples of RDF triples describing a single vehicle in a scenario at a sampled time instant. Subject is the assigned ID, *car1*, of the vehicle. The vehicle is a car, a collision warning has not been detected, the vehicle is not giving way to another vehicle, it is approaching the intersection from the right of the ego-vehicle, and it is turning left.

Subject	Predicate	Object
car1	hasType	Car
car1	hasCollisionWarning	False
car1	giveWay	False
car1	approachFrom	Right
car1	isTurning	Left

necessary, removing them reduces both computation required when reasoning and unnecessary effort in result review.

4   Experiment

4.1   Experimental Setup

The simulated set of scenarios included a total of 108 scenarios in which 27 scenarios were two-vehicle scenarios and 81 scenarios were three-vehicle scenarios. The scenarios were created by defining starting points and behaviors for each individual vehicle.

The simulator used was CARLA. CARLA is a simulator being developed for autonomous driving research [4]. Specifically, CARLA 0.9.2 was used due to it introducing a new traffic scenario engine. This engine was used to implement vehicle behaviors, including turning right, driving straight across, and two different left turns due to the intersection where scenarios took place being rectangle rather than a square.

While the scenarios were ran, the state of the simulation was sampled at a regular sampling rate resulting in multiple samples from each scenario. These snapshots of the scenario state were then abstracted into a format matching the used vocabulary by detecting abstract states and events in the data offered by the simulator. The scenarios were considered complete once the ego-vehicle had exited the intersection as any events taking place in the intersection after this point have no relevance for ego-vehicle behavior.

The abstracted snapshots were formatted as Resource Description Framework (RDF)-graphs and stored as one dataset. An example of the RDF-format is shown in Table 3 which contains the RDF-triples concerning one vehicle in the scenario at a single time instant. The vehicle has been assigned ID *car1*, it is of type *Car*, a collision warning has not been issued, it is not giving way to another vehicle, it is approaching the intersection from the right of the ego-vehicle, and it is turning left. This particular state of a vehicle could be captured from the scenario shown in Fig. 3.

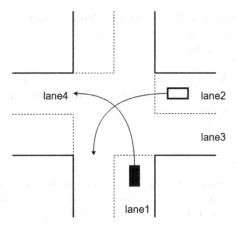

Fig. 3. Visualization of {Ego-vehicle: Left ∧ Right-vehicle: Left ⇒ Stop}. Ego-vehicle depicted in black is turning left while another vehicle is approaching the intersection from the right of the ego-vehicle. The other vehicle is turning left. Thus, ego-vehicle must give way to the other vehicle.

4.2 Generated Rules

The rules extracted from the created dataset using association rule learning are shown in Table 4. Each member of a rule body first states the vehicle it describes followed by the intended action of that vehicle. Figure 3 visualizes the scenario described in the first rule with the ego-vehicle marked with black. These rules are the correct rules matching traffic rules in an uncontrolled four-way intersection. Additionally, the set of rules is of full coverage for the chosen scope. Notably, each rule only involves the ego-vehicle and one other vehicle as do real-world traffic rules. This is due to the chained nature of right-of-way. It is sufficient to give way to one vehicle at a time. Once that vehicle has exited the intersection, the situation is assessed again to see if giving way to another vehicle is necessary.

Translation to SWRL. To enable the use of the rules in the ontology-based decision-making system, the rules must be converted to SWRL format with vocabulary described in the ADAS ontology. This is done to ensure compatibility between different systems by adhering to a shared baseline vocabulary. Let us inspect the first rule in Table 4 and convert it as an example. This rule describes a scenario state visualized in Fig. 3 where ego-vehicle is indicated by black. This rule can be written in SWRL-format as

1. $MyCar(?ego) \land Vehicle(?vehicle)$
2. $\land Intersection(?int) \land RoadSegment(?road1)$
3. $\land Lane(?lane1) \land Lane(?lane2) \land Lane(?lane3)$
4. $\land isRunningOn(?ego, ?lane1) \land isRunningOn(?vehicle, ?lane2)$
5. $\land turnRightTo(?lane1, ?lane3)$

6. $\land hasLane(?road1, ?lane2) \land hasLane(?road1, ?lane3)$
7. $\land TurnLeft(?ego) \land TurnLeft(?vehicle)$
8. $\Rightarrow Stop(?ego) \land giveWay(?ego, ?vehicle)$

where lines 1 to 3 declare class variables. Line 4 places the involved vehicles on lanes. Lines 5 and 6 ensure that turning right from ego-vehicle position leads to the road the other vehicle is running on. Line 7 describes the intended actions of the vehicles. Finally, line 8 states that the ego-vehicle should stop and give way to the other vehicle.

Table 4. The ruleset generated with association rule learning. The rules are in the desired format and all pruning steps have been applied. The rules are correct and reflect traffic rules in an uncontrolled four-way intersection. *Support* ≥ 0.01, *confidence* $\geq$ 0.9, and *length* ≤ 5.

Supp	Conf	Rule
0.09	1.00	$\textbf{\textit{Ego : Left}} \land \textbf{\textit{Right : Left}} \Rightarrow \textbf{\textit{Stop}}$
0.08	1.00	$\textbf{\textit{Ego : Left}} \land \textbf{\textit{Right : Straight}} \Rightarrow \textbf{\textit{Stop}}$
0.04	1.00	$\textbf{\textit{Ego : Left}} \land \textbf{\textit{Opposite : Straight}} \Rightarrow \textbf{\textit{Stop}}$
0.05	1.00	$\textbf{\textit{Ego : Left}} \land \textbf{\textit{Opposite : Right}} \Rightarrow \textbf{\textit{Stop}}$
0.06	1.00	$\textbf{\textit{Ego : Straight}} \land \textbf{\textit{Right : Left}} \Rightarrow \textbf{\textit{Stop}}$
0.02	1.00	$\textbf{\textit{Ego : Straight}} \land \textbf{\textit{Right : Straight}} \Rightarrow \textbf{\textit{Stop}}$
0.01	1.00	$\textbf{\textit{Ego : Straight}} \land \textbf{\textit{Right : Right}} \Rightarrow \textbf{\textit{Stop}}$

On line 7 of the above SWRL-rule, *TurnLeft(?ego)* indicates the intention of the ego-vehicle to cross the intersection by turning left. This can be reasoned from the path planned for the ego-vehicle. In other words, it is a result of another rule. Using the same variable names as above and adhering to the illustration in Fig. 3, the rule producing *TurnLeft(?ego)* is

1. $MyCar(?ego) \land Lane(?lane1) \land Lane(?lane4) \land Intersection(?int)$
2. $isRunningOn(?ego, ?lane1) \land turnLeftTo(?lane1, ?lane4)$
3. $nextPathSegment(?lane1, ?int) \land nextPathSegment(?int, ?lane4)$
4. $\Rightarrow TurnLeft(?ego)$

where line 1 declares class variables. Line 2 establishes the current lane ego-vehicle is running on and the lane the ego-vehicle would be running on after a left turn. Line 3 ties the planned vehicle path to the path from *lane1* to *lane4* through *int*. If this conjunction evaluates to true, line 4 then states the vehicle is planning to turn left.

The rest of the rules in Table 4 are similar to the first rule with only the vehicles and their directions varying. As such, the rest of the rules can be translated into SWRL-format in a manner similar to the first one.

5   Conclusion

In this paper, we proposed an approach for using machine learning to generate a set of logical rules for use in ontology-based decision-making systems. Through this approach, we successfully created a set of correct rules describing vehicle behavior in a set of scenarios taking place in an uncontrolled four-way intersection. The expressive power of the ADAS ontology was sufficient for describing the chosen scenarios. However, the vocabulary is currently heavily dependent on existing map-data. Facilitating vehicle control in previously unknown environments requires expansion of the ontology or integration of Simultaneous Localization and Mapping (SLAM) techniques.

In conclusion, the proposed approach shows promise while requiring further work to expand it outside the scope of traffic scenarios inspected in this paper. Importantly, this work is laying the foundation for future work on the way towards enabling the use of ontology-based decision-making in practical autonomous driving applications.

Expanding on this research involves dealing with more data, imperfect data, and scenarios more difficult to express with logical rules. As such, the expressive power of the ontology as well as the scalability and robustness of the rule learning approach remain as key points to evaluate. In the future, we will work towards expanding the set of rules to cover a wider slice of traffic situations.

References

1. Agrawal, R., Imieliński, T., Swami, A.: Mining association rules between sets of items in large databases. SIGMOD Rec. **22**(2), 207–216 (1993)
2. Agrawal, R., Srikant, R.: Fast algorithms for mining association rules in large databases. In: Proceedings of 20th International Conference on Very Large Data Bases, pp. 487–499. Morgan Kaufmann (1994)
3. Bojarski, M., et al.: End to end learning for self-driving cars. arXiv:1604.07316v1 (2016)
4. Dosovitskiy, A., Ros, G., Codevilla, F., Lopez, A., Koltun, V.: CARLA: an open urban driving simulator. In: Proceedings of the 1st Annual Conference on Robot Learning, pp. 1–16 (2017)
5. Geiger, A., Lenz, P., Stiller, C., Urtasun, R.: Vision meets robotics: the KITTI dataset. Int. J. Robot. Res. **32**(11), 1231–1237 (2013)
6. Horrocks, I., Patel-Schneider, P.F., Boley, H., Tabet, S., Grosofand, B., Dean, M.: SWRL: a semantic web rule language combining OWL and RuleML. W3C Member Submission (2004)
7. Ichise Laboratory: Advanced driver assistant system ontology. http://ri-www.nii.ac.jp/ADAS/index.html
8. Zhao, L., Ichise, R., Liu, Z., Mita, S., Sasaki, Y.: Ontology-based driving decision making: a feasibility study at uncontrolled intersections. IEICE Trans. Inf. Syst. **100**, 1425–1439 (2017)
9. Zhao, L., Ichise, R., Mita, S., Sasaki, Y.: Core ontologies for safe autonomous driving. In: Proceedings of the ISWC Poster and Demonstrations Track (2015)

Attention-Based Direct Interaction Model for Knowledge Graph Embedding

Bo Zhou[1,2(✉)], Yubo Chen[1], Kang Liu[1,2], and Jun Zhao[1,2]

[1] National Laboratory of Pattern Recognition, Institute of Automation, Chinese Academy of Sciences, Beijing 100190, China
{bo.zhou,yubo.chen,kliu,jzhao}@nlpr.ia.ac.cn
[2] University of Chinese Academy of Sciences, Beijing 100049, China

Abstract. Knowledge graph embedding aims at learning low-dimensional representations for entities and relations in knowledge graph. Previous knowledge graph embedding methods usually assign a score to each triple in order to measure the plausibility of it. Despite of the effectiveness of these models, they ignore the fine-grained (matching signals between entities and relations) clues since their scores are mainly obtained by manipulating the triple as a whole. To address this problem, we instead propose a model which firstly produces diverse features of entity and relation by multi-head attention and then introduces the interaction mechanism to incorporate matching signals between entities and relations. Experiments show that our model achieves better link prediction performance than multiple strong baselines on two benchmark datasets WN18RR and FB15k-237.

Keywords: Knowledge graph embedding · Link prediction · Attention-based · Direct interaction

1 Introduction

Knowledge graphs can be treated as large knowledge bases (KBs) which comprise structured triples in the form of $(entity, relation, entity)$. There are many KBs, such as Freebase [2] DBpedia [9] and YAGO [15] which can greatly benefit many natural language processing applications such as question answering, relation extraction and machine reading comprehension. However, these KBs are incomplete in a certain degree, which means many valid facts can't be found in the KBs. Therefore, many researches have been focused on the task of *knowledge base completion* which aims at predicting the tail entity when given the head entity and relation, or vice versa.

In order to perform the *knowledge base completion* task, different methods have been proposed over recent years. Roughly, these can be divided into two categories [18], one is *Translational Distance Models* and they measure the plausibility of a fact as the distance between the two entities, usually after a translation carried out by the relation. The other is *Semantic Matching Models* and

© Springer Nature Singapore Pte Ltd. 2020
X. Wang et al. (Eds.): JIST 2019, CCIS 1157, pp. 100–108, 2020.
https://doi.org/10.1007/978-981-15-3412-6_10

they measure plausibility of facts by matching latent semantics of entities and relations embodied in their vector space representations.

These models can learn good representations for entities and relations in KBs and perform well in knowledge base completion task. Despite of the effectiveness, they ignore the fine-grained clues (matching signals between entities and relations) since their scores are mainly obtained by manipulating the triple as a whole. Take the model ConvE [4] for example, for each fact triple (h, r, t), the concatenation of embeddings of h and r is input to CNN to obtain different feature maps, which will be concatenated and projected to a vetor of the same size as entity embedding of t. Then logit for each entity will be obtained by dot product between the projected vector and the corresponding entity embedding. The ConvE simply extracts a vector from embeddings of h and r and the dot product can only capture linear relationships.

To address this problem, we instead propose a model which incorporates multi-head attention and interaction mechanisms. First, diverse features of head entity and relation are produced by multi-head attention. Then we introduce the interaction mechanism to calculate matching scores between these features and entities and these interaction scores will be further processed to obtain logit for each entity. Besides, we include a nonlinear transformation to better evaluate the dot product.

In summary, our contributions in this paper are as follows:

- We propose a model which leverages the interaction mechanism to directly calculate the interaction signals between different feature vectors and embeddings of entities.
- We utilize multi-head attention to produce diverse features and nonlinear transformation to better evaluate the dot product.
- We evaluate our model on two benchmark datasets and our model achieves better link prediction performance than multiple strong baselines.

2   Related Work

Translational Distance Models utilize additive functions over embeddings to obtain a score. TransE [3] is the first model introducing translation-based embedding, in which both entities and relations are represented as real vectors of the same length. It assumes the relation $\boldsymbol{h} + \boldsymbol{r} \approx \boldsymbol{t}$ and minimizes the distance score $f_r(h, t) = \|\boldsymbol{h} + \boldsymbol{r} - \boldsymbol{t}\|_{1/2}$. In order to better model the 1-to-N, N-to-1 and N-to-N relations which can't be well dealt with in TransE, TransH [19] introduces relation-specific hyperplanes. TransR [10] introduces relation-specific spaces instead of hyperplanes which is similar to TransH. TransD [7] decomposes the relation-specific matrix in TransR into product of two vectors in order to reduce the number of parameters. By leveraging sparse relation-specific matrix, TranSparse [8] also reduces the parameters in TransR. There are also some works taking the uncertainty in knowledge graph into account, in these methods entities and relations are modeled as random vectors [6].

Semantic Matching Models use product-based functions over embeddings to obtain a score. RESCAL [13] represents each entity as a vector and each ralation as a matrix which defines the score of a triple by $f_r(h, t) = \boldsymbol{h}^\top \boldsymbol{M}_r \boldsymbol{t}$ rather than the translational distance in TransE. DistMult [20] replaces the relation matrix in RESCAL with a diagonal matrix in order to reduce the number of parameters. By introducing complex-valued embeddings, ComplEx [16] extends DistMult which can better model asymmetric relations. There are also some works utilizing neural netwok to calculate the score for each triple. In MLP [5], embeddings of entities and relations are first mapped into hidden representations, then the score is obtained by dot product. ConvKB [12] uses CNN to produce feature maps and then computes the score by dot product.

3   The Proposed Model

A knowledge graph $\mathcal{G}$ can be seen as a set which contains valid triples (head entity, relation, tail entity) denoted as (h, r, t) such that $h, t \in \mathcal{E}$ and $r \in \mathcal{R}$ where $\mathcal{E}$ is a set of entities and $\mathcal{R}$ is a set of relations. Each embedding model aims to define a score for a triple such that valid triples get higher scores than invalid ones. Table 1 gives score functions of some previous SOTA models.

Table 1. The score functions in previous SOTA models. $\langle \boldsymbol{v}_h, \boldsymbol{v}_r, \boldsymbol{v}_t \rangle = \sum_i \boldsymbol{v}_{h_i} \boldsymbol{v}_{r_i} \boldsymbol{v}_{t_i}$ denotes a tri-linear dot product.

Model	The score function $f(h, r, t)$
TransE	$-\|\boldsymbol{v}_h + \boldsymbol{v}_r - \boldsymbol{v}_t\|_{1/2}$
ComplEx	$Re\left(\langle \boldsymbol{v}_h, \boldsymbol{v}_r, \overline{\boldsymbol{v}}_t \rangle\right)$
DistMult	$\langle \boldsymbol{v}_h, \boldsymbol{v}_r, \boldsymbol{v}_t \rangle$
MLP	$\boldsymbol{w}^\top \tanh\left(\boldsymbol{M}^1 \boldsymbol{h} + \boldsymbol{M}^2 \boldsymbol{r} + \boldsymbol{M}^3 \boldsymbol{t}\right)$
ConvE	$\mathbf{f}(\text{vec}(f([\overline{\mathbf{r}}, \overline{\mathbf{h}}] * \boldsymbol{\Omega}))\mathbf{W})\mathbf{t}$
RotatE	$-\|\mathbf{h} \circ \mathbf{r} - \mathbf{t}\|^2$

We have a lookup table for entities $\boldsymbol{E} \in \mathbb{R}^{|\mathcal{E}| \times d}$ named entity table and a lookup table for relations $\boldsymbol{R} \in \mathbb{R}^{|\mathcal{R}| \times d}$ named relation table, where d denotes the embbeding size.

Given a triple (h, r, t), we first use h and r to look up the entity table and relation table to get their corresponding embeddings denoted as a matrix $\boldsymbol{L} = [\boldsymbol{v}_h, \boldsymbol{v}_r] \in \mathbb{R}^{d \times 2}$. Then, we use the multi-head attention [17]. Given a matrix of n query vectors $\boldsymbol{Q} \in \mathbb{R}^{n \times d}$, keys $\boldsymbol{K} \in \mathbb{R}^{n \times d}$ and values $\boldsymbol{V} \in \mathbb{R}^{n \times d}$, the multi-head attention computes the attention scores based on the following equation:

$$\begin{cases} \boldsymbol{F} = \text{MultiHead}(\boldsymbol{Q}, \boldsymbol{K}, \boldsymbol{V}) = \text{Concat}\left(\text{head}_1, \ldots, \text{head}_h\right) \boldsymbol{W}^O \\ \text{head}_i = \text{Att}\left(\boldsymbol{Q}\boldsymbol{W}_i^Q, \boldsymbol{K}\boldsymbol{W}_i^K, \boldsymbol{V}\boldsymbol{W}_i^V\right) = f\left(\frac{(\boldsymbol{Q}\boldsymbol{W}_i^Q)(\boldsymbol{K}\boldsymbol{W}_i^K)^T}{\sqrt{d}}\right)(\boldsymbol{V}\boldsymbol{W}_i^V) \end{cases} \quad (1)$$

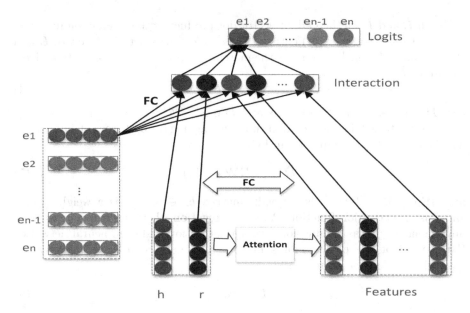

e1 e2   en-1 en   Logits

Interaction

FC

e1

e2

FC

en-1

en

h   r

Attention

Features

Fig. 1. Illustration of the model with direct interaction. In the picture FC is abbreviation for fully connected layer and for convenience we only show the interaction for e1.

here Q, K, V are the same matrix and equal to L^T, f is softmax and $\frac{1}{\sqrt{d}}$ is the scaling factor. The output of attention layer is a matrix denoted as $F \in \mathbb{R}^{2 \times d}$. We use $\frac{k}{2}$ multi-head attention layers, so after concatenating outputs of these attention layers with L, we obtain input matrix $I \in \mathbb{R}^{d \times (k+2)}$ (Fig. 1).

Alternatively, we also replace the multi-head attention layer with CNN to obtain the input matrix I. Specifically, the embedding matrix L is input to a convolutional neural network to get differernt feature maps. Specifically, we have k filters and each is of shape $[f_h, 2]$. Thus each filter will produce a feature map of size $[d + 2n_p - f_h + 1, 1]$, where n_p is the number of zero padding which ensures the height of each feature map equals d. Concatenating these k feature maps with L, we obtain input matrix $I \in \mathbb{R}^{d \times (k+2)}$.

After obtaining the input matrix I by multi-head attention or CNN, it's input to a fully connected layer (FC):

$$\bar{I} = f \left(I^T W_i + b_i \right) \tag{2}$$

here $W_i \in \mathbb{R}^{d \times d}$ is a weight matrix, $b_i \in \mathbb{R}^d$ is a weight vector and f is an activation function.

The entity table E is also input to an FC:

$$\bar{E} = f \left(E W_e + b_e \right) \tag{3}$$

here $W_e \in \mathbb{R}^{d \times d}$ is a weight matrix, $b_e \in \mathbb{R}^d$ is a weight vector and f is an activation function.

With $\bar{E}$ and $\bar{I}$, we then adopt vector dot product as the interaction function. It's easy to see that the (i, j) entry of D is the dot product of ith row of $\bar{E}$ and jth column of $\bar{I}$, which represents the matching score between ith entity and jth feature of $\bar{I}$:

$$D = \bar{E}\bar{I} \tag{4}$$

here D is called interaction matrix and $D \in \mathbb{R}^{|\mathcal{E}| \times (k+2)}$.

In order to get logits for all entities, we aggregate each row of interaction matrix D. First, D is input to an FC:

$$\bar{D} = f\left(DW_d + b_d\right) \tag{5}$$

here $W_d \in \mathbb{R}^{(k+2) \times (k+2)}$ is a weight matrix, $b_e \in \mathbb{R}^{(k+2)}$ is a weight vector and f is an activation function. As for aggregation, there are different ways to implement it such as summation, average, attention and even neural networks. Here we adopt dot product for simplicity and more complicated aggregation strategies are left for future work:

$$l = \bar{D}w_a \tag{6}$$

where $w_a \in \mathbb{R}^{(k+2) \times 1}$ is trainable parameter and $l \in \mathbb{R}^{|\mathcal{E}| \times 1}$ is logits for all entities. It's easy to see that the ith entry of l is the logit of the ith entity, which is a weighted sum of all the matching scores for the entity although the weight is not normalized. We then normalize the logits l into probability:

$$p = \text{sigmoid}\left(l\right) \tag{7}$$

We choose binary classification loss as our loss function and we optimize our model by minimizing the total loss $\mathcal{L}_{loss}$:

$$\mathcal{L}_{loss} = -\sum_{i=1}^{N} \sum_{j=1}^{|\mathcal{E}|} \left(l_i^j \log\left(p_i^j\right) + \left(1 - l_i^j\right) \log\left(1 - p_i^j\right)\right) \tag{8}$$

4   Experiments

4.1   Datasets

Our experiments are conducted on two benchmark datasets: WN18RR and FB15k-237. WN18RR is a subset of WN18 derived from Wordnet [11] which is a KB whose entities (termed synsets) correspond to senses of words, and relationships between entities define lexical relations. Compared with WN18, WN18RR dose not suffer inverse relation test leakage. FB15k-237 is a subset of FB15k derived from Freebase [2] which is a huge and growing KB for common facts with around 1.9 billion triplets. Unlike FB15k, FB15k-237 does not contain inverse relations. In our experiments, we use the same train/valid/test sets split as in [4]. The detailed statistics of WN18RR and FB15k-237 are showed in Table 2.

4.2 Baselines

We compare our model with several previous methods. Our baselines include DistMult, ComplEx, R-GCN [14], ConvE [4] and A2N [1], some of them are strong baselines. We report the results of DistMult, ComplEx, R-GCN and ConvE from [4]. The result of A2N is reported from [1].

Table 2. Statistics of the experimental datasets.

Dataset	$|\mathcal{E}|$	$|\mathcal{R}|$	#Triples in train/valid/test		
WN18RR	40943	11	86835	3034	3134
FB15k-237	14541	237	272115	17535	20466

4.3 Evaluation Metrics

The purpose of *link prediction* or *KB completion* task [3] is to predict the missing entity given the relation and the other entity in the valid triple, i.e, predicting h giving (r, t) or predicting t giving (h, r). The results are then evaluated based on the rankings of the scores calculated by the score function.

Specifically, for each valid triple, we first replace the head entity or tail entity randomly by all the other entity in $\mathcal{G}$ to produce a set of corrupted triples, i.e., the negative triple sets corresponding to the valid triple. Then all the scores of corrupted triples together with the valid triple are calculated by the score function and the results are ranked based on these scores to get a ranking list. We employ common metrics to evaluate the ranking list: mean reciprocal rank (MRR) (i.e., the reciprocal mean rank of the correct test triples), mean rank (MR) (i.e., the mean rank of the correct test triples), Hits@10 (i.e., the proportion of the correct test triples ranked in top 10 predictions), Hits@3 and Hits@1.

As pointed out in [3], the above corrupted triple set for each test triple may contain some valid triples in $\mathcal{G}$ and these valid triples may be ranked above the test triple which will influence the results. To avoid this, we follow [3] to remove from the corrupted triple set all the triples that appear in $\mathcal{G}$. The former is called Raw setting and the latter is called Filter setting. We then evaluate results with MR, MRR, Hits@10, Hits@3 and Hits@1 on the new ranking list.

4.4 Training Protocol

The Bernoulli trick is used to generate the head or tail entities when producing negative facts, i.e., with probably p the head entity of a test triple is replaced and with probably $1 - p$ the tail entity is replaced. We compute MR, MRR, Hits@1, Hits@3 and Hits@10 in Filter setting.

In our experiment, the dimension d of entities and relations are set to 200. All the lookup tables are initialized by uniform distribution between $\left[-\frac{6.0}{\sqrt{200}}, \frac{6.0}{\sqrt{200}}\right]$. The number of multi-head attention is 5 and for each attention layer, we set head number to 2. The filters of CNN are initialized by a uniform distribution $\left[-\frac{1}{\sqrt{22}}, \frac{1}{\sqrt{22}}\right]$. The number of filters for CNN is 8 and the filter size is $[2, 11]$. In order to keep the size of feature maps, zero padding of shape $[0, 5]$ is used. We also use Dropout after the CNN and the dropout rate is 0.1. We choose ReLU as the activation function f. The label smoothing is also used to reduce over-fitting and the ratio is set to 0.1. In order to make the training process better, the trick of learning rate decay is utilized. For both datasets, the batch size is 128. The Adam optimizer is used to train our model. The initial learning rate 0.001 for both datasets. We run our model on both datesets to 1000 epochs and the validation set is used to select the best model in these epochs to do test set evaluation.

4.5   Experimental Results

Results are summarized in Tables 3 and 4. Table 3 compares the performance of our model with results of previous models, from which we can see that our attention-based model outperforms all baselines on FB15k-237 in terms of all the evaluation metrics. This shows the effectiveness of our model. However, compared with attention-based model, the CNN-based model performs worse on FB15k-237.

On WN18RR, our attention-based model achieves best performance as for MR and MRR. In terms of Hits@10, Hits@3 and Hits@1, our attention-based model obtains comparable peformance with ComplEx and A2N. Once again the CNN-based model performs worse compared with attention-based model on WN18RR. We ascribe this to the better capability of capturing the internal structure of entities and relations and muti-head mechanism of our attention-based model.

Table 3. Results on WN18RR and FB15k-237. Best results are in bold.

Model	WN18RR					FB15k-237				
			Hits					Hits		
	MR	MRR	@10	@3	@1	MR	MRR	@10	@3	@1
DistMult	5110	.43	.49	.44	.39	254	.241	.419	.263	.155
ComplEx	5261	.44	**.51**	**.46**	.41	339	.247	.428	.275	.158
R-GCN	-	-	-	-	-	-	.248	.417	.258	.153
ConvE	5277	.46	.48	.43	.39	246	.316	.491	.350	.239
A2N	-	.45	**.51**	**.46**	**.42**	-	.317	.486	.348	.232
Ours (CNN)	5423	.43	.44	.41	.38	271	.310	.471	.334	.229
Ours (Attention)	**5005**	**.47**	.48	.44	.39	**240**	**.331**	**.499**	**.357**	**.248**

In Table 4, we study the influence of number of muti-head attention in our attention-based model on FB15k-237. We compare number of 1, 3 and 5 and report the corresponding performance in terms of MRR, Hits@10 and Hits@1. From the table we see that as the number increases the performance tends to get better in general, which coincides with our intuition. But taking into account model complexity and computing efficiency, we set the number of muti-head attention to 5 in our attention-based model.

Table 4. The influence of number of multi-head attention on FB15k-237.

Num of attention	MRR	Hits@10	Hits@1
1	.320	.487	.239
3	.328	.495	.249
5	.331	.499	.248

5   Conclusion

In this paper, we propose a novel model for the knowledge graph embedding task. The model leverages the interaction mechanism to directly calculate the interaction signals between different feature vectors and embeddings of entities. Meanwhile, the model utilizes multi-head attention to produce diverse features and nonlinear transformation to better evaluate the dot product. Experiments show that our model achieves better performance in link prediction task than multiple strong baselines on two benchmark datasets WN18RR and FB15k-237. In the future, we plan to incorporate more complicated interaction and aggregation mechanisms to better model the knowledge embedding task.

Acknowledgments. This work is supported by the National Natural Science Foundation of China (No. 61533018), the Natural Key R&D Program of China (No. 2017YFB1002101), the National Natural Science Foundation of China (No. 61806201) and the independent research project of National Laboratory of Pattern Recognition. This work was also supported by CCF-Tencent Open Research Fund.

References

1. Bansal, T., Juan, D.C., Ravi, S., McCallum, A.: A2N: attending to neighbors for knowledge graph inference. In: Proceedings of the 57th Conference of the Association for Computational Linguistics, pp. 4387–4392 (2019)
2. Bollacker, K., Evans, C., Paritosh, P., Sturge, T., Taylor, J.: Freebase: a collaboratively created graph database for structuring human knowledge. In: Proceedings of the 2008 ACM SIGMOD International Conference on Management of Data, pp. 1247–1250. ACM (2008)

3. Bordes, A., Usunier, N., Garcia-Duran, A., Weston, J., Yakhnenko, O.: Translating embeddings for modeling multi-relational data. In: Advances in Neural Information Processing Systems, pp. 2787–2795 (2013)
4. Dettmers, T., Minervini, P., Stenetorp, P., Riedel, S.: Convolutional 2D knowledge graph embeddings. In: Thirty-Second AAAI Conference on Artificial Intelligence (2018)
5. Dong, X., et al.: Knowledge vault: a web-scale approach to probabilistic knowledge fusion. In: Proceedings of the 20th ACM SIGKDD International Conference on Knowledge Discovery and Data Mining, pp. 601–610. ACM (2014)
6. He, S., Liu, K., Ji, G., Zhao, J.: Learning to represent knowledge graphs with Gaussian embedding. In: Proceedings of the 24th ACM International on Conference on Information and Knowledge Management, pp. 623–632. ACM (2015)
7. Ji, G., He, S., Xu, L., Liu, K., Zhao, J.: Knowledge graph embedding via dynamic mapping matrix. In: Proceedings of the 53rd Annual Meeting of the Association for Computational Linguistics and the 7th International Joint Conference on Natural Language Processing (Volume 1: Long Papers), vol. 1, pp. 687–696 (2015)
8. Ji, G., Liu, K., He, S., Zhao, J.: Knowledge graph completion with adaptive sparse transfer matrix. In: Thirtieth AAAI Conference on Artificial Intelligence (2016)
9. Lehmann, J., et al.: DBpedia-a large-scale, multilingual knowledge base extracted from Wikipedia. Semant. Web **6**(2), 167–195 (2015)
10. Lin, Y., Liu, Z., Sun, M., Liu, Y., Zhu, X.: Learning entity and relation embeddings for knowledge graph completion. In: Twenty-Ninth AAAI Conference on Artificial Intelligence (2015)
11. Miller, G.A.: WordNet: a lexical database for English. Commun. ACM **38**(11), 39–41 (1995)
12. Nguyen, D.Q., Nguyen, T.D., Nguyen, D.Q., Phung, D.: A novel embedding model for knowledge base completion based on convolutional neural network. arXiv preprint arXiv:1712.02121 (2017)
13. Nickel, M., Tresp, V., Kriegel, H.P.: A three-way model for collective learning on multi-relational data. ICML **11**, 809–816 (2011)
14. Schlichtkrull, M., Kipf, T.N., Bloem, P., van den Berg, R., Titov, I., Welling, M.: Modeling relational data with graph convolutional networks. In: Gangemi, A., et al. (eds.) ESWC 2018. LNCS, vol. 10843, pp. 593–607. Springer, Cham (2018). https://doi.org/10.1007/978-3-319-93417-4_38
15. Suchanek, F.M., Kasneci, G., Weikum, G.: YAGO: a core of semantic knowledge. In: Proceedings of the 16th international conference on World Wide Web, pp. 697–706. ACM (2007)
16. Trouillon, T., Welbl, J., Riedel, S., Gaussier, É., Bouchard, G.: Complex embeddings for simple link prediction. In: International Conference on Machine Learning, pp. 2071–2080 (2016)
17. Vaswani, A., et al.: Attention is all you need. In: Advances in Neural Information Processing Systems, pp. 5998–6008 (2017)
18. Wang, Q., Mao, Z., Wang, B., Guo, L.: Knowledge graph embedding: a survey of approaches and applications. IEEE Trans. Knowl. Data Eng. **29**(12), 2724–2743 (2017)
19. Wang, Z., Zhang, J., Feng, J., Chen, Z.: Knowledge graph embedding by translating on hyperplanes. In: Twenty-Eighth AAAI Conference on Artificial Intelligence (2014)
20. Yang, B., Yih, W.T., He, X., Gao, J., Deng, L.: Embedding entities and relations for learning and inference in knowledge bases. arXiv preprint arXiv:1412.6575 (2014)

Discovering Hypernymy Relationships in Chinese Traffic Legal Texts

Peng Gao[1,2], Xiang Zhang[1,2,3(✉)], and Guilin Qi[2]

[1] Research Center for Judicial Big Data, Supreme Court of China, Nanjing, China
[2] School of Computer Science and Engineering, Southeast University, Nanjing, China
[3] School of Cyber Science and Engineering, Southeast University, Nanjing, China
{gao_peng,x.zhang,gqi}@seu.edu.cn

Abstract. Currently, Knowledge Graph is playing a crucial rule in some knowledge-based applications, such as semantic search and data integration. Due to the particularity of the vocabulary and language pattern in the Chinese legal domain, the exploration of hierarchical legal knowledge structures is still challenging. In this paper, we first explore a combination of pattern-based and linguistic-rule-based approach in helping experts to identify hypernymy relationships in large-scale traffic legal corpus. Using these relationships as ground truths, we then propose a supervised hypernymy classification of candidate term pairs using an attention-based bidirectional LSTM model, in which a global context of each candidate is defined as the feature for classification. We compare the performance of our approach with state-of-art baselines on real-world data. The evaluation results show that our approach is quite effective in finding Chinese hypernym-hyponym in the traffic legal domain.

Keywords: Hypernymy relations · Legal texts · Global context

1 Introduction

Knowledge Graph has developed rapidly in recent years, especially in the economic, medical, and legal fields. In the legal field, China has launched several Legal Knowledge Graph projects in the past two years and the purpose of which is to extract legal named entities from legal texts, establish the relationship between entities and construct the Legal Knowledge Graph [2], to assist automatic legal question-answering, legal decision-making, and other intelligent systems.

Hypernymy relationship plays a fundamental role in the construction of Legal Knowledge Graphs. It characterizes the hierarchical legal knowledge structures embedded in entities in the legal domain. A lot of research work has been carried out in finding hypernymy relationships in the open domain, including manually-constructed thesaurus like WordNet [7] and HowNet [5], and automatic-extracted thesaurus such as stated in [9]. In the domain-specific area, there are studies on manual construction of UMLS Metathesaurus in the medical domain [3], which

© Springer Nature Singapore Pte Ltd. 2020
X. Wang et al. (Eds.): JIST 2019, CCIS 1157, pp. 109–116, 2020.
https://doi.org/10.1007/978-981-15-3412-6_11

includes enormous hierarchical medical concepts, and automatic extraction of hypernymy relationships in the domain of tourism as stated in [11]. However, there is no relevant research that can automatically extract the hypernymy relationship in Chinese legal text. This task is challenging due to the particularity of the vocabulary and language pattern in Chinese legal texts. Besides, existing works usually assume that a pair of candidate entities co-occur in a sentence, and the local context between these entities are good indicators for hypernymy classification. However, we observe that the task of discovering hypernymy relationship in Chinese legal text suffers from the problem of data sparsity: most of the entity pairs that have a hypernymy relationship do not show a co-occurrence in a sentence in Chinese legal corpus. The lack of local context in the legal domain brings a barrier to the feature engineering of hypernymy discovery.

In this paper, we propose our approach to automatically identifying hypernymy relationships between legal entities in a crawled corpus of Chinese road traffic regulations. The main contributions of this work are in particular: (1) We propose a combination of pattern-based and linguistic-rule-based approach in helping experts to identify hypernymy relationships as ground truths in large-scale traffic legal corpus of crawled regulation texts; (2) In order to alleviate the lack of local context, We construct a Sentence Graph from the corpus to capture a global context between a pair of candidate legal entities, which provides rich features to the hypernymy classification; (3) We propose an attention-based bidirectional LSTM model for a supervised hypernymy classification. Experimental results demonstrate that the global context based on Sentence Graph is effective in finding Chinese hypernym-hyponym in the traffic legal domain.

2 Related Works

There have been several works to address the problem of hypernymy detection, which can be categorized into path-based approaches and distributional approaches. A path-based approach identifies the hypernymy relationship through a lexical-syntactic path that joins the occurrence of pairs of entities in a large corpus. Snow's work [8] learned to detect hypernymy relationship by a neural network model. The limitation of this approach is caused by the data sparsity. It usually requires co-occurrence of term pairs in a sentence, which can not be fulfilled in many scenarios. In recent years, the distributional approach focus on supervised methods, in which entity pairs are represented by a feature vector, i.e. the contexts with which each entity occurs separately in the corpus. In these methods, a classifier is trained on these vectors to predict hypernymy. Different from previous approaches, we construct a Sentence Graph from a Chinese traffic legal corpus, which is used to extract the local and global context to solve the problem of data sparsity.

3 Discovering Hypernymy Relationships in Legal Corpus

We demonstrate our approach of hypernymy discovery in Fig. 1. As the input of our approach, we've crawled a corpus of Chinese traffic legal text from several websites, which is shown in Table 1. In the step of pre-processing, all the Chinese named entities are extracted from the corpus, and entities in the legal domain are identified. A pre-trained Chinese word embedding of each entity defined in [6] is utilized to train an SVM classifier with a set of human annotation to correctly distinguish legal entities from non-legal. Here We omit the details of entity classification because this topic is not the focus of this paper. In the second step, human experts will manually annotate pairs of entities with hypernymy relationship with the help of a combination of pattern-based and linguistic-rule-based approach for selecting candidate pairs. Human annotations of entity pairs are divided into a training set and a testing set. In step 3 of context generation, a sentence Graph is generated from the corpus to offer rich context information for hypernymy classification. In the last step, an attention-based bidirectional LSTM model is trained with human-annotated training data, and the model classifies hypernymy relationships according to the context information of testing entity pairs.

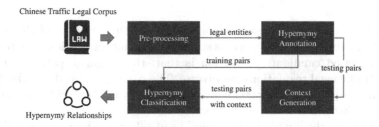

Fig. 1. The Workflow of discovering hypernymy relationships in traffic legal corpus

Table 1. Statistics of the source websites of our corpus

Website	#articles	#sentences
search.chinalaw.gov.cn/search2.html	4,346	303,326
www.gov.cn/zhengce/zc_flfg.htm	38,325	38,325
china.findlaw.cn/jiaotongshigu/jiaotongfa/	25,600	263,383
www.chinacourt.org/law.shtml	1,055	37,307
policy.mofcom.gov.cn/law/index.shtml	776	45,707
www.66law.cn/laws/jiaotongshigu/	18,675	815,891

3.1 Hypernymy Annotation

For the supervised classification of hypernymy relationships, it is necessary to build a high-quality training set of hypernymy entity pairs. It will be extremely burdensome for human annotators to manually discover hypernymy entities in the enormous legal corpus. We define a pattern-based approach to the automatic extraction of candidate entity pairs by introducing six pattern rules, as stated in Table 2. The text in bold is the pattern text, and text in red and blue represents hyponym and hypernym respectively.

Table 2. Pattern-based approach to the discovering of candidate entities.

Pattern	Example
x 以及其他 y	...公交车、小轿车**以及其他**机动车...
x 或者其他 y	...驾驶证、身份证**或者其他**有效证件...
y 比如 x	...违章行为，**比如**违章停车、超速、逆行等。
y 包括 x	..危险路段，**包括**急弯、陡坡、临崖、临水。
y，甚至 x	有以下行为将受到扣分、拘留的处罚，**甚至**刑事处罚。
x 是一种 y	保险**是一种**经济制度，同时也是一种法律关系。

Candidate pairs of entities are supposed to have hypernymy relationships in the legal domain, but the correctness still needs human verification. The problem of pattern-based candidate extraction is that: the language patterns used in Chinese traffic legal regulations are diverse. The patterns defined in Table 2 only help human experts to verify 903 pairs of hypernymy entities, which is too small to form an effective training set.

According to the linguistic right-hand head rule in modern Chinese [4], compound words in Chinese usually has the headword on the right side of the compound. For example, "公共停车场" is a compound word of "公共" and "停车场", and the headword of this compound is the right-hand word "停车场". Since the compound word is usually the semantic hyponym of the headword, We heuristically utilize this linguistic rule to enlarge the candidate hypernymy entities. All compound words in the legal domain are extracted from the corpus, and each compound word together with its headword forms a candidate pair. After human verification, we successfully add 10,027 pairs of hypernymy entities into the training set. A similar approach is adopted in [10].

3.2   Context Generation

Due to the problem of data sparsity, a large part of the candidate pairs do not co-occur in the same sentence in the corpus. In the last step, a total number of 20,562 candidate pairs are extracted, in which 13,880 pairs (most of them are compound words and headwords) occur in different sentences. The lack of local context (words connecting two entities in the same sentence) of two entities leads to the problem of feature sparsity in hypernymy classification.

To alleviate this problem, we define a model of Sentence Graph in Fig. 2, where x and y are two entities in a candidate pair, the white circles represent sentences containing x, dark circles represent sentences containing y, and grey circles represent sentences containing both x and y. The edge between each sentence stands for shared words between two sentences. The local context is the words in the grey circle that connect both x and y, and the global context is the words on the edges that connecting a sentence of x and a sentence of y. Comparing to the sparse local context, the global context of candidate pairs provides richer information on how two entities are related in the whole corpus.

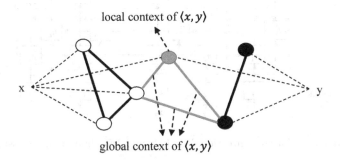

Fig. 2. Local and global context of candidate pairs in the Sentence Graph

3.3 Hypernymy Classification

Each entity pair is represented in the sequence of hypernym, hyponym, with local and global context, which is a sequence of words, denoted as $x = (x_1, x_2, ..., x_t)$. The model we used for hypernymy classification is shown in Fig. 3. The first layer of the model is the embedding layer, pre-trained Chinese word embeddings are used to represent the input sequence and we get the outputs of the embedding layer: $(e_1, e_2, ..., e_t)$. Then, we employ the bidirectional LSTM as the second layer, in which the hidden state is $\overrightarrow{h}_1, \overrightarrow{h}_2, ..., \overrightarrow{h}_{t-1}, \overrightarrow{h}_t$ (arrow indicates the direction of the LSTM is forward). In this setting, the hidden state of the word e_i corresponds to $h_i = [\overrightarrow{h}_i; \overleftarrow{h}_i](i = 1, 2, ..., t)$.

In the hidden layer, the hidden states $\overrightarrow{h}_t$ and $\overleftarrow{h}_t$ are concatenated as a sequence representation. The significance of each word in classification is different. Hence the attention mechanism is been employed. We calculate the corresponding weights for each word by the attention mechanism and then weighted the sum of the hidden states of all the words according to the weight, and the result of the summation h_b is also taken as part of the sequence feature.

As shown in Fig. 3, V_l represents the category vector and the number of categories is two, $a_i(i = 1, 2, ..., t)$ represents the similarity between the hidden state of the i word and the category vector, which is the weight of the i word, the similarity formula is [1].

Besides, S is a parameter matrix that calculates generalized similarity, When it is a unit array, the similarity of h_i and V_l has degenerated into the inner

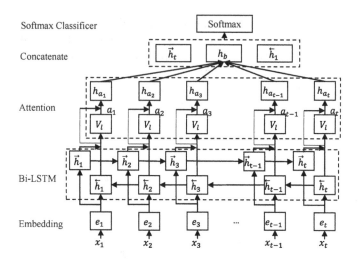

Fig. 3. Attention-based bidirectional LSTM model for hypernymy classification

product. $a = (a_1, a_2, ..., a_t)$ represents the weight vector. According to Eq. 1 we can discover that it has been normalized, The resulting weighted feature vector h_b is Eq. 2. And then h_b together with LSTM forward and backward results, the result expressed in Eq. 3 represents the information of sequence. Finally, a softmax classifier in the output layer will produce the classification result.

$$a_i = \frac{e^{h_i^T M_{V_l}}}{\sum_{j=1}^{t} e^{h_i^T M_{V_l}}} \tag{1}$$

$$h_b = \sum_{i=1}^{t} a_i h_i \tag{2}$$

$$s = [h_b, \overrightarrow{h}_t, \overleftarrow{h}_1] \tag{3}$$

4   Evaluation

We publish all the original corpus and the train/test dataset on our GitHub website[1], as well as the source code of our project. We extract 23,623 entities in the traffic legal domain from the corpus. Three experts in the legal domain manually verify a total number of 10,937 entity pairs (903 pairs from pattern-based approach, 10,027 from the linguistic-rule-based approach) with hypernymy relationship in our corpus. Besides, we use the rule of compound entities, which is similar to [10] and extend the data set to 14,477 entity pairs. We do a negative sampling from the pairs that fail in human verification. The ratio of positive and negative samples is set to 1:1.

---

[1] https://github.com/wds-seu/HITT/.

We perform a standard random splitting with 60% train, 20% test and 20% validation sets. The overall dataset contains 21,860 entity pairs, in which the number of train, test, and validation is 13,116:4,372:4,372.

We compare our model with several robust neural networks for hypernymy classification, which include fastText, CNN and RNN models. Due to limited space, here we omit the detail structures of these models, which can be found on our Github website. Table 3 displays the performance of our model against the baselines. The score of the table is the accuracy of the test set. In addition to using several robust neural network models, we conduct comparative experiments with four sets of input features: for "no context", only word embedding of entities are treated as features; for "local" and "global context", only local or global context is represented as features for classification; in "local + global", a combined context is exploited as features. From Table 3, it is obvious that our model achieves better performance against all baseline models. Besides, our model with the global context is the best in discovering hypernymy relationships.

In contrast to entity pairs without context, entity pairs with a global context conveys more information, which can boost the performance of the classification model. Compared to entity pairs with the local context, the number of entity pairs with local context is 13,880 of total of 20,562 pairs, in the meantime, the number of entity pairs with global context is 20,551 pairs. So the global context can boost the performance of classification. For the entity pairs with both local and global context, the model performance is declining. This phenomenon shows that comparing to rich global context extracted from the Sentence Graph, sparse local context provides very limited and sometimes misleading information for hypernymy classification.

Table 3. Accuracy scores of different models, w/o local and global context.

Feature	fastText	CNN	RNN	Our model
no context	0.5619	0.8232	0.8342	0.8466
local context	0.5232	0.8191	0.8164	0.8181
global context	**0.6744**	**0.8403**	**0.8429**	**0.8626**
local + global context	0.5018	0.8060	0.8337	0.8262

5 Conclusion and Future Work

In this paper, we present a pipeline approach for finding hypernymy relationships in a Chinese legal corpus. We propose a combination of pattern-based and linguistic-rule-based approach for efficiently selecting and annotating hypernymy pairs of entities. A notion of global context is defined to deal with the data sparsity. We use an attention-based Seq2Seq model for the hypernymy classification.

Experiments show that our model performs well on real legal text with rich feature embedding in the global context.

In the future, we will investigate a fine-grained classification of hypernymy relationships, which will distinguish more subtle semantic relations between entities, such as broader/narrower/equivalency, etc.

Acknowledgement. The work is partially funded by the Judicial Big Data Research Centre, School of Law at Southeast University, and is also supported by the National Natural Science Foundation of China under grant U1736204, and the National Key Research and Development Program of China under grant 2018YFC0830201.

References

1. Bahdanau, D., Cho, K., Bengio, Y.: Neural machine translation by jointly learning to align and translate. arXiv preprint arXiv:1409.0473 (2014)
2. Bi, S., Huang, Y., Cheng, X., Wang, M., Qi, G.: Building Chinese legal hybrid knowledge network. In: Douligeris, C., Karagiannis, D., Apostolou, D. (eds.) KSEM 2019. LNCS (LNAI), vol. 11775, pp. 628–639. Springer, Cham (2019). https://doi.org/10.1007/978-3-030-29551-6_56
3. Bodenreider, O.: The unified medical language system (UMLS): integrating biomedical terminology. Nucleic Acids Res. **32**(suppl-1), D267–D270 (2004)
4. Ceccagno, A., Basciano, B.: Compound headedness in Chinese: an analysis of neologisms. Morphology **17**(2), 207–231 (2007)
5. Dong, Z., Dong, Q., Hao, C.: HowNet and the computation of meaning (2006)
6. Li, S., Zhao, Z., Hu, R., Li, W., Liu, T., Du, X.: Analogical reasoning on Chinese morphological and semantic relations. arXiv preprint arXiv:1805.06504 (2018)
7. Miller, G.A.: Wordnet: a lexical database for English. Commun. ACM **38**(11), 39–41 (1995)
8. Snow, R., Jurafsky, D., Ng, A.Y.: Learning syntactic patterns for automatic hypernym discovery. In: Advances in Neural Information Processing Systems, pp. 1297–1304 (2005)
9. Wang, C., Fan, Y., He, X., Zhou, A.: Predicting hypernym-hyponym relations for Chinese taxonomy learning. Knowl. Inf. Syst. **58**, 585–610 (2018)
10. Wang, Q., Xu, C., Zhou, Y., Ruan, T., Gao, D., He, P.: An attention-based Bi-GRU-CapsNet model for hypernymy detection between compound entities. In: 2018 IEEE International Conference on Bioinformatics and Biomedicine (BIBM), pp. 1031–1035. IEEE (2018)
11. Xiao-Jun, M.A., Guo, J.Y., Xian, Y.T., Mao, C.L., Yan, X., Zheng-Tao, Y.U.: Entity hyponymy acquisition and organization combining word embedding and bootstrapping in special domain. Computer Science (2018)

Multi-task Learning for Attribute Extraction from Unstructured Electronic Medical Records

Ming Du, Minmin Pang, and Bo Xu[✉]

School of Computer Science and Technology, Donghua University, Shanghai, China
{duming,xubo}@dhu.edu.cn, 2171780@mail.dhu.edu.cn

Abstract. Electronic medical records have been widely used in hospitals to store patient information in a digital format, which is convenient to reuse the patient's medical data and make it become the data of teaching and scientific research. It is also convenient to analyze and mine the patient's data, so as to provide the basis for medical research. However, most of the existing methods are based on structured data of electronic medical records, and researches on unstructured texts are very rare, which would lose a lot of important information. In this paper, we focus on attribute extraction from the unstructured text of electronic medical records, and propose a multi-task learning model to jointly learn related tasks to help improve the generalization performance of all the tasks. Specifically, we use an end-to-end neural network model to extract different attribute values from the same unstructured text. We take each sentence/segment of the text as an instance. For each instance, we first use the pre-trained word embedding to better initialize our neural network models, then we fine-tune them by using our domain corpus to capture domain specific semantics/knowledge. Considering that the importance of different instances for attribute extractors is not equal, we also use an attention mechanism to select the most important instances for those attribute extractors. Finally, our model use multi-task learning by solving multiple multi-class classification problems simultaneously. Experimental results show the effectiveness of our method.

Keywords: Electronic medical records · Attribute extraction · Multi-task learning

1 Introduction

With the development of information technology and hospital information systems, many hospitals have used electronic medical records (EMR) to store patient information, which are unstructured text and valuable resources for

This paper was sponsored by National Natural Science Foundation of China (No. 61906035), Shanghai Sailing Program (No. 19YF1402300), and the Initial Research Funds for Young Teachers of Donghua University (No. 112-07-0053019).

© Springer Nature Singapore Pte Ltd. 2020
X. Wang et al. (Eds.): JIST 2019, CCIS 1157, pp. 117–128, 2020.
https://doi.org/10.1007/978-981-15-3412-6_12

medical research, such as identifying adverse drug reaction and making early judgments about the patients' symptoms [11].

However, most of the existing methods are based on structured data of electronic medical records, and researches on unstructured texts are very rare, which would lose a lot of important information. For example, in Fig. 1, there are three Chinese pathology reports of colorectal cancer (CRC) specimens. These reports are unstructured text and contain a large amount of descriptive information about the specimen, including the status of some cancer indicators. In order to get more complete information from electronic medical records, we need to extract structured information from unstructured text, such as the status of some cancer indicators.

ID	Sentence
1	"直肠癌根治标本"：腺癌，中分化，溃疡型，肿瘤大小6.0×4.0×1.5cm，浸润至肠肌壁外纤维脂肪组织，未见肯定的脉管瘤栓及神经侵犯；另见绒毛状管状腺瘤伴低级别上皮内瘤变，直径0.3cm；标本上切缘、另送"下切缘"及基底切缘均见癌累及；肠旁淋巴结0/13枚未见癌转移。
2	"乙状结肠肿瘤"：中分化腺癌，溃疡型，瘤体大小5.0×3.0×1.5cm，浸润至外膜外，未见明确的神经侵犯，上下切端均未见癌组织累及，肠旁淋巴结3/20枚见癌转移。
3	"胃癌根治标本"：低分化腺癌，大小4.2×2.5cm，侵透胃壁全层至纤维脂肪组织。脉管内癌栓，神经见侵犯。小弯侧淋巴结11/12枚、大弯侧淋巴结3/3枚见癌转移；上切端未见癌组织累及，"第12组淋巴结"2枚未见肿瘤。基底切缘见癌累及。

ID	Cancer involved in Upper Margin (CUPM,上切端癌累及情况)	Cancer involved in Bottom Margin (CBOM,下切端癌累及情况)	Cancer involved in Base Margin (CBAM,基底切端癌累及情况)	Nerve Invasion (NI,侵犯神经情况)	Vascular Invasion (VI,侵犯脉管情况)
1	YES(是)	YES(是)	YES(是)	NO(否)	NO(否)
2	NO(否)	NO(否)	UNKNOWN(未知)	NO(否)	UNKNOWN(未知)
3	NO(否)	UNKNOWN(未知)	YES(是)	YES(是)	YES(是)

Fig. 1. An example of Chinese pathological reporting of colorectal cancer (CRC) specimens and some extracted attribute values about the status of some cancer indicators.

In this paper, we propose to extract attribute values from the unstructured text of electronic medical records. Specifically, we focus on extract the status of some cancer indicators from cancer specimens, including whether the cancer is involved in the upper/bottom/base margins, whether it has invaded the nerves or vascular, etc. The status of cancer indicators has three categories: {YES, NO, and UNKNOWN}. It is a typical classification problem. We propose a multi-task learning method to jointly learn related tasks to solve multiple classification problems simultaneously. We take each sentence/segment of the text as an instance, and use an end-to-end neural network model to extract the attribute values from the same unstructured text. For each instance, we first use the pre-trained word embedding to initialize our neural network models, then we fine-tune them by using our domain corpus to capture domain specific semantics/knowledge. Considering that the importance of different instances for different attribute extractors is not equal. We also use an attention mechanism to select the most important instances for different attribute extractors. Finally, our model use multi-task learning to get better result and reduce the risk of over-fitting by sharing useful information. At the same time, due to the limitation of data imbalance, we have made a distinction of different importance for the loss contribution of each task.

Our contributions can be summarized as follows.

- Firstly, limited by the data insufficient problem, we propose a multi-task learning method to extract different attribute values from unstructured text of electronic medical records.
- Secondly, we fine-tune the pre-trained word embedding by our electronic medical records to capture domain specific semantics/knowledge and use an attention mechanism to select the most important instances for those attribute extractors.
- Finally, the experimental results show that our multi-task learning models perform better than the single task models, indicating that our model can improve the generalization performance of all tasks.

The rest of this paper is organized as follows. In Sect. 2, we formalize the problem and give an overview of our proposed model. In Sect. 3, we describe the detail of our multi-instance learning model for attribute value extraction. In Sect. 4, we describe our experimental settings for evaluation and discuss the results. In Sect. 5, we review the related work. Finally, we conclude this work in Sect. 6.

2 Overview

In this section, we first formulate our problem, and then introduce our framework.

2.1 Problem Formulation

As mentioned, our task is to extract the status of some cancer indicators from cancer specimens, including whether the cancer is involved in the upper, bottom and base margins, whether it has invaded the nerves or vascular, etc. The status of cancer indicators has three categories: {YES, NO, UNKNOWN}.

In this paper, we treat the attribute value extraction task as a *multi-class classification* problem. Let E be the set of cancer specimens, S_e be the sentences of cancer specimen $e \in E$ in the Chinese pathological reporting. For each cancer specimen $e \in E$, our goal is to use attribute extractor a_i to infer the status v_i of cancer indicators i from S_e.

2.2 Solution Framework

We use multi-task learning to jointly train several attribute extractor for the text. We take the text (divided into sentences S_e) of specimen e as input, getting an attribute extractor a_i of every cancer indicators i, and predict value/result v_i.

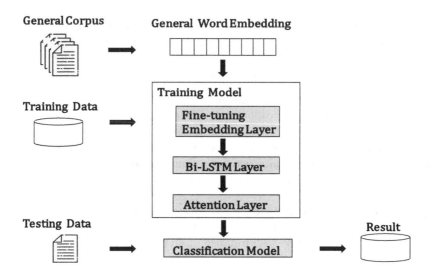

Fig. 2. Framework of the multi-task learning method for attribute value extraction from the unstructured text of electronic medical records.

The framework is shown in Fig. 2. We use an end-to-end neural network model to extract the attribute values from multiple instances of the text. For each instance, we first use the pre-trained word embedding to better initialize our neural network models, then we fine-tune them by using our domain corpus to capture domain specific semantics/knowledge. After that, we use BiLSTM layer to consider both the left and right contexts jointly for a better instance representation. And, we use an attention layer to select the most important instance for different attribute extractors. Finally, multi-task learning was used in output layer, jointly learning related tasks to solve multiple multi-class problems simultaneously.

3   Method

In this section, we mainly present the implementations of our multi-task learning neural network model to solve the problem of extracting the status of some cancer indicators from cancer specimens. Figure 3 shows an example of using multi-task learning to extract the status of some cancer indicators from cancer specimens. And cancer indicators include CUPM, CBOM, CBAM, NI, and VI (Cancer involved in Upper Margin, Cancer involved in Bottom Margin, Cancer involved in Base Margin, Nerve Invasion, and Vascular Invasion).

3.1   Embedding Layer

As shown in Fig. 3, for each cancer specimen $e \in E$, we split the text into N sentences/segments as an instance of the cancer specimen, then divide the

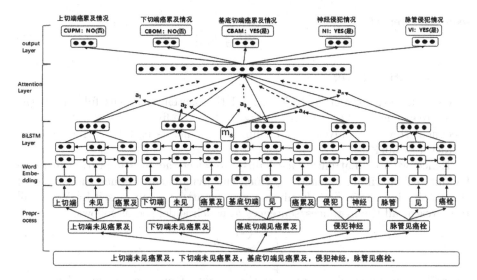

Fig. 3. An example of using multi-task learning to extract the status of some cancer indicators from cancer specimens. And cancer indicators include CUPM, CBOM, CBAM, NI, and VI (Cancer involved in Upper Margin, Cancer involved in Bottom Margin, Cancer involved in Base Margin, Nerve Invasion, and Vascular Invasion).

sentence into M words. N, M are the number of sentences and words. To avoid manual feature engineering efforts, we use the pre-trained word embedding which are trained on large-scale general corpus, such as Tencent Embedding [10] and Word2vec [7]. However, the performance of using general word embedding only in our situation is limited, since pre-trained word embedding on general corpus do not capture domain specific semantics/knowledge [9]. For example, "the upper margin" is not exist in any publicly Chinese pre-trained word embedding, which would affect the extraction effect of the attribute extractor of CUPM.

Hence, in this paper, we first use the pre-trained word embedding to better initialize our models, then we fine-tune them by using our electronic medical records corpus.

3.2 BiLSTM Layer

Then we use BiLSTM layer to consider both the left and right contexts jointly for a better sentence/instance representation [19]. For each sentence S_{ei}, we use a hidden vector h_i to represent it:

$$h_i = [h_{i,1}, h_{i,2}, ..., h_{i,j}, ...h_{i,w}] \tag{1}$$

where $h_{i,j}$ is the hidden vector representation of the j-th word of sentence S_{ei}, which concatenating the forward and backward LSTM along with a non-linear transformation σ. One with the standard sequence, and the other with the sequence reversed:

$$h_{i,j} = \sigma([\overrightarrow{h_{i,j}}, \overleftarrow{h_{i,j}}]) \tag{2}$$

3.3   Attention Layer

In our attribute extraction task, not all the sentences are useful for all the attribute extractors. For example in Fig. 3, there are five sentences in the cancer specimen. However, only the first Chinese sentence is useful for the attribute extractor of CUPM.

Hence, we use an attention mechanism to select the most important instance for different attribute extractors, which can dynamically reduce the weight of those noisy instances. Specifically, we use the attention proposed by Yang [16] to represent all the instances/sentences h, which is defined as follows:

$$h = \sum_i \alpha_i h_i \tag{3}$$

where h_i is instance of i, and α_i is the weight of instance h_i, and defined as follows:

$$\alpha_i = \frac{\exp(\mathbf{m_i}^T m_s)}{\sum_i \exp(\mathbf{m_i}^T m_s)} \tag{4}$$

$$m_i = \tanh(w_s h_i + b_s) \tag{5}$$

where m_s and m_i are the instance/sentence level context vectors, which can be randomly initialized and jointly learned during the training process [16].

3.4   Multi-task Output Layer

Since we study the problem of extracting the status of some cancer indicators from cancer specimens, our model use multi-task learning. The representation of all instances h are ultimately fed into different output layers. And, we use softmax function to obtain multi-class results.

$$P_c = softmax(w_c h + b_c) \tag{6}$$

where P_c is prediction probabilities for task c, w_c is the weight parameters, b_c is the bias vector.

3.5   Model Training

For training the model, we use categorical cross-entropy as loss function and the stochastic gradient descent (SGD) as optimizer. And due to the limitation of data imbalance, it will cause a serious imbalance of loss contribution. Therefore, we assign different weights to the contribution of the loss function of each task to the final loss.

$$Loss = \sum_{c=1}^{C} \gamma_c L(t_c, P_c) \tag{7}$$

$$L(t, P) = -\sum_{i=1}^{N}\sum_{j=1}^{M} t_{i,j} \log P_{i,j} \tag{8}$$

where γ_c is the weights for each task c respectively, C is the sum of tasks, $P_{i,j}$ is the probability result, $t_{i,j}$ is the true result, N denotes the number of training samples and M is the class number.

Table 1. Performance of different methods for single task models.

Embedding	Learning models	CUPM	CBOM	CBAM	NI	VI
Tencent embedding	TEXT-CNN	0.48	0.47	0.59	0.69	0.65
	TEXT-LSTM	0.50	0.49	0.63	0.70	0.66
	TEXT-BiLSTM	0.53	0.51	0.65	0.74	0.69
	MI-BiLSTM	0.55	0.56	0.69	0.77	0.73
	MI-BiLSTM-ATT	0.64	0.60	0.72	0.79	0.76
Word2vec embedding	TEXT-CNN	0.50	0.55	0.61	0.69	0.69
	TEXT-LSTM	0.56	0.58	0.65	0.73	0.72
	TEXT-BiLSTM	0.57	0.61	0.67	0.76	0.73
	MI-BiLSTM	0.59	0.60	0.72	0.80	0.77
	MI-BiLSTM-ATT	0.67	0.62	0.77	0.81	0.79
Fine-tuning embedding	TEXT-CNN	0.59	0.59	0.63	0.70	0.73
	TEXT-LSTM	0.63	0.63	0.68	0.73	0.75
	TEXT-BiLSTM	0.65	0.68	0.72	0.79	0.76
	MI-BiLSTM	0.68	0.74	0.78	0.82	0.80
	MI-BiLSTM-ATT	**0.73**	**0.79**	**0.81**	**0.84**	**0.82**

4   Experiments

In this section, we describe the experimental details. All experiments are performed on a server with Intel(R) Xeon(R) E5-2620 2.40 GHz CPU and NVIDIA GeForce GTX 1080Ti, running Windows Server 2016 and 64 GB memory.

4.1   Data

In our experiment, we collect electronic medical records from a hospital. We ask ten volunteers to label the data. Finally, we get 11,818 labeled records with five cancer indicators. We randomly selected 80% of them as training data, and the remaining 20% as test data. Our task is to extract the status of five cancer indicators, including {CUPM, CBOM, CBAM, NI, and VI} (cancer involved in upper margin, cancer involved in bottom margin, cancer involved in base margin, nerve invasion, and vascular invasion). And the status of cancer indicators has three labels, including: {YES, NO, and UNKNOWN}.

4.2   Baselines

We compare our method and its variants with three embedding methods, including Tencent mmbedding [10] which are pre-trained on 8 million Chinese words and phrases, word2vec embedding [7] which produce word embedding from the training data, and fine-tuning embedding which fine-tune Tencent embedding by using the training data.

Table 2. Performance of different methods for multi-task models.

Embedding	Learning models	CUPM	CBOM	CBAM	NI	VI
Tencent embedding	MT-TEXT-CNN	0.50	0.58	0.62	0.71	0.73
	MT-TEXT-LSTM	0.57	0.60	0.64	0.74	0.75
	MT-TEXT-BiLSTM	0.58	0.61	0.67	0.75	0.77
	MT-MI-BiLSTM	0.60	0.61	0.70	0.80	0.79
	MT-MI-BiLSTM-ATT	0.65	0.67	0.74	0.83	0.80
Word2vec embedding	MT-TEXT-CNN	0.56	0.61	0.79	0.80	0.79
	MT-TEXT-LSTM	0.61	0.62	0.80	0.82	0.80
	MT-TEXT-BiLSTM	0.84	0.82	0.80	0.83	0.80
	MT-MI-BiLSTM	0.87	0.84	0.81	0.82	0.81
	MT-MI-BiLSTM-ATT	0.92	0.88	0.83	0.85	0.84
Fine-tuning embedding	MT-TEXT-CNN	0.62	0.65	0.81	0.83	0.80
	MT-TEXT-LSTM	0.68	0.67	0.81	0.85	0.80
	MT-TEXT-BiLSTM	0.86	0.83	0.82	0.85	0.81
	MT-MI-BiLSTM	0.88	0.85	0.83	0.85	0.82
	MT-MI-BiLSTM-ATT	**0.93**	**0.89**	**0.83**	**0.86**	**0.86**

4.3   Learning Models

Our learning models are divided into two departments, including single task models and multi-task models. Single task models get a multi-class result and multi-task models obtain five multi-class results. In the experiment setup for multi-task models, the loss weight of five attribute extractors are 0.385, 0.385, 0.039, 0.039, and 0.154.

- TEXT-CNN [4] and MT-TEXT-CNN. TEXT-CNN takes the whole text as input and consists of word embedding layer and CNN layer. MT-TEXT-CNN is the multi-task version.
- TEXT-LSTM [6] and MT-TEXT-LSTM. TEXT-CNN takes the whole text as input and consists of word embedding layer and LSTM layer. MT-TEXT-LSTM is the multi-task version.
- TEXT-BiLSTM and MT-TEXT-BiLSTM. TEXT-BiLSTM takes the whole text as input and consists of word embedding layer and BiLSTM layer. MT-TEXT-BiLSTM is the multi-task version.

- MI-BiLSTM and MT-MI-BiLSTM. MI-BiLSTM treats each sentence of the whole text as an instance, and takes all the instances as input, and consists of word embedding layer and BiLSTM layer. MT-MI-BiLSTM is the multi-task version.
- MI-BiLSTM-ATT and MT-MI-BiLSTM-ATT. MI-BiLSTM-ATT treats each sentence of the whole text as an instance, and takes all the instances as input, and consists of word embedding layer, BiLSTM layer and attention layer. MT-MI-BiLSTM-ATT is the multi-task version.

4.4 Performance

We use *accuracy* metric to evaluate the performance of different learning models. The comparison results are shown in Tables 1 and 2.

The first observation is that, *by using the same embedding method, different learning models would achieve different performance*. The details are as follows:

- Firstly, compared to the single task methods, multi-task neural network models perform better than single task ones, which demonstrates the predictive power of multi-task nerual models.
- Secondly, MT-MI-BiLSTM and MT-MI-BiLSTM-ATT perform better than MT-TEXT-BiLSTM, which demonstrates the effectiveness of our multi-instance learning strategy.
- Thirdly, MT-MI-BiLSTM-ATT performs better than MT-MI-BiLSTM, which demonstrates that the attention measure is very useful to select the most important instances.

The second observation is that, *by using the same learning method, different embedding methods would also achieve different performance*. The details are as follows:

- Firstly, the Tencent Embedding method achieve the worst performance, which demonstrates that pre-trained word embedding on general corpus do not capture domain specific semantics/knowledge.
- Secondly, the Fine-tuning Embedding method achieve the best performance, demonstrating the effectiveness of our embedding strategy.

4.5 Application

Our method is very useful for the standardization of electronic medical records. Because doctors are more inclined to use natural language to write electronic medical records. Due to the diversity of natural language, the contents written by different doctors are not the same. Therefore, tools are needed to normalize the records written by different doctors. Our standardization process consists of two steps. The first step is to extract the corresponding attribute values through the extractors (which is the focus of this paper). In the second step, the corresponding text is generated based on the attribute value pairs. The application is shown in the Fig. 4. Currently, we can normalize the electronic medical records extracted by five attribute extractors. In the future, we will extract more different types of attributes.

5   Related Work

In this section, we review and summarize the works that are most relevant to our research. These include works in named entity recognition, entity typing, text classification and multi-task learning. Named entity recognition is a task that classifies an entity mention in a sentence into a predefined set of types [8]. Recent works have focused on a large set of fine-grained types [1,5,17], since their types are not mutually exclusive, they cast the problem as multi-label classification problems. However, most of them use hand-crafted features, such as *Head, POS, Word Shape, Length, Brown Cluster*, etc, which requires great human effort. [1] proposes the neural network model for named entity recognition. But these methods only apply to a single sentence.

Fig. 4. The application is used for attribute extraction tasks related to electronic medical records.

Entity typing is a task that classifies an entity in knowledge bases into a predefined set of types. Recently, many works have been proposed to use text corpus to infer entity types. Specifically, we split the corpus into sentences, and propose a multi-task learning model to infer its types from all the sentences of the abstract text [13–15]. But they only focus on the types of entities in sentences, instead of the types of the sentences.

Text classification is a classical natural language task that classifies text according to a certain classification system. Recent works have focus on using neural network model for classification tasks. CNN is widely used in text classification tasks [18]. Recurrent Neural Network (RNN) based on long short-term memory (LSTM) also is used for classification tasks. However, those neural network model consider the entire context of a text to get a classification result. Our model extract different attribute values from a text.

Multi-task neural networks were also used in many applications related to NLP. Firat et al. [3] improved the performance on neural machine translation which can make use of cross-lingual information. And multi-task learning has been used in classification by jointly training related tasks [2,6,12]. In contrast to previous approach, our proposed methods is to train multi-task classifier models on deep features for attribute classification, thus obtaining better results.

6 Conclusion

In this paper, we study the problem of extracting attribute values from the unstructured text of electronic medical records. Since we treat the attribute value extraction task as multiple *multi-class classification* problem, we propose a multi-task learning method to jointly learn related tasks to help improve the generalization performance of all the tasks. At the same time, we use an end-to-end neural network model to complete this task. Firstly, we take each sentence/segment of the text as an instance. For each instance, we use the pre-trained word embedding to better initialize our neural network models. Secondly, considering the pre-trained word embedding is trained on large-scale general corpus, we fine-tune it by using our domain corpus to capture domain specific semantics/knowledge. Thirdly, we use BiLSTM layer to obtain a better instance representation and use an attention layer to select the most important instances for different attribute extractors. Finally, multi-task learning was used in output layer to extract the status of some cancer indicators. Experimental results show the effectiveness of our method.

References

1. Dong, L., Wei, F., Sun, H., Zhou, M., Xu, K.: A hybrid neural model for type classification of entity mentions. In: Proceedings of the 24th International Conference on Artificial Intelligence, pp. 1243–1249 (2015)
2. Fanhe, X., Guo, J., Huang, Z., Qiu, W., Zhang, Y.: Multi-task learning with knowledge transfer for facial attribute classification. In: IEEE International Conference on Industrial Technology, ICIT 2019, pp. 877–882 (2019)
3. Firat, O., Cho, K., Bengio, Y.: Multi-way, multilingual neural machine translation with a shared attention mechanism. In: NAACL HLT 2016, The 2016 Conference of the North American Chapter of the Association for Computational Linguistics: Human Language Technologies, pp. 866–875 (2016)

4. Kim, Y.: Convolutional neural networks for sentence classification. In: Proceedings of the 2014 Conference on Empirical Methods in Natural Language Processing, EMNLP 2014, pp. 1746–1751 (2014)
5. Ling, X., Weld, D.S.: Fine-grained entity recognition. In: Proceedings of the Twenty-Sixth AAAI Conference on Artificial Intelligence, pp. 94–100 (2012)
6. Liu, P., Qiu, X., Huang, X.: Recurrent neural network for text classification with multi-task learning. In: Proceedings of the Twenty-Fifth International Joint Conference on Artificial Intelligence, IJCAI 2016, pp. 2873–2879 (2016)
7. Mikolov, T., Chen, K., Corrado, G.S., Dean, J.: Efficient estimation of word representations in vector space. CoRR, pp. 1–12 (2013)
8. Ren, X., El-Kishky, A., Ji, H., Han, J.: Automatic entity recognition and typing in massive text data. In: Proceedings of the 2016 International Conference on Management of Data, pp. 2235–2239 (2016)
9. Sarma, P.K., Liang, Y., Sethares, B.: Domain adapted word embeddings for improved sentiment classification. In: Proceedings of the 56th Annual Meeting of the Association for Computational Linguistics, ACL 2018, Volume 2: Short Papers, pp. 37–42 (2018)
10. Song, Y., Shi, S., Li, J., Zhang, H.: Directional skip-gram: explicitly distinguishing left and right context for word embeddings. In: Proceedings of the 2018 Conference of the North American Chapter of the Association for Computational Linguistics: Human Language Technologies, Volume 2 (Short Papers), pp. 175–180. Association for Computational Linguistics (2018)
11. Sun, W., Cai, Z., Li, Y., Liu, F., Fang, S., Wang, G.: Data processing and text mining technologies on electronic medical records: a review. J. Healthc. Eng. **2018**, 1–9 (2018)
12. Tian, B., Zhang, Y., Wang, J., Xing, C.: Hierarchical inter-attention network for document classification with multi-task learning. In: Proceedings of the Twenty-Eighth International Joint Conference on Artificial Intelligence, IJCAI 2019, pp. 3569–3575 (2019)
13. Xu, B., et al.: METIC: multi-instance entity typing from corpus. In: Proceedings of the 27th ACM International Conference on Information and Knowledge Management, pp. 903–912 (2018)
14. Yaghoobzadeh, Y., Adel, H., Schütze, H.: Noise mitigation for neural entity typing and relation extraction. In: Proceedings of the 15th Conference of the European Chapter of the Association for Computational Linguistics: Volume 1, Long Papers, vol. 1, pp. 1183–1194 (2017)
15. Yaghoobzadeh, Y., Schütze, H.: Corpus-level fine-grained entity typing using contextual information. In: Proceedings of the 2015 Conference on Empirical Methods in Natural Language Processing, pp. 715–725 (2015)
16. Yang, Z., Yang, D., Dyer, C., He, X., Smola, A.J., Hovy, E.H.: Hierarchical attention networks for document classification. In: HLT-NAACL, pp. 1480–1489 (2016)
17. Yosef, M.A., Bauer, S., Hoffart, J., Spaniol, M., Weikum, G.: HYENA: hierarchical type classification for entity names. In: 24th International Conference on Computational Linguistics, pp. 1361–1370 (2012)
18. Zhang, X., Zhao, J., LeCun, Y.: Character-level convolutional networks for text classification. In: Advances in Neural Information Processing Systems, vol. 28, pp. 649–657 (2015)
19. Zheng, G., Mukherjee, S., Dong, X.L., Li, F.: OpenTag: open attribute value extraction from product profiles. In: Proceedings of the 24th ACM SIGKDD International Conference on Knowledge Discovery and Data Mining, pp. 1049–1058. ACM (2018)

Uncertain Ontology-Aware Knowledge Graph Embeddings

Khaoula Boutouhami$^{(\boxtimes)}$, Jiatao Zhang, Guilin Qi$^{(\boxtimes)}$, and Huan Gao

School of Computer Science and Engineering, Southeast University, Nanjing, China
kboutouhami@gmail.com,1193744197@qq.com,{qgi,gh}@seu.edu.cn

Abstract. Much attention has recently been given to knowledge graphs embedding by exploiting latent and semantic relations among entities and incorporating the structured knowledge they contain into machine learning. Most of the existing graph embedding models can only encode a simple model of the data, while few models are designed for ontology rich knowledge graphs. Furthermore, many automated knowledge construction tools produce modern knowledge graphs with rich semantics and uncertainty. However, there is no graph embedding model which includes uncertain ontological information into graph embedding models. In this paper, we propose a novel embedding model UOKGE (Uncertain Ontology-aware Knowledge Graph Embeddings), which learns embeddings of entities, classes, and properties on uncertain ontology-aware knowledge graphs according to confidence scores. The proposed method preserves both structures and uncertainty of knowledge in the embedding space. Specifically, UOKGE encodes each entity in a knowledge graph as a point of n-dimensional vector, each class as a n-sphere and each property as 2n-sphere in the same semantic space. This representation allows for the natural expression of uncertain ontological triples. The preliminary experimental results show that UOKGE can robustly learn representations of uncertain ontology-aware knowledge graphs when evaluated on a benchmark dataset.

Keywords: Ontology-aware knowledge graph · Knowledge graphs · Embedding · Uncertainty

1 Introduction

Knowledge Graphs (KGs) play an essential role in many fields, such as Semantic Web Search, Question Answering, and Information Retrieval. The advantage of using KGs is their ability to represent knowledge in a format that is easier to grasp by a user. Knowledge graphs can be categorized into two views: (i) a simple model of knowledge graph which is essentially a set of binary relational data and (ii) the ontology-aware knowledge graph which contains specific semantics for classes and properties in a knowledge graph. Moreover, a knowledge graph can be turned into an uncertain knowledge graph by annotating the triples with a weight that expresses uncertainty.

© Springer Nature Singapore Pte Ltd. 2020
X. Wang et al. (Eds.): JIST 2019, CCIS 1157, pp. 129–136, 2020.
https://doi.org/10.1007/978-981-15-3412-6_13

Recently, knowledge graph embedding models have the potential of becoming a fundamental tool for incorporating the structured knowledge representations in Knowledge graphs into machine learning. These models learn to capture latent representations of triples in a knowledge graph by mapping the entities and the relations of triples into a low-dimensional vector space. Various approaches have been proposed for knowledge graph embeddings. Among them, translation-based models perform efficiently for large graphs with high accuracy. The first model in this sub-field was TransE model [1] which learns vector embeddings h, r and t which satisfy $r \approx t - h$. Thereafter, TransH model [12], TransR model [8] and TransD model [5], etc are proposed to solve the problem of TransE model when modeling 1-to-N, N-to-1, and N-to-N relations. All of the previously mentioned models do not learn embedding representations on uncertain knowledge graphs, where the uncertainty is represented in terms of a confidence score. UKGE model [2] is proposed to capture uncertainty information in multi-relational representation learning.

Nowadays, modern KGs are often enriched by rich ontological triples. In this context, EmbedS model [3] is proposed to explore the problem of graph embedding on ontology-rich KGs which considers RDFS classes and other ontological information as first-class citizens, providing a geometrical interpretation for triples and ontology assertions.

One of the major limitations of the existing models is that they do not include uncertain ontological information into graph embedding models. Although uncertain and rich ontological triples often accompany the KGs. In general, the uncertainty of knowledge is valuable because it shows its degree of reliability. One of the consequences of ignoring the confidence score of the knowledge is that noisy knowledge can degrade the quality of the embedding representations.

In this paper, we propose a novel embedding method for the semantic representation of uncertain ontology-aware, to deal with the uncertainty of triples in ontology-aware KGs. To the best of our knowledge, there has been no previous work on learning embeddings for uncertain ontology-aware Knowledge Graphs. Specifically, we consider the unsolved problem of graph embedding on uncertain ontology-aware knowledge graphs where the simplest languages RDFS expresses the rich ontological triples, and the uncertainty degree is treated as the confidence score for a triple. We use the spherical representation to encode entities, classes, and properties in the same coordinate space. This representation allows for a natural expression of uncertainty associated with RDFS ontological constraints. We provide preliminary results that show UOKGE to be comparable to state-of-the-art graph embedding techniques when measured on a benchmark dataset.

2   Related Work

Various approaches have been proposed to handle the task of link prediction in knowledge graph embeddings. The key idea is to encode a given set of triples into a low-dimensional vector space. Various approaches for knowledge graph embeddings have been proposed [11]. Among them, translation-based models. TransE model [1] is one of the most popular models, which interprets relationships as translations operating on the low-dimensional embeddings of the entities. Despite its conceptual simplicity and its efficiency, this model cannot deal with reflexive one-to-many, many-to-one, and many-to-many. A large number of approaches have been proposed in recent years, including TransH model [12] which projects entities on a hyper-plane before applying the translation and TransR model [8], which builds entity and relation embeddings in separate entity space and relation spaces. In order to distinguish between concepts and instances and regard both as entities to make a simplification, TransC model [9] is proposed which embeds instances, concepts, and relations in the same space to deal with the transitivity of isA relations. Most of the proposed models considered the knowledge graph as nothing than a set of binary relations, with no special semantics while modern RDF data are often enriched by rich ontological information. Embeds model [3] is proposed to explore the problem of training graph embedding on ontology-rich knowledge graphs by considering RDFS classes and other ontological information as first-class citizens. EmbedS model uses the spherical representation to encode the entities, classes, and relationships, thus provide a geometrical interpretation of the embedding space. Also, it offers the possibility of a new mode of triple classification based on the geometrical interpretation of the embedding space.

3   Problem Formulation

In this section, we define the uncertain ontology-rich KG embedding problem by first introducing the definition of uncertain ontology-aware KGs.

Definition 1. *Uncertain ontology-aware KGs*
An uncertain ontology-aware KGs is a finite set of weighted triples of the form $\langle l, s_l \rangle$. For each pair $\langle l, s_l \rangle$, $l = (h, r, t)$ is a triple that can be an ordinary relation or can be one of the following relation: Type, Subclass, Domain, Range, Subproperty, and $s_l \in (0, 1]$ indicates the confidence score of the knowledge.

In this work, we assume that only the set of triples that are not wholly uncertain and not wholly certain are considered ($0 < s_l < 1$) and interpret the confidence score as *a weight* of the triple. If we consider $\forall s_l, s_l = 1$ then we represent an ontology-aware KGs.

Example 1. We consider the following uncertain ontology-rich graph data:

$G = \{\ \langle (John, type, Loyal), \delta_1 \rangle \qquad\qquad \langle (Discount, sc, Loyal), \delta_2 \rangle$
$\qquad\ \langle (NeedBased, sc, Discount), \delta_3 \rangle \qquad \langle (Loyal, dom, satisfiedBy), \delta_4 \rangle$
$\qquad\ \langle (FidelityS, range, satisfiedBy), \delta_5 \rangle \quad \langle (John, satisfiedBy, Gifts), \delta_6 \rangle \}$

The triple $\langle (Discount, sc, Loyal), \delta_2 \rangle$ states that "a Discount customer may be a Loyal customer with a confidence score equal to δ_2.

Definition 2. *Problem*
Given an uncertain ontology-aware KG denoted by G, the problem of uncertain ontology-aware KGs embedding aims to represent each entity as a point of n-dimensional, class as n-sphere and properties as $2n$-sphere.

4 Our Approach

In this section, we propose our model for uncertain ontology-aware KG embeddings. The proposed model UOKGE encodes the knowledge graph structure according to the confidence of triple.

4.1 Framework

Consider an uncertain RDFs dataset G, and let E, C, and P be the sets of entities, classes, and properties. The problem of uncertain ontology-rich knowledge graphs embedding is modeled as follow:

- Each instance $e_i \in E$ is represented as a point of n-dimensional vector of parameters (i.e. variables $e_i = (e_{i_1}, \ldots, e_{i_n})$),
- Each class $c_i \in C$ is represented as a sphere $s_i(c_i, \rho_i)$ where $c_i = (c_{i_1}, \ldots, c_{i_n})$ is the centre of the sphere and the parameter ρ_i is its radius and
- Each property $p_i \in P$ is represented as a sphere $s_i((p_i^d, p_i^r), \varrho_i)$, where (p_i^d, p_i^r) are the centre of the sphere, p_i^d represent the domain and p_i^r represent the range. The parameter ϱ_i represent its radius.

For what follows, we first define a mapping function σ which allows changing the scale from $\mathbb{R}$ to $[0, 1]$ defined as follow:

$$\sigma(x) = 1 - \frac{2}{1 + e^{2.x}} \tag{1}$$

In this work, we have six kinds of triples and define different gap functions for them, respectively:

- **Uncertain type triple** $t = \langle (e_i, type, c_i), s_l \rangle \in E \times \{type\} \times C$.

$$Gap(t) = 1 - \sigma(\max(0, \| e_i - c_i \|_2 - \rho_i)) \tag{2}$$

- **Uncertain data triple** $t = \langle (e_i, p, e_j), s_l \rangle \in E \times P \times E$.

$$Gap(t) = 1 - \sigma(\max(0, \| e_i - p^d \|_2 + \| e_j - p^r \|_2 - \varrho)) \tag{3}$$

- **Uncertain subclass triple** $t = \langle (c_i, sc, c_j), s_l \rangle \in C \times \{sc\} \times C$.

$$Gap(t) = 1 - \sigma(\max(0, \| c_i - c_j \|_2 - \rho_j + \rho_i)) \tag{4}$$

- **Uncertain domain triple** $t = \langle (p_i, dom, c_i), s_l \rangle \in C \times \{dom\} \times P$. The gap function is:

$$Gap(t) = 1 - \sigma(\max(0, \| p_i^d - c_i \|_2 - \varrho_i)) \tag{5}$$

- **Uncertain range triple** $t = \langle (p_i, range, c_i), s_l \rangle \in C \times \{range\} \times P$. The gap function is:

$$Gap(t) = 1 - \sigma(\max(0, \| p_i^r - c_i \|_2 - \varrho_i)) \tag{6}$$

- **Uncertain sub-property triple** $t = \langle(p_i, sp, p_j), s_l\rangle \in P \times \{sp\} \times P$. The gap function is:

$$Gap(t) = 1 - \sigma(\max(0, \| p_i^d - p_j^d \|_2 + \| p_i^r - p_j^r \|_2 - (\varrho_i - \varrho_j))) \quad (7)$$

In experiments, we enforce constrains as $\| e \|_2 \leq 1, \| c \|_2 \leq 1, \| p \|_2 \leq 1, \| \rho \|_2 \leq 1$ and $\| \varrho \|_2 \leq 1$.

4.2 Objective Formalization

In this subsection, we present the objective function of uncertain ontology-aware KG embeddings.

The goal of the objective function $\mathcal{L}_*$ is to minimize the mean squared error (MSE) between the confidence score s_l and our gap Gap(t) for each triple t, $\mathcal{L}_*$ is defined as follows:

$$\mathcal{L}_* = \sum_{t \in \mathcal{T}} | Gap(t) - s_l |^2 \quad (8)$$

where $*$ is one of the precise form of triples and $\mathcal{T}$ is the set of relation facts. The overall objective function is a combinations of all the objective functions:

$$\mathcal{L} = \mathcal{L}_{type} + \mathcal{L}_{data} + \mathcal{L}_{sc} + \mathcal{L}_{dom} + \mathcal{L}_{range} + \mathcal{L}_{sp} \quad (9)$$

We use Gradient-Based Optimization to optimize our model. The spherical representation allows a geometrical interpretation. By embedding entities as single n-dimensional vectors, classes as regions of the euclidean space and properties as pairs of points, we are modeling them as points, as n-spheres and 2n-spheres respectively and we are representing the uncertainty of the triple (h,r,t) as a gap the reflect its confidence degree. The higher the confidence degree is, the lower the uncertainty is, the closer the head h to the tail t is. For instance, given type triple $t = \langle(e_i, type, c_i), s_l\rangle$, the point e_i should be outside the sphere c_i with a gap equal to its confidence score. Actually, there are two other relative position:

- The point e_i is far from the sphere c_i (For example $s_l = 0.95$ and $Gap(t) = 0.24$, see Fig. 1a). In this condition, the point need to get closer.
- The point e_i is near from the sphere c_i (For example $s_l = 0.65$ and $Gap(t) = 1$, Fig. 1b). In this condition, the point need to get far.

5 Preliminary Experimental Results

In this section, we present a preliminary experimental evaluation of the proposed model. We evaluate our models on two tasks: confidence prediction and triples classification. An exhaustive experimental evaluation will be left for future work.

Fig. 1. The relative positions between the point e_i and the sphere c_i

Most previous work used NL27 and PPI5k for evaluation. But these two datasets are not suitable for our model because NL27 and PPI5k mainly consists of relation facts. Therefore, we use another popular knowledge graph **CN15K**, which is a sub-graph of the commonsense KG ConceptNet. This sub-graph contains 15,000 entities and 241,158 uncertain relation.

We considered the following baselines in our comparison: EmbedS [3] and complEx [10], UKGE [2] and URGE [6].

5.1 Confidence Prediction

This task aim to predict confidence scores of unknown triples. For each uncertain triples, we predict the confidence score and report the mean square error (MSE).

$$MSE = \frac{1}{n} \sum_{i=1}^{n} (y_i - x_i)^2 \tag{10}$$

$$MAE = \frac{1}{n} \sum_{i=1}^{n} abs(y_i - x_i) \tag{11}$$

Where: y_i is the confidence score, x_i the predicted score, $(y_i - x_i)^2$ is the squares of the errors and $abs(y_i - x_i)$ is the absolute Error (Table 1). The obtained results are depicted in Table 2.

Table 1. Examples of confidence prediction

Head	Relation	Tail	Confidence	Predicted confidence
Stromboli	Type	Stratovolcano	0.525878	0.507512
Bowl	Subclassof	Containerful	0.892709	0.875841
Patient	Subclassof	Person	0.709293	0.744984

From Table 2, we can see that the results are very encouraging. Our model outperform the baseline URGE and UKGE.

Table 2. Mean squared error (MSE) and mean absolute error (MAE)

Metrics	MSE	MAE
URGE	0.063	0.201
UKGE	0.0119	0.0739
UOKGE	**0.0096**	**0.0682**

5.2 Triple Classification

This task can be viewed as a binary classification task. It aims to judge whether a triple t is strong or not. In an uncertain ontology-aware KG, a triple is considered strong if its confidence score s_l is above a specific threshold ζ, otherwise weak. We followed a procedure that is similar to the protocol in [12]. We also assure that the number of generated negative triples should be equal to that of positive triples. For each dataset, we set the confidence threshold ζ and divide the test cases into two groups, strong and weak, by their confidence scores. Here we set $\zeta = 0.7$ for $CN15k$. A given triple t, if its confidence score is above than ζ, it will be classified as positive, otherwise negative (Table 3).

Table 3. Experimental results on triple classification

Metrics	Accuracies (%)
complEx	60.1
EmbedS	91.1
URGE	76.0
UKGE	91.9
UOKGE	**95.5**

The experimental results are very encouraging: we can observe that UOKGE model outperform all baseline models.

6 Conclusion and Future Work

In this paper, we developed the new problem of training graph embeddings on uncertain ontology-rich datasets. We propose a model which includes uncertain ontological information into graph embedding models. Preliminary experimental results show that the model can perform at state-of-the-art levels on standard benchmark datasets.

One meaningful future work is an exhaustive experimental evaluation on relation fact ranking for standard benchmark datasets and uncertain ontology-rich datasets. We also plan to demonstrate with a downstream application such as fact validation in order to show the further contribution of our approach, propose an approach that combines the logic rule-based methods and the ontology-rich knowledge graph embedding methods, explore more expressive model instead of spheres to represent classes and properties and study knowledge graph reasoning consider one of formalism for representing uncertainty: probability theory [7], fuzzy sets [13], possibility theory [4].

Acknowledgements. Research presented in this paper was partially supported by the National Key Research and Development Program of China under grants (2018YFC0830200, 2017YFB1002801), the Natural Science Foundation of China grants (U1736204).

References

1. Bordes, A., Usunier, N., Garcia-Duran, A., Weston, J., Yakhnenko, O.: Translating embeddings for modeling multi-relational data. In: Proceedings of NIPS, pp. 2787–2795 (2013)
2. Chen, X., Chen, M., Shi, W., Sun, Y., Zaniolo, C.: Embedding uncertain knowledge graphs. In: Proceedings of AAAI, pp. 3363–3370 (2019)
3. Diaz, G.I., Fokoue, A., Sadoghi, M.: EmbedS: scalable, ontology-aware graph embeddings. In: Proceedings of EDBT, pp. 433–436 (2018)
4. Dubois, D., Prade, H.: Possibility theory, probability theory and multiple-valued logics: a clarification. Ann. Math. Artif. Intell. **32**(1–4), 35–66 (2001). https://doi.org/10.1023/A:1016740830286
5. Ji, G., He, S., Xu, L., Liu, K., Zhao, J.: Knowledge graph embedding via dynamic mapping matrix. In: Proceedings of ACL, pp. 687–696 (2015)
6. Hu, J., Cheng, R., Huang, Z., Fang, Y., Luo, S.: On embedding uncertain graphs. In: Proceedings of CIKM, pp. 157–166 (2017)
7. Kallenberg, O.: Foundations of modern probability. Springer, New York (2006). https://doi.org/10.1007/b98838
8. Lin, Y., Liu, Z., Sun, M., Liu, Y., Zhu, X.: Learning entity and relation embeddings for knowledge graph completion. In: Proceedings of AAAI (2015)
9. Lv, X., Hou, L., Li, J., Liu, Z.: Differentiating concepts and instances for knowledge graph embedding. In: Proceedings of EMNLP, pp. 1971–1979 (2018)
10. Trouillon, T., Welbl, J., Riedel, S., Gaussier, É., Bouchard, G.: Complex embeddings for simple link prediction. In: Proceedings of ICML, pp. 2071–2080 (2016)
11. Wang, Q., Mao, Z., Wang, B., Guo, L.: Knowledge graph embedding: a survey of approaches and applications. IEEE Trans. Knowl. Data Eng. **29**(12), 2724–2743 (2017)
12. Wang, Z., Zhang, J., Feng, J., Chen, Z.: Knowledge graph embedding by translating on hyperplanes. In: Proceedings of AAAI (2014)
13. Zadeh, L.A.: Fuzzy sets. Inf. Control **8**(3), 338–353 (1965)

Investigating Schema Definitions Using RDFS and OWL 2 for RDF Databases in Life Sciences

Atsuko Yamaguchi[1]([✉])[iD], Tatsuya Kushida[2,3][iD], Yasunori Yamamoto[1][iD], and Kouji Kozaki[4][iD]

[1] Database Center for Life Science, Research Organization of Information and Systems, 178-4-4 Wakashiba, Kashiwa, Chiba 277-0871, Japan
{atsuko,yy}@dbcls.rois.ac.jp
[2] BioResource Research Center, RIKEN, Tsukuba, Japan
tatsuya.kushida@riken.jp
[3] National Bioscience Database Center, Japan Science and Technology Agency, Tokyo, Japan
[4] Faculty of Information and Communication Engineering, Osaka Electro-Communication University, Neyagawa, Japan
kozaki@osakac.ac.jp

Abstract. With the development of measuring instruments, life science databases are becoming larger and more heterogeneous. As a step towards providing integrated databases, many life science databases have been published as Linked Open Data (LOD). To utilize such databases efficiently, it is desirable that the schema, such as class–class relations, can be acquired in advance from SPARQL Protocol and RDF Query Language (SPARQL) endpoints. However, a SPARQL query to obtain the schema from a SPARQL endpoint often fails because it is time consuming and places an excessive load on the server. On the other hand, many datasets include the definitions using standard vocabularies, such as RDF Schema 1.1 and OWL 2. If the database schema is properly described and provided using RDF Schema 1.1 or OWL 2, it is no longer necessary to obtain it by exhaustively crawling the SPARQL endpoints. Therefore, we investigated the extent of the schema definitions in life sciences databases, focusing on seven specific patterns related to properties using RDF Schema 1.1 or OWL 2. We found that for some datasets, the patterns of domain and range definitions using RDF Schema 1.1, are relatively well defined for properties. However, there are few patterns using OWL 2 as schema definitions for properties. Additionally, we validated RDF datasets by restricting the patterns of domain and range definitions of RDF Schema 1.1. Subsequently, we found that RDF datasets follow these restrictions.

Keywords: Linked Open Data · RDF Schema · OWL 2 · Ontology · Schema validation

© Springer Nature Singapore Pte Ltd. 2020
X. Wang et al. (Eds.): JIST 2019, CCIS 1157, pp. 137–144, 2020.
https://doi.org/10.1007/978-981-15-3412-6_14

1   Introduction

In accordance with recent progress in measurement instruments, life sciences data have been rapidly accumulated in the form of databases. To obtain scientific knowledge from these large and heterogeneous databases, they should be integrated. Therefore, many life science databases have been published as Linked Open Data (LOD) and provided through a web API called a SPARQL endpoint that accepts queries written in SPARQL Protocol and RDF Query Language (SPARQL). However, many biologists, particularly experimental biologists, are not familiar with the semantic web technologies, and therefore, it is difficult for them to obtain required data from LOD. Therefore, a system to suggest a query for data from LOD specific to user requirements, such as PSurfer [1], is necessary. To suggest a query in a feasible time using a system, the schema, such as a list of classes, or properties, and class–class relations of each dataset in LOD, should be obtained in advance. However, if a system obtains the schema of datasets by exhaustively crawling SPARQL endpoints, it often fails because of a time out error of a SPARQL endpoint because of the large size and time-consuming nature of RDF datasets in life sciences.

On the other hand, vocabularies of RDF Schema 1.1 (RDFS) [2] and the OWL 2 Web Ontology Language (OWL 2) [3] are widely used to express a data model for an RDF dataset. Therefore, if RDFS or OWL 2 restrictions, such as `rdfs:domain`, `rdfs:range`, `owl:Restriction`, of each dataset in LOD are properly defined and the dataset follows these restrictions, it should be possible to obtain the schema efficiently because our crawler can skip over SPARQL queries related to these restrictions.

Therefore, as an initial step, we investigated the extent to which schema are defined using RDFS or OWL 2 in RDF datasets and how an RDF dataset follows the restrictions provided. In this study, we investigated the two points described above by focusing on seven specific patterns using RDFS or OWL 2, which could be useful for a crawler in obtaining the schema by narrowing the search space for an RDF dataset.

2   Methods

In this study, we did not consider all words in RDFS and OWL 2 because our purpose was an efficient acquisition of schema using a crawler to SPARQL endpoints by narrowing the search space using restrictions related to classes and properties. Therefore, we focused on the following seven patterns of restrictions of RDFS and OWL 2 that are useful to obtain schema related to classes and properties.

```
(1) ex:property rdfs:domain ex:Domain.
(2) ex:property rdfs:range ex:Range.
(3) ex:property rdfs:range xsd:(datatype).
(4) ex:Class1 rdfs:subClassOf ex:Class3.
    ex:Class3 ex:p owl:Restriction;
              owl:onProperty ex:property;
              owl:someValuesFrom ex:Class2.
(5) ex:Class1 rdfs:subClassOf ex:Class3.
    ex:Class3 ex:p owl:Restriction;
              owl:onProperty ex:property;
              owl:someValuesFrom xsd:(datatype).
(6) ex:Class1 rdfs:subClassOf ex:Class3.
    ex:Class3 ex:p owl:Restriction;
              owl:onProperty ex:property;
              owl:allValuesFrom ex:Class2.
(7) ex:Class1 rdfs:subClassOf ex:Class3.
    ex:Class3 ex:p owl:Restriction;
              owl:onProperty ex:property;
              owl:allValuesFrom xsd:(datatype).
```

To investigate the present restrictions for these seven patterns in life science RDF datasets, we used a list of SPARQL endpoints provided by YummyData [4]. For each of these endpoints, we first investigated the extent to which the schema were defined using the seven aforementioned patterns for properties in the RDF datasets. To this end, we computed a set P of all properties, a set $P(RDFS)$ of properties having restrictions (1) and (2)/(3), and a set $P(OWL)$ of properties having restrictions (4), (5), (6) or (7), by sending SPARQL queries. For example, for a property ex:property, we can obtain restrictions with patterns (4) and (5) by the following SPARQL query.

```
SELECT ?c1 ?c2 WHERE{
    ?c1 rdfs:subClassOf ?s .
    ?s ?p owl:Restriction ;
       owl:onProperty ex:property ;
       owl:someValuesFrom ?c2.}
```

2.1 Validation Policies and Methods

By investigating the properties processing the seven restriction patterns (1)–(7), we obtained a set of restrictions for RDF datasets. To apply these restrictions to a search system, it was vital that an RDF dataset follows these restrictions. Therefore, for each SPARQL endpoint, we tried to validate RDF datasets using these restrictions. As reported in Sect. 3.1, the restrictions collected from SPARQL endpoints were predominantly patterns (1), (2), or (3). Therefore, we focused on these patterns for validating RDF datasets.

However, RDF Schema 1.1 does not provide vocabulary usage. In fact, in Sect. 4 named "Using the Domain and Range vocabulary" of [2], it has been stated that "RDF Schema provides a mechanism for describing this information, but does not say whether or how an application should use it." Therefore, we needed to determine our own validation policy, which was suited to our purpose.

For the restriction pattern (1) `ex:property rdfs:domain ex:Domain`, ideally, for all triples using `ex:property` as predicates, any subjects of the triples should be an instance of `ex:Domain`. However, a subject may be typed using a different class or may even not be typed using any class in an RDF dataset. In [5], both these cases were validated to be false. However, our purpose of `rdfs:domain` use was to narrow search space in order for a crawler to obtain the schema for a SPARQL query. Therefore, we did not have to consider the subject that was not typed using any class to be false because the class of the subject can be easily inferred from the restriction `ex:property rdfs:domain ex:Domain` to be `ex:Domain`. By contrast, a subject that is typed using a different class may hinder search efficiency because a query that searches for instances in the other class would be suggested to the user. Theoretically, if the other class is a subclass of `ex:Domain`, the subject does not violate the restriction. However, many-step inference may be too time-consuming for the system to suggest a SPARQL query. Therefore, we determined that an inference of a single step of `rdfs:subClassOf` was viable for validation.

In conclusion, for a restriction `ex:property rdfs:domain ex:Domain`, and a triple `ex:subject ex:property ex:object`, we regard `ex:subject` to be validated by the restriction when the RDF dataset includes (A) a triple `ex:subject rdf:type ex:Domain`, (B) two triples `ex:subject rdf:type ex:(SubClass)`, and `ex:(SubClass) rdfs:subClassOf ex:Domain`, or (C) no triple `ex:subject rdf:type ex:(Class)`. Furthermore, we regard `ex:subject` to violate the restriction when the RDF dataset includes (D) a triple `ex:subject rdf:type ex:(Class)` and `ex:(Class)`, which is neither `ex:Domain` nor `rdfs:subClassOf ex:Domain`.

The validation policy for pattern (2) was formulated in a similar fashion. For pattern (3), we simply determined the object to be validated if the datatype is `xsd:(datatype)`.

3   Experimental Result

3.1   Rate of Properties with Restrictions

We denote the size of P, $P(RDFS)$, and $P(OWL)$ by $\#P$, $\#P(RDFS)$, and $\#P(OWL)$, respectively. Figure 1 shows the total numbers of $\#P$, $\#P(RDFS)$, and $\#P(OWL)$ for 47 SPARQL endpoints that are shown on the x-axis of Fig. 2. The x-axis of Fig. 1 indicates the sets of properties and the y-axis indicates the total number of properties. It can be seen that the size of $P(OWL)$ is negligibly small.

Figure 2 shows the size of P, $P(RDFS)$, and $P(OWL)$ for each of the 47 SPARQL endpoints. The x-axis indicates SPARQL endpoints sorted by $\#P$ and the y-axis indicates the total number of properties. Note that the y-axis is a logarithmic scale because the number of properties varies greatly between

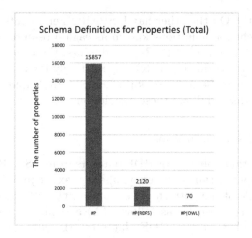

Fig. 1. Total number of the sizes of P, $P(RDFS)$, and $P(OWL)$.

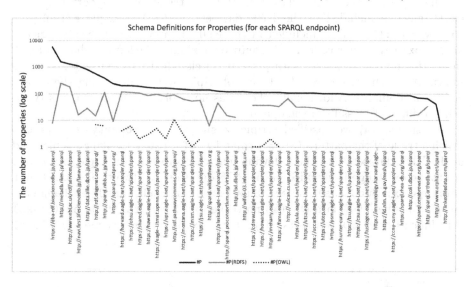

Fig. 2. Sizes of P, $P(RDFS)$, and $P(OWL)$ for each SPARQL endpoint

SPARQL endpoints. It can be seen that the ratio of $P(RDFS)$ and $P(OWL)$ to P varied depending on SPARQL endpoints.

For example, the SPARQL endpoint with the largest number of properties provides an RDF dataset for the Life Science Database (LSDB) archive [6], which is a service to collect, preserve, and provide databases generated by life science researchers in Japan. As of September 2019, the LSDB archive includes 1467 databases. The RDF dataset needs 5606 properties to store heterogeneous databases. However, few schema definitions are provided for the RDF dataset although many resources in the RDF dataset are typed using `rdf:type`. Therefore, for this dataset, restrictions (1)–(7) would not help a crawler in obtaining the schema efficiently. On the other hand, SPARQL endpoints related to eagle-i [7] have common schema definitions known as eagle-i resource ontology (ERO). For datasets provided by these SPARQL endpoints, the ratio of properties having restrictions (1)–(7) defined in ERO was relatively high. Therefore, for these datasets, a crawler may be able to skip some SPARQL queries related to the properties if the datasets follows these restrictions.

3.2   Validation by Restrictions

Based on our validation policies, for RDF datasets from a SPARQL endpoint, we first classified a triple `ex:subject ex:property ex:object` in the RDF datasets to which a triple of the pattern (1) `ex:property rdfs:domain ex:Domain` is included into four categories as follows: (A) a triple `ex:subject rdf:type ex:Domain` is included in the RDF datasets, (B) two triples `ex:subject rdf:type ex:(SubClass).` and `ex:(SubClass) rdfs:subClassOf ex:Domain` are included in the RDF datasets, (C) no triple `ex:subject rdf:type ex:(Class)` is included in the RDF datasets, and (D) a triple `ex:subject rdf:type ex:(Class)` is included in the RDF datasets, where `ex:(Class)` is neither `ex:Domain` nor `rdfs:subClassOf ex:Domain`. The left bar chart of Fig. 3 shows the number of triples with pattern (1) classified into four categories. As shown in the chart, nearly all subjects of triples were typed using the classes defined as domains. Additionally, there was no triple whose subject was typed using a different class from the domain.

In a similar way, we classified a triple `ex:subject ex:property ex:object` to which a triple of the pattern (2) `ex:property rdfs:range ex:Range` is included in the RDF datasets into the following four categories: (A) a triple `ex:object rdf:type ex:Range` is included in the RDF datasets, (B) two triples `ex:object rdf:type ex:(SubClass)` and `ex:(SubClass) rdfs:subClassOf ex:Range` are included in the RDF datasets, (C) no triple `ex:object rdf:type ex:(Class)` is included in the RDF datasets, (D) a triple `ex:object rdf:type ex:(Class)`

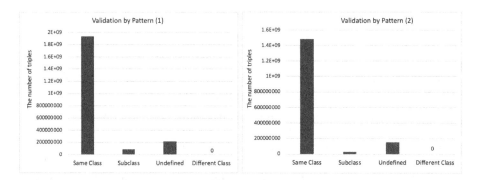

Fig. 3. The number of triples with patterns (1) and (2) classified into four categories. Y-axis indicates the number of triples, and x-axis indicates categories (A) Same Class, (B) Subclass, (C) Undefined, and (D) Different Class.

is included in the RDF datasets, where ex:(Class) is neither ex:Range nor
rdfs:subClassOf ex:Range. The bar chart on the right in Fig. 3 shows the
number of triples with pattern (2) classified into four categories. Similar to the
pattern (1), objects of triples were nearly always typed using the classes defined
as ranges, and there was no triple whose object was typed using a different class
from the range.

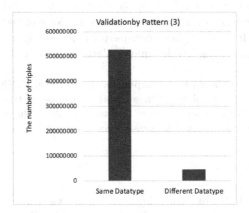

Fig. 4. The number of triples with pattern (3) classified into two categories. Y-axis
indicates the number of triples, and x-axis indicates categories (A) Same Datatype,
and (B) Different Datatype.

For a property with pattern (3) of ex:property rdfs:range xsd:(datatype),
we classified a triple ex:subject ex:property ex:object into two categories: (A)
the datatype of ex:object is xsd:(datatype) or (B) the datatype of ex:object
is not xsd:(datatype). Figure 4 shows the number of triples with pattern (3) classified into two categories. It can be seen that, although almost all datatype for the
objects are correctly attached to literals, some datatypes of objects were wrong.

4   Conclusion

In this study, we investigated two points, the extent to which the schema is
defined using RDFS and OWL 2 in RDF datasets and how an RDF dataset
follows the restrictions provided with the datasets. We focused on seven specific
patterns that can be used by a crawler to obtain a schema more efficiently by
narrowing the search space.

For the first point, although the ratio of $P(RDFS)$ and $P(OWL)$ to P greatly
varies between SPARQL endpoints, $P(RDFS)$ relatively covers P depending on
a SPARQL endpoint. If the RDF datasets follow the restrictions of patterns (1),
(2) and (3), the restriction can be used by a crawler to narrow down the search
space. On the other hand, the ratio of $P(OWL)$ is negligibly small.

To validate RDF datasets by restrictions of patterns (1), (2) and (3), we determined validation policies for our purpose. We defined four categories (A) Same Class, (B) Subclass, (C) Undefined and (D) Different Class of triples, whose predicates have domain or range class definitions in RDF datasets. From our experimental result, all triples were validated by restrictions (1) and (2) because we determined a triple in (A), (B) and (C) to be true for our purpose. For pattern (3), we defined two categories (A) Same Datatype and (B) Different Datatype. As a result, some triples violated the restrictions of datatypes although most triples followed them. Therefore, the restrictions of patterns (1) and (2) can be safely used for search, however, pattern (3) restrictions should be dealt with carefully because some triples may violate the restrictions.

Acknowledgments. This work was supported by JSPS KAKENHI grant numbers 17K00434 and by the National Bioscience Database Center of the Japan Science and Technology Agency. We also acknowledge the participants of the NBDC/DBCLS Bio-Hackathon 2019, who participated in a discussion on a validation method.

References

1. Yamaguchi, A., Toh, H.: Implementing LOD surfer as a search system for the annotation of multiple protein sequence alignment. In: Ichise, R., Lecue, F., Kawamura, T., Zhao, D., Muggleton, S., Kozaki, K. (eds.) JIST 2018. LNCS, vol. 11341, pp. 418–426. Springer, Cham (2018). https://doi.org/10.1007/978-3-030-04284-4_29
2. RDF Schema 1.1. https://www.w3.org/TR/rdf-schema/
3. OWL 2 Web Ontology Language Document Overview. https://www.w3.org/TR/owl2-overview/
4. Yamamoto, Y., Yamaguchi, A., Splendiani, A.: YummyData: providing high-quality open life science data. Database **2018**(1), bay022 (2018)
5. Polikoff, I.: From OWL to SHACL in an automated way. https://www.topquadrant.com/2018/05/01/from-owl-to-shacl-in-an-automated-way/
6. Life Science Database Archive. https://dbarchive.biosciencedbc.jp/
7. eagle-i. https://www.eagle-i.net/

RQE: Rule-Driven Query Expansion to Solve Empty Answers in SPARQL

Xinze Lyu and Wei Hu[⊠]

State Key Laboratory for Novel Software Technology,
Nanjing University, Nanjing, China
xinzelyu@outlook.com, whu@nju.edu.cn

Abstract. A branch of question answering approaches translates natural language questions to SPARQL queries. The empty answer problem exists even when we have properly-translated ones, due to the heterogeneity and incompleteness of knowledge graphs. Existing methods use similarities, ontologies or embeddings to relax failed queries and obtain approximate answers, but they may lose efficacy in approximating simple queries with only one or two constraints because of their low accuracy and suitability for over-constrained ones. In this paper, we propose a rule-driven query expansion approach to expand failed queries for obtaining more accurate approximate answers. Specifically, we first automatically build high-quality rule sets for predicates in failed queries with rule learning techniques. Then, we use the learned rules to expand failed queries to get approximate answers and explain the reasons why we choose these answers. We develop two datasets to evaluate the effectiveness and efficiency of our approach and the results show that our approach achieves better results than several approaches based on similarities, ontologies and embeddings in approximating simple queries.

Keywords: Question answering · SPARQL query expansion · Empty answer · Rule learning

1 Introduction

A typical way to build question answering systems [13,23] is to translate the natural language questions to SPARQL queries and retrieve results by accessing an RDF knowledge graph (KG). Sometimes, the generated SPARQL queries may fail to retrieve any answer. We believe that 3 cases may cause this problem: (1) Answers to the questions are inexistent in the real world. For example, the answer for *"Who are the children of Leonardo DiCaprio?"* is empty because Leonardo has no child. (2) The generated SPARQL queries have syntactic error or wrong node/predicate linking. We conclude this as failures to reflect the intentions of questions. This is the most common case and, in the cross field of natural language processing and database, many works like entity (node) linking [20], relation (predicate) linking [7] and NLIDB [16] try to improve the quality of

© Springer Nature Singapore Pte Ltd. 2020
X. Wang et al. (Eds.): JIST 2019, CCIS 1157, pp. 145–160, 2020.
https://doi.org/10.1007/978-981-15-3412-6_15

translated SPARQL queries. But can we get meaningful answers as long as the questions are valid and the translated SPARQL queries reflect their intentions precisely? Not really. The empty-answer query Q1 of Table 1 shows an example, the question *"Who is the advisor of Yann LeCun?"* is obviously valid and meaningful, Q1 is elaborately constructed to reflect the intension of the question precisely, but it retrieves an empty answer. This is the third situation, (3) the questions and translated SPARQL queries are free from (1) and (2), but there is no clear match for the queries in a KG.

Finding empty result is a correct phenomenon in case (1). Plenty of works in question answering are devoted to case (2), meanwhile case (3) is rarely mentioned. In this paper, we assume that the queries generated by question answering systems are free from cases (1) and (2), i.e., we focus on solving case (3).

Table 1. SPARQL query examples

Q1	SELECT ?advisor WHERE		
	(1) dbr:Yann_LeCun	dbo:doctoralAdvisor	?advisor
Q2	SELECT ?film ?actor WHERE		
	(1) ?film	dbo:starring	?actor
	(2) ?actor	dbo:residence	dbr:Province_of_New_York
Q3	SELECT ?advisor ?student WHERE		
	(1) dbr:Yann_LeCun	dbo:doctoralAdvisor	?advisor
	(2) ?student	dbo:doctoralAdvisor	dbr:Yann_LeCun
Q4	SELECT ?company WHERE		
	(1) ?company	rdf:type	dbo:Company
	(2) ?company	dbo:industry	dbr:Electronics
	(3) dbr:IPhone	dbp:developer	?company
Q5	SELECT ?company WHERE		
	(1) ?company	dbo:regionServed	dbr:Asia
	(2) ?company	dbo:location	dbr:Italy
Q6	SELECT ?o1,?o2 WHERE		
	(1) ?x	dbo:regionServed	?o1
	(2) ?x	dbo:location	?o2

Case (3) Analysis. Before giving solutions, we analyze the causes of case (3) first. We take DBpedia [1] as the queried KG here. The **incompleteness** of a KG is the main factor causing case (3). *"dbr:Geoffrey_Hinton"*[1] is a correct

---

[1] Predefined Namespace Prefixes: dbr ← http://dbpedia.org/resource/, dbo ← http://dbpedia.org/ontology/, dbp ← http://dbpedia.org/property/, rdf ← http://www.w3.org/1999/02/22-rdf-syntax-ns.

answer for Q1 because Yann LeCun used to be a postdoctor of Geoffrey Hinton, but they are only linked by *"dbo:notableStudent"*.

Q1 shows the absence of predicates, but note that another situation is the absence of nodes. Not every advisor of Yann LeCun is recorded in DBpedia [1], so they cannot all be retrieved by only accessing DBpedia, the additional resources like text corpus are needed. In this paper, we do not consider the absence of nodes because of its complexity.

The **heterogeneity** of the KG is another factor. Specifically, KGs can describe the same predicate with multiple ways. For example, in our opinion, it is appropriate to translate *"the advisors of"* into *"dbo:doctoralAdvisor"* or *"dbo:academicAdvisor"*. But when we try to answer *"Who is the advisor of Isaac Newton?"*, only using *"dbo:academicAdvisor"* can retrieve answers. It seems to be a translating problem belonging to case (2), but we argue that it belongs to case (3). Different from *"dbr:Isaac_Newton"*, some entities (like *"dbr:Max_Planck"*) are only linked with their advisors by *"dbo:doctoralAdvisor"*. Relaxing empty-answer queries is a promising way to help these queries get correct answers.

Some studies on query relaxation try to approximate generated SPARQL queries by replacing nodes/predicates with similar ones [8] or using ontology [18] to reform failed queries, but these methods may change the intention of the original failed queries and yield too many irrelevant results. In recent years, embedding techniques [11,22] are used to relax SPARQL queries and approximate failed queries in a continuous vector space. This method is plagued by the quality of embeddings for a very large dataset like DBpedia [1]. It is also a challenge to maintain the embeddings of a large dataset dynamically because the dataset may be updated. Their common problem is that they are more suitable to approximate over-constrained SPARQL queries. For simple queries with only one or two triple patterns, which is more common in current question answering datasets [2,3,17,21]. Their relaxations do not work well.

In this paper, we try to solve case (3) by the reasoning with rules over a KG to get approximate results. Specifically, we focus on simple queries with only one or two triple patterns, which are hard for current query relaxation works to give satisfactory approximate answers.

Motivating Example, Challenges and Solutions. First, we describe the motivating example in Fig. 1 to solve case (3). If we do not know who is the advisor (*doctoralAdvisor*) of Yann LeCun, we could find the man/woman whose students (*notableStudent*) include Yann LeCun. The *"notableStudent"* is a rule of *"doctoralAdvisor"* because we can infer *"doctoralAdvisor"* between two people once knowing they hold *"notableStudent"*. We no longer force *"?advisor"* to satisfy *"dbo:dcotoralAdvisor"* with *"dbr:Yann_LeCun"*, an answer is retrieved as long as it satisfies at least one of rules of *"dbo:doctoralAdvisor"*.

We face two challenges when we use rules to expand queries. First, how to maintain a high-quality rule set of moderate size? In DBpedia, the rules for a predicate (like *"dbo:birthPlace"*) may be more than 10 thousand, it is time consuming if we apply all the rules to search approximate answers. Also, some rules are spurious and only correct in some special cases. These spurious ones

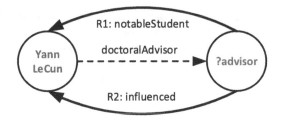

Fig. 1. Query graph to find the advisors of Yann LeCun

should be filtered as soon as possible. Then, how to determine confidence of a triple $\langle s, p, o \rangle$ inexistent in the KG by leveraging the rules of p.

To cope with the above two issues, we use support proportion and precision under partial completeness assumption (PCA) [9] to delete low-quality rules. To give confidence of a triple $\langle s, p, o \rangle$, we construct rule feature vector following the idea in [15] and design a completeness-aware training procedure by using embedding method (like TransE [4]) to generate **soft labels** for training data.

Contributions. We summarize our main contributions as follows:

1. We apply rule learning techniques to solve the empty-answer problem of SPARQL queries.
2. We design a completeness-aware training procedure to leverage rules to give confidence for triples.
3. We construct empty-answer queries dataset EmptyQ by analyzing and imitating questions from real-world question answering datasets [2,3,21]. We also extract two datasets from a subgraph of DBpedia [1] by using patterns of failed queries. The experiments show that our method outperforms three query relaxation methods in accuracy and interpretability.

2 Preliminaries

RDF Knowledge Graph (KG). Following the definition in [5,6], a KG $\mathcal{G}$ is a set of RDF triples. An RDF triple $\langle s, p, o \rangle$ consists of three components: subject s, predicate p, and object o. We call the set of subjects and objects of $\mathcal{G}$ together nodes, which is denoted as $\mathcal{N}$. The set of predicates is denoted as $\mathcal{P}$. In this paper, we only consider the situation that $\forall n \in \mathcal{N}$, n is an IRI. To facilitate rule finding, we add inverse triple $\langle o, p^{-1}, s \rangle$ to the KG for every $\langle s, p, o \rangle$.

Basic Graph Pattern (BGP). Following the definition in [12], we define $\mathcal{V}$ as the set of query variables where $\mathcal{V}$ is disjoint from $\mathcal{N}$ and $\mathcal{P}$. A triple pattern is a member of the set $(\mathcal{N} \cup \mathcal{V}) \times (\mathcal{P} \cup \mathcal{V}) \times (\mathcal{N} \cup \mathcal{V})$. For example, $\langle Gates, found, ?company \rangle$ is a triple pattern where $?company$ is a query variable. A BGP $\mathcal{B}$ is a set of triple patterns. In this paper, we confine a triple pattern to be $\langle s, p, o \rangle$ with only s or o that can be replaced by a query variable v because it is found that the questions to fetch predicates are very rare after surveying some famous question answering datasets like WebQuestions [2], SimpleQuestions [3], QALD [17] and LC-Quad [21]. We also focus on simple SPARQL queries whose BGPs only contain one or two triple patterns.

Rules. In this paper, we aim to mine and use rules in the form of Eq. (1). Technically, these are Horn rules on binary predicates. The left part (rule head) is a predicate and can be inferred by the right part (rule body) which is a sequence of one or more predicates.

$$locationCountry(x, y) \Leftarrow locationCity(x, z) \land country(z, y) \qquad (1)$$

An rule r is a sequence of predicates $\{p_0, ..., p_k\}$, two nodes s and o hold r when there are nodes $\{n_0, ..., n_{k-1}\}$ can connect s and o as $s \xrightarrow{p_0} n_0 \xrightarrow{p_1} ...n_{k-2} \xrightarrow{p_{k-1}} n_{k-1} \xrightarrow{p_k} o$, which is recorded as $r(s, o) \in \mathcal{G}$, meanwhile, $r(s, o) \notin \mathcal{G}$ means that there are no nodes that can connect s and o with $\{p_0, ..., p_k\}$. The number of the predicates in rule body is the length of the rule.

Partial Completeness Assumption (PCA) Confidence. The Closed World Assumption (CWA) assumes that any triple inexistent in a KG does not hold in the real world. For a rule r_i of predicate p (rule head is p), the precision under CWA $P_{cwa}(r_i)$ of r_i is calculated as Eq. (2). CWA will categorize some correct triples as wrong ones, so it is not very precise. AMIE [10] calculates precision of rules under the Partial Completeness Assumption (PCA) which holds the idea that if the KG knows some p-predicates of s, then it knows all p-predicates of s, so it neglects (s, o) whose s does not contain any p-predicates and the PCA precision $P_{pca}(r_i)$ of r_i is calculated as Eq. (3), this metric has proven to be useful in rule mining [9,10]. Under PCA, recall and F-score of r_i are calculated by Eqs. (4) and (5), respectively.

$$P_{cwa}(r_i) = \frac{\#(s, o) : r_i(s, o) \in \mathcal{G} \land p(s, o) \in \mathcal{G}}{\#(s, o) : r_i(s, o) \in \mathcal{G}} \qquad (2)$$

$$P_{pca}(r_i) = \frac{\#(s, o) : r_i(s, o) \in \mathcal{G} \land p(s, o) \in \mathcal{G}}{\#(s, o) : \{\exists o' : r_i(s, o) \in \mathcal{G} \land p(s, o') \in \mathcal{G}\}} \qquad (3)$$

$$R_{pca}(r_i) = \frac{\#(s, o) : r_i(s, o) \in \mathcal{G} \land p(s, o) \in \mathcal{G}}{\#(s, o) : p(s, o) \in \mathcal{G}} \qquad (4)$$

$$F_{pca}(r_i) = \frac{2 \cdot P_{pca}(r_i) \cdot R_{pca}(r_i)}{P_{pca}(r_i) + R_{pca}(r_i)} \qquad (5)$$

3   Related Work

In this section, we analyze limitations of three types of query relaxation works.

Similarity-Based Method (SB). It replaces certain nodes or predicates in failed queries with similar ones to obtain approximate answers. The core component of this method is to calculate a high-quality similarity between nodes/predicates. The main difficulty of this method is how to define "similar".

Assume that we try to obtain LeCun's students and advisors by Q3 in Table 1. If we try to replace *"dbr:Yann_LeCun"*, we should choose LeCun's classmates for constraint (1) (to search LeCun's advisors); but for constraint (2) (to search LeCun's students), LeCun's colleagues are more proper choices. Similar nodes should be chosen according to the situations, but existing methods like [8] just choose nodes under a fixed similarity ranking.

Ontology-Based Method (OB). This method [18] follows RDFS rules in Table 2 (which is got from [18]) to relax queries. Given an ontology $\mathcal{K}$, this method computes the extended reduction $extRed(\mathcal{K})$ of $\mathcal{K}$ first and then assign different cost to Rules (2), (4), (5) and (6) before using them to relax failed queries. For example, relaxing constraint (1) of Q1 in Table 1 with Rule (6) can get *"?advisor rdf:type dbo:Person"*, many irrelevant results are retrieved and it is hard to rank them because they are retrieved by the same relaxation, which means they have the cost. That is the main problem of this method.

Table 2. RDFS rules

Group A (Subproperty)	(1) $\dfrac{(a,sp,b)(b,sp,c)}{a,sp,c}$	(2) $\dfrac{(a,sp,b)(X,a,Y)}{(X,b,Y)}$
Group B (Subclass)	(3) $\dfrac{(a,sc,b)(b,sc,c)}{(a,sc,c)}$	(4) $\dfrac{(a,sc,b)(X,type,a)}{(X,type,b)}$
Group C (Typing)	(5) $\dfrac{(a,dom,c)(X,a,Y)}{(X,type,c)}$	(6) $\dfrac{(a,range,c)(X,a,Y)}{(Y,type,c)}$

Embedding-Based Methods (EB). These methods train embeddings of a KG [11,22] and use the projection in vector space to approximate results. They process Q2 in Table 1 like Eqs. (6) and (7), where $vec(\cdot)$ represents the embedding of a node or predicate.

$$vec(?actor) = vec(dbr{:}Province\_of\_New\_York) - vec(dbo{:}residence) \quad (6)$$

$$vec(?film) = vec(?actor) - vec(dbo{:}starring) \quad (7)$$

We can note that *"?actor"* is only restrained to be a "person" that lives in the Province of New York, it has nothing to do with "actor". The embedding-based methods need an anchor point to achieve the embedding of another points, *"?actor"* cannot be influenced by *"dbo:starring"* because *"?film"* is a variable.

The Common Problem and Analysis. We believe that these methods are particular suitable for over-constrained failed queries. Q4 in Table 1 is a typical over-constrained failed query that we collect from the released resource of [22]. We can infer that *"?company"* is *"dbr:Apple_Inc."* only with constraint (3), while constraints (1) and (2) are redundant.

SB and OB are low-precision methods (see our experiments in Sect. 5). Theoretically, they retrieve approximate answers by alleviating the effect of some constraints. For example, OB can relax constraints (2) to *"?company rdf:type dbo:Company"* using Rule (5) in Table 2 (The domain of *"dbo:industry"* is *"dbo:Company"*) and helps Q4 get *"dbo:Apple_Inc."*. In fact, OB's relaxation deletes constraints (2) and changes the intension of original queries. For queries with only one triple pattern, changing the original intention is highly unlikely to succeed because there is no other triple pattern to constrain the target node. Our method uses rules that can infer expanded predicates to maintain the intensions of original queries as much as possible, so our method has better accuracy in dealing with simple failed queries, which is shown in experiments in Sect. 5.

As an EB method, the working [22] mentions that it is designed to solve over-constrained ones. We think that EB always cannot reach accurate embeddings of results with only one or two triple patterns due to the low quality of embedding generated by the current embedding methods.

4 Rule-Driven Query Relaxation (RQE)

Overview. RQE consists of two sub-tasks: (1) learning rule in a KG; (2) recommending answers to empty-answer queries based on rules learned.

To cope with these two tasks, we develop two modules, a rule learning module and an approximate answer recommendation module. The rule learning module has two goals: the first one is to derive separate predicate-rule sets of different predicates, which are sets of useful rules for target predicates in a KG; based on the predicate-rule sets derived, the second goal is to build separate predicate models of different predicates to give the confidence of whether a node pair holds some predicates. The approximate answers recommendation module first uses predicate-rule sets to search candidate results. Then it ranks them using the predicate models. Finally, it gives explanation for ranked answers using rules.

4.1 Rule Learning Module

Given a predicate p, the aim of rule learning module is to derive predicate-rule set R_p and predicate model M_p.

Deriving Predicate-Rule Set. For any node pair $\langle s, o \rangle$ which holds predicate p in the KG $\mathcal{G}$, we consider the paths linking s and o as the rules that can be used to infer p, Fig. 1 shows two rules of predicate *"dbo:doctoralAdvisor"* in DBpedia. We cannot use the rules directly because some rules are of low quality, just like R2 in Fig. 1 (It is hardly true that A is B's advisor just because A influences B). There are two requirements for any rule r of R_P: (1) r should be accurate, which means node pairs linked by r are more likely to hold p than not hold. (2) r should have high recall rate, which means that the more node pairs holding p can also be linked by r, the better. First, following the idea in [15], we keep rules that are supported by at least a fraction α of training node pairs, as well as being of length no more than β. In our experiments, we set α to 0.01 and β to 3, which means that the maximum number of predicates in rule body of a rule is 3. Then, under PCA, we calculate the PCA F-score of each rule as Eq. (5) and keep top-k rules to construct R_P. In this paper, we set k as 1000.

Generating Predicate Model. Given predicate p, the aim of predicate model M_p is to decide the confidence that a node pair $\langle s, o \rangle$ holds the predicate p based on the predicate-rule set $R_p = \{r_0, r_1, ..., r_n\}$.

Given any node pair $\langle s, o \rangle$, we first use the same way in Path Ranking Algorithm (PRA) [15] to generate rule feature vectors. The rule feature vector of $\langle s, o \rangle$ with respect to R_p is defined as Eq. (8), where each entry of $F(s, o|R_p)$ represents the encoded value of r_i in R_p.

$$F(s, o|R_p) = [y(o|s, r_0), ..., y(o|s, r_n)]^\top \tag{8}$$

$$y(o|s, r) = \begin{cases} 1, & r(s, o) \in \mathcal{G} \\ 0, & \text{otherwise} \end{cases} \tag{9}$$

Then we design a completeness-aware training procedure. Generally speaking, during training, node pairs that hold predicate p is considered as positive data and those do not hold predicate p are negative ones, this way to construct negative data may be wrong sometimes because some negative data are just not recorded in the KG but existent in the real world. To deal with this problem, we use embedding method to get the representation of our KG. The representation of the KG works as a "oracle" to be aware of the situation of every node and their completeness. With the help of embeddings, we design a function $l(s, p, o)$ to generate a **soft label** for training data as Eq. (10), where $vec(\cdot)$ represents the embedding generated by TransE[2] [4] in our experiments.

$$l(s, p, o) = \begin{cases} 1, & \langle s, p, o \rangle \in \mathcal{G} \\ simi(o|s, p), & \text{otherwise} \end{cases} \tag{10}$$

$$simi(o|s, p) = \frac{1 + cosimi(vec(s) + vec(p), vec(o))}{2} \tag{11}$$

$$cosimi(vec(a), vec(b)) = \frac{vec(a) \cdot vec(b)}{||vec(a)|| \, ||vec(b)||} \tag{12}$$

Given training data $\{(s, o)_i\}$, we can get $\{(F(s, o|R_p), l(s, p, o))_i\}$. The objective function to minimize is as Eq. (13), where W is the parameter to estimate, $conf(s, p, o|W)$ is the predicted confidence that node pair $\langle s, o \rangle$ holds predicate p and λ control l2-regularization to prevent overfitting.

$$Loss(W) = \sum_{\{(s,o)_i\}} \left(l(s, p, o)_i - conf(s, p, o|W)_i \right)^2 + \lambda|W|_2 \tag{13}$$

$$conf(s, p, o|W) = \frac{1}{1 + e^{-value(s,p,o|W)}} \tag{14}$$

$$value(s, p, o|W) = WF(s, o|R_p) = w_0 y(o|s, r_0) + ... + w_n y(o|s, r_n) \tag{15}$$

---

[2] Implementation: https://github.com/thunlp/OpenKE/tree/OpenKE-PyTorch.

Implementation Details

1. Based on the consideration of high efficiency, we sample a subgraph of the whole KG to conduct rule learning module in our experiments. Taking DBpedia for example, intuitively, we believe that the rules of *"dbo:birthPlace"* for Americans are almost the same as those for most people in the world. So, we sample nodes within two steps from *"dbr:United_States"* to develop a dataset which describes the knowledge only related to the United States.
2. Each predicate has separate predicate-rule set and predicate model. To generate predicate-rule set of p, we sample at most N node pairs $\langle s, o \rangle$ which hold p to mine rules, these N node pairs also make up positive data to train predicate model of p. To generate negative data, we construct $\langle s, o' \rangle$ that does not hold P for every $\langle s, o \rangle$ belonging to positive data, where o' is randomly chosen from nodes that appeared in positive data (Sampling o' from the whole KG will easily generate meaningless negative data, for example, using *McDonald* to replace *Japan* to construct negative data $(s, birthPlace, McDonald)$). In our experiments, N is set to 1000.

4.2 Approximate Answers Recommendation Module

For a failed query Q, it has several triple patterns $TP(Q) = \{tp_0, ..., tp_n\}$, we expand predicates of every triple pattern tp_i with its learned rules and get $TP'(Q) = \{tp'_0, ..., tp'_n\}$, we fetch candidates $Cand_Q$ by Eq. (16),

$$Cand_Q = \bowtie_{i=0}^{n} query(tp'_i, \mathcal{G}) \tag{16}$$

$$query(tp'_i, \mathcal{G}) = \{\langle s, o \rangle | \exists r \in R'_p, r(s, o) \in \mathcal{G}\}, p \in tp_i \tag{17}$$

$$R'_p = \{p, R_p\} \tag{18}$$

where $query(tp'_i, \mathcal{G})$ is the results queried by tp'_i from KG $\mathcal{G}$ and $\bowtie$ is the natural join on variables shared by triple patterns. The variables of Q are $\mathcal{V}(Q) = \{v^1, .., v^k\}$, the queried results are $Cand_Q = \{(v_i^1, ..., v_i^k)\}$. We calculate the confidence of every result $conf(Q, (v_i^1, ..., v_i^k))$ as Eq. (19), where $(tp_j, (v_i^1, ..., v_i^k))$ means that we use nodes in $(v_i^1, ..., v_i^k)$ to replace corresponding variables in tp_j and W_p means the parameter of p model.

$$conf(Q, (v_i^1, ..., v_i^k)) = \prod_{j=1}^{n} conf(tp_j, (v_i^1, ..., v_i^k)) \tag{19}$$

$$conf(tp_j, (v_i^1, ..., v_i^k)) = conf(s, p, o | W_p), (s, p, o \in tp_j) \tag{20}$$

Then we rank answers in $Cand_Q$, we display confidence c and rules for every triple pattern tp_i. The explanation for Q1 in Table 1 is shown in Table 3.

Table 3. Approximate results of querying the advisors of Yann LeCun

Result	Yann_LeCun, doctoralAdvisor Geoffrey_Hinton	c: 0.66
Rules	dbr:Yann_LeCun → **dbo:notableStudent**$^{-1}$ → dbr:Geoffrey_Hinton	

5   Experimental Evaluation

5.1   Dataset

DBO. We conduct our experiments on mapping-based objects of DBpedia version 2016-10[3] (only English version) [1], which is denoted as DBO in this paper. DBO consists of high-quality data using mapping-based extraction and includes 5900558 nodes, 661 predicates and 18746174 triples.

EmptyQ. A dataset which contains 25 empty-answer SPARQL queries with one or two triple patterns. Focusing on simple SPARQL queries, we analyze questions and corresponding SPARQL queries in a question answering dataset LC-QuAD [21]. There are three types of simple SPARQL queries: (1) BGP has one variable and one triple pattern; (2) BGP has one variable and two triple patterns and (3) BGP has two variable and two triple patterns, like Q1, Q5 and Q2 in Table 1 respectively. We imitate the style of questions in LC-QuAD and develop 10 empty-answer queries for type (1) and (2) respectively, 5 empty-answer queries for type (3). The constructed queries are denoted as Ei ($i \in [1, 25]$), E1–E10 are of type (1), E11–E20 are of type (2) and E21–E25 are of type (3). The set of them are denoted as EmptyQ. EmptyQ contains 15 different predicates and 28 different nodes, which are considered as EmptyQ$_P$ and EmptyQ$_N$ respectively.

OneCons and TwoCons. It is hard to construct simple and meaningful empty-answer SPARQL queries. Some works [8,22] construct 20–40 empty-answer queries and evaluate the results by hiring people. The results may not reflect the ability of algorithms accurately due to the contingency and randomness of the constructed dataset. So, we extract two datasets OneCons and TwoCons from DBO to make evaluations on a larger scale.

To construct OneCons, we consider SPARQL queries whose BGPs only contain one triple pattern and one variable like Q1 in Table 1. For every p_i in EmptyQ$_P$, we extract 1000 distinct nodes $\{s_j\}$ which hold predicate p_i at random and record corresponding nodes $(o_0, ..., o_k)$ as the standard answers for every $\langle s_j, p_i, ?x \rangle$. OneCons is as Eq. (21).

$$\text{OneCons} = \{YQ_{p_i}\}, p_i \in \text{EmptyQ}_P \tag{21}$$

$$YQ_{p_i} = \{\langle s_j, p_i, (o_0, .., o_k)_j \rangle\}, j \in [0, 999] \tag{22}$$

For SPARQL queries whose BGPs have two triple patterns and one variable like Q5 in Table 1, EmptyQ has 10 SPARQL queries of this type (E11–E20),

---

[3] https://wiki.dbpedia.org/downloads-2016-10.

so we extract 1000 testing data for every one. Taking Q5 for example, we randomly collect 1000 distinct pairs $\{\langle o_j^1, o_j^2 \rangle\}$ by executing Q6 in Table 1. For every $\langle o_j^1, o_j^2 \rangle$, we fetch a set of results $(x_0, ..., x_k)_j$ by replacing $?o_1$, $?o_2$ with o_j^1 and o_j^2 respectively and executing Q6 again. The testing data for Q5 is as Eq. (23) and TwoCons is as Eq. (24) (E17 is ignored because it has the same predicates with E13).

$$TQ_{(p_1, p_2)} = \{\langle p_1, o_j^1, p_2, o_j^2, (x_0, .., x_k)_j \rangle\}, j \in [0, 999] \qquad (23)$$

$$\text{TwoCons} = \{TQ_{(p_1, p_2)_i}\}, (p_1, p_2)_i \in \{\text{E11}-\text{E16}, \text{E18}-\text{E20}\} \qquad (24)$$

EmptyQ, OneCons and TwoCons can be downloaded[4].

5.2 Baselines and Implementation

We use SB [8], OB [18] and EB [11,22] as our baselines. These 3 methods do not use external resources like text, which are the same as our method and suitable for comparison. Also, we remove completeness-aware training procedure to construct another baseline RQE_c.

We reimplement similar nodes/predicates searching methods of [8]. This method is based on statistical language models [19] and use the Jensen–Shannon divergence to measure distance between different nodes/predicates. It uses similar nodes/predicates to replace nodes/predicates in failed queries, and the distance between the reformed query and the original failed query is the sum of the distance spent to replace nodes/predicates in the original query. For each failed query, we keep top-10 reformed queries whose distance to the original queries are under 0.5 and use these reformed queries to fetch approximate results.

For OB, we reimplement the method from [18] to develop extended reduction ontology of DBpedia ontology[5]. We assign 0.1 as the cost to Rules (2), (4) and 0.2 to Rules (5), (6) when using them to reform failed queries. This method always yields too many results when it is applied to simple queries, so we only keep at most 10 results with the lowest cost. Also, nodes in DBO usually do not have predicate "rdf:type", so we query the whole DBpedia when OB relaxes a query to the one with "rdf:type".

For EB, we consider the methods proposed in [11] and [22]. [22] has similarity training and approximating procedures with [11] while the latter one uses TransE [4] as geometric projection operator. We use code released from [22] to train the embeddings of DBO. Then, we use the trained embeddings and triple patterns of BGP to obtain approximate embedding of the target node. The similarity between the target node and other nodes is computed by the cosine similarity $cosimi(vec(t), vec(o))$ as Eq. (12), where the $vec(\cdot)$ represent the embeddings of nodes. We also keep 10 results for every variable in BGP with the highest similarity value.

---

[4] https://tinyurl.com/y65pvr2p.
[5] https://wiki.dbpedia.org/downloads-2016-10#ontology.

We remove **soft labels** to test the impact of our completeness-aware training procedure, which is denoted as RQE_c. Now, the label of a training triple $\langle s, p, o \rangle$ is 1 if $\langle s, p, o \rangle \notin \mathcal{G}$ or 0 otherwise. Codes for baselines and our model can be found on github[6].

5.3 Evaluation Setting

For **metric**, the hits@10 is used for the evaluation on EmptyQ, we judge the correctness of the retrieved results by searching their information on the Internet. A answer for queires with two variables (E21–E25) are considered as correct if and only if the retrieved nodes for two variables are both correct.

The hits@10, mean reciprocal rank (MRR) and average time (Time) are used for the evaluation on OneCons and TwoCons. The data of these two datasets can be considered as SPARQL queries and the corresponding answers can be found in the KG. We only consider the first correct answer to compute MRR.

For **parameters**, we implement our training procedure on the basis of PyTorch[7]. We use Adam [14] to optimize the object function. The learning rate, l2-regularization parameter λ and batch size are 0.001, 0.001 and 128 respectively. Every model is trained 1000 epochs. The embeddings we use to generate soft label are of size 100 and trained 1000 epochs.

Table 4. Evaluation on OneCons

	hits@10			MRR			Time/s		
	EB	RQE	RQE$_c$	EB	RQE	RQE$_c$	EB	RQE	RQE$_c$
award	0.078	**0.147**	**0.147**	0.041	0.117	**0.118**	0.973	**0.027**	0.028
origin	0.016	**0.765**	0.663	0.011	**0.627**	0.503	1.029	**0.492**	0.502
owner	0.089	**0.548**	**0.548**	0.045	**0.504**	**0.504**	0.966	**0.022**	0.023
starring	0.097	**0.631**	**0.631**	0.05	**0.462**	**0.462**	1.031	**0.012**	0.016
location	0.068	**0.613**	0.59	0.037	**0.495**	0.464	**1.153**	1.247	1.305
product	0.094	**0.568**	0.566	0.055	0.441	**0.445**	0.985	**0.296**	0.307
timeZone	0.001	**0.961**	0.959	0.0002	0.839	**0.842**	0.967	**0.039**	0.052
publisher	0.063	**0.296**	**0.296**	0.031	**0.269**	**0.269**	0.973	**0.001**	**0.001**
residence	0.024	**0.821**	0.803	0.015	**0.732**	0.699	**0.998**	5.437	6.132
birthPlace	0.031	**0.732**	0.688	0.017	**0.576**	0.561	**0.972**	1.443	1.514
deathPlace	0.026	**0.755**	0.682	0.016	**0.621**	0.526	**0.971**	3.4	4.447
regionServed	0.017	**0.782**	0.76	0.011	**0.626**	0.588	**0.97**	5.041	5.225
locationCountry	0.002	**0.869**	0.84	0.001	**0.753**	0.736	0.973	**0.325**	0.417
foundationPlace	0.02	**0.898**	0.888	0.014	**0.813**	0.793	**0.967**	8.132	8.32
doctoralAdvisor	0.023	**0.633**	0.632	0.014	**0.602**	0.599	**0.971**	0.265	0.341
Average	0.043	**0.668**	0.646	0.024	**0.565**	0.541	**0.993**	1.745	1.909

---

[6] https://github.com/xzlyu/RQE.
[7] https://pytorch.org/.

5.4   Evaluation on EmptyQ

Answers retrieved can be downloaded[8]. SB fails to get any correct answer for all queries of EmptyQ and finds no answer in 24 of 25 queries. OB only succeeds in E10. For queries other than E10, OB retrieves no answer or thousands of answers with the same cost, which is hard to select the top-10. So, besides their precision are low, we think that they are not practical to relax simple queries. SB and OB are not evaluated on OneCons and TwoCons.

EB also gets no correct answer for all 25 queries. But compared with SB and OB, it can give a complete rank list of approximate answers. Answers retrieved by EB are more closer to correct answers than that of SB and OB. We think that it is at least a useful method in practice and worth evaluating on OneCons and TwoCons.

RQE gets correct answers for 17 of 25 queries, hits@10 is 0.68, which is much better than SB, OB and EB. This demonstrates RQE has big advantages in dealing with simple queries. Also, we display rules to explain the reasons why some answers are retrieved, it improves the interpretability of our method.

5.5   Evaluation on OneCons and TwoCons

The evaluation results on OneCons and TwoCons are shown in Tables 4 and 5. The best results on each test item are highlighted in bold.

Firstly, we compare EB and RQE to discuss the ability of the method we proposed. On OneCons, the performance of EB is far behind that of RQE in hits@10 and MRR, while RQE has achieved the best result. On average, RQE improves 0.625 and 0.541 in hits@10 and MRR respectively. Evaluation on TwoCons has the similar situation, except for E11, EB performs badly compared with RQE. That demonstrates that our method has better ability than EB in getting approximate answers of simple SPARQL queries.

EB has more advantages in time consumption, especially in TwoCons. We think that the time consumption of EB and RQE on OneCons are both acceptable, EB's lead is negligible by 0.752 seconds on average. EB is about 30 seconds faster on average than RQE on TwoCons, which is a big advantage, but we think that it is not very meaningful due to the bad performance of EB.

Secondly, we compare the performance of RQE and RQE_c to discuss the impact of completeness-aware training procedure. The hits@10 of RQE is equal or better than that of RQE_c on all the test items. As for MRR, RQE performs better than RQE_c on the most test items of OneCons and TwoCons, even on 4 test items that RQE_c is better, RQE is just 0.004 (product) behind at most. The completeness-aware training procedure proved to be effective.

The time consumption of RQE and RQE_c are very close because these two methods have the same procedure in searching and ranking approximate answers.

---

[8] https://tinyurl.com/y65pvr2p.

Table 5. Evaluation on TwoCons

	hits@10			MRR			Time/s		
	EB	RQE	RQE$_c$	EB	RQE	RQE$_c$	EB	RQE	RQE$_c$
E11	**0.065**	0.018	0.018	**0.045**	0.016	0.016	**2.881**	48.747	46.731
E12	0.03	**0.458**	0.406	0.016	**0.361**	0.327	**2.924**	47.403	46.445
E13	0.059	**0.321**	0.318	0.037	**0.259**	0.259	**2.861**	15.661	15.448
E14	0.0	**0.885**	0.76	0.0	**0.769**	0.684	**2.989**	28.629	28.512
E15	0.005	**0.436**	0.435	0.005	0.362	**0.363**	**2.989**	46.558	48.366
E16	0.066	**0.888**	0.885	0.035	**0.837**	0.827	**2.445**	16.479	16.553
E18	0.018	**0.356**	0.347	0.009	**0.248**	0.245	**2.418**	22.23	22.301
E19	0.004	**0.175**	0.093	0.001	**0.118**	0.06	**2.758**	55.105	55.437
E20	0.074	**0.822**	**0.822**	0.042	**0.779**	0.777	**2.425**	19.898	19.996
Average	0.036	**0.484**	0.454	0.021	**0.417**	0.395	**2.743**	33.412	33.31

6   Conclusions

Devoted to simple failed SPARQL queries, we use rule learning techniques to expand them and reason results of high quality. To make rule mining efficiently and generate rules of high quality, we sample a subgraph and calculate F-score under the PCA to filter rules. To achieve accurate confidence that a triple holds, we design a completeness-aware procedure. The experimental results show that our method achieves much better performance than SB, OB and EB. Also, our completeness-aware procedure is effective. As far as our performance is concerned, the time consumption is acceptable. Also, our method can be an additional module to question answering system to give them improvements.

In the future, we will optimize our model to support expansion with more rules efficiently. Some predicates also cannot be predicted only by rules, we consider rule representation with embedding or rule learning over multiple KGs.

Acknowledgments. This work is funded by the National Natural Science Foundation of China (No. 61872172), and the Key R&D Program of Jiangsu Science and Technology Department (No. BE2018131).

References

1. Auer, S., Bizer, C., Kobilarov, G., Lehmann, J., Cyganiak, R., Ives, Z.: DBpedia: a nucleus for a web of open data. In: Aberer, K., et al. (eds.) ISWC 2007, ASWC 2007. LNCS, vol. 4825, pp. 722–735. Springer, Heidelberg (2007). https://doi.org/10.1007/978-3-540-76298-0_52
2. Berant, J., Chou, A., Frostig, R., Liang, P.: Semantic parsing on freebase from question-answer pairs. In: Proceedings of the 2013 Conference on Empirical Methods in Natural Language Processing, pp. 1533–1544 (2013)

3. Bordes, A., Usunier, N., Chopra, S., Weston, J.: Large-scale simple question answering with memory networks. arXiv preprint arXiv:1506.02075 (2015)
4. Bordes, A., Usunier, N., Garcia-Duran, A., Weston, J., Yakhnenko, O.: Translating embeddings for modeling multi-relational data. In: Advances in Neural Information Processing Systems, pp. 2787–2795 (2013)
5. Brickley, D., Guha, R.V., McBride, B.: RDF schema 1.1. W3C recommendation **25**, 2004–2014 (2014)
6. World Wide Web Consortium, et al.: RDF 1.1 concepts and abstract syntax (2014)
7. Dubey, M., Banerjee, D., Chaudhuri, D., Lehmann, J.: Earl: joint entity and relation linking for question answering over knowledge graphs. arXiv preprint arXiv:1801.03825 (2018)
8. Elbassuoni, S., Ramanath, M., Weikum, G.: Query relaxation for entity-relationship search. In: Antoniou, G., et al. (eds.) ESWC 2011. LNCS, vol. 6644, pp. 62–76. Springer, Heidelberg (2011). https://doi.org/10.1007/978-3-642-21064-8_5
9. Galárraga, L., Teflioudi, C., Hose, K., Suchanek, F.M.: Fast rule mining in onto-logical knowledge bases with AMIE+. VLDB J. - Int. J. Very Large Data Bases **24**(6), 707–730 (2015)
10. Galárraga, L.A., Teflioudi, C., Hose, K., Suchanek, F.: Amie: association rule mining under incomplete evidence in ontological knowledge bases. In: Proceedings of the 22nd International Conference on World Wide Web, pp. 413–422. ACM (2013)
11. Hamilton, W., Bajaj, P., Zitnik, M., Jurafsky, D., Leskovec, J.: Embedding logical queries on knowledge graphs. In: Advances in Neural Information Processing Systems, pp. 2030–2041 (2018)
12. Harris, S., Seaborne, A., Prud'hommeaux, E.: SPARQL 1.1 query language. W3C recommendation 21(10), 778 (2013)
13. Hu, S., Zou, L., Yu, J.X., Wang, H., Zhao, D.: Answering natural language questions by subgraph matching over knowledge graphs. IEEE Trans. Knowl. Data Eng. **30**(5), 824–837 (2017)
14. Kingma, D.P., Ba, J.: Adam: a method for stochastic optimization. arXiv preprint arXiv:1412.6980 (2014)
15. Lao, N., Mitchell, T., Cohen, W.W.: Random walk inference and learning in a large scale knowledge base. In: Proceedings of the Conference on Empirical Methods in Natural Language Processing, pp. 529–539. Association for Computational Linguistics (2011)
16. Li, F., Jagadish, H.: Constructing an interactive natural language interface for relational databases. Proc. VLDB Endow. **8**(1), 73–84 (2014)
17. Lopez, V., Unger, C., Cimiano, P., Motta, E.: Evaluating question answering over linked data. Web Semant.: Sci. Serv. Agents World Wide Web **21**, 3–13 (2013)
18. Poulovassilis, A., Wood, P.T.: Combining approximation and relaxation in semantic web path queries. In: Patel-Schneider, P.F., et al. (eds.) ISWC 2010. LNCS, vol. 6496, pp. 631–646. Springer, Heidelberg (2010). https://doi.org/10.1007/978-3-642-17746-0_40
19. Rosenfeld, R.: Two decades of statistical language modeling: where do we go from here? Proc. IEEE **88**(8), 1270–1278 (2000)
20. Shen, W., Wang, J., Han, J.: Entity linking with a knowledge base: issues, techniques, and solutions. IEEE Trans. Knowl. Data Eng. **27**(2), 443–460 (2015)
21. Trivedi, P., Maheshwari, G., Dubey, M., Lehmann, J.: LC-QuAD: a corpus for complex question answering over knowledge graphs. In: d'Amato, C., et al. (eds.) ISWC 2017. LNCS, vol. 10588, pp. 210–218. Springer, Cham (2017). https://doi.org/10.1007/978-3-319-68204-4_22

22. Wang, M., Wang, R., Liu, J., Chen, Y., Zhang, L., Qi, G.: Towards empty answers in SPARQL: approximating querying with RDF embedding. In: Vrandečić, D., et al. (eds.) ISWC 2018. LNCS, vol. 11136, pp. 513–529. Springer, Cham (2018). https://doi.org/10.1007/978-3-030-00671-6_30
23. Zheng, W., Yu, J.X., Zou, L., Cheng, H.: Question answering over knowledge graphs: question understanding via template decomposition. Proc. VLDB Endow. **11**(11), 1373–1386 (2018)

Aspect-Level Sentiment Analysis of Online Product Reviews Based on Multi-features

Binhui Wang[(⊠)], Ruiqi Wang, Shujun Liu, Yanyu Chai,
and Shusong Xing

College of Software, Nankai University, Tianjin, China
{wangbh,xings}@nankai.edu.cn, harrywang966@gmail.com,
liushujun1223@gmail.com, Kristin5339@gmail.com

Abstract. Aspect-level sentiment analysis aims to identify the sentiment polarity of fine-grained opinion targets. Existing methods are usually performed on structured standard datasets. We propose a model for a specific dataset which has a complex structure. First, we utilize some matching rules to extract implicit aspects, then we use the extracted aspect words to segment the corpus into samples. Finally, we propose a set of methods to construct data-based features, and try to fuse multi-features for classifier training. Experiments show that the method integrated three features has the highest F1 score, and the sentiment analysis results are more accurate.

Keywords: Aspect-level sentiment analysis · Feature fusion · Implicit aspect

1 Introduction

Aspect-based sentiment analysis is a fine-grained task in sentiment analysis, which aims to extract opinion targets from opinion text and identify the corresponding sentiment polarity. For example, in sentence "The machine is slow to boot up and occasionally crashes completely", the target "boot up" should be extracted first, then the emotional polarity will be recognized as negative.

Traditional methods for aspect-based sentiment analysis are often employ hand-crafted features to train sentiment classifier. In recent years, benefiting from the automatic feature extraction of neural networks, deep learning models have consistently achieved state of art performance in sentiment analysis field, e.g., Long Short Term Memory (LSTM) together with attention mechanism [1, 2] are utilized to extract aspects, and double embedding technology [3] is employed to improve the performance of target extraction on product reviews text. However, these methods based on sequence labeling are mostly used for explicit aspect extraction. In consideration of the particularity of the data set we use, we propose an implicit aspect recognition method which is simple but efficient.

Neural network models are suitable for downstream tasks of sentiment analysis, which have been testified in previous study. Ma et al. [4] proposed a bidirectional attention mechanism that could interactively learn the attention weights on aspect and context terms. Fan et al. [5] designed a multi-grained attention network for sentiment classification, in which the context and aspects were fused by the attention mechanism.

© Springer Nature Singapore Pte Ltd. 2020
X. Wang et al. (Eds.): JIST 2019, CCIS 1157, pp. 161–169, 2020.
https://doi.org/10.1007/978-981-15-3412-6_16

Li et al. [6] proposed a hierarchical attention network to generate the target-specific representations of contextual words for improving the performance of sentiment polarity classification. These approaches proved that the interaction between aspects and the contexts is an effective way of sentiment analysis. However, one of the assumptions that these methods depend is that the aspects in datasets should be represented explicitly.

In many situations, a large amount of implicit aspects is involved in datasets, especially the domain specific contents. It would not be a suitable operation that applies the learning models of attention mechanisms directly on the datasets because the relationships between target words and contextual words may not be explicitly observed. This is the case with the dataset we have setup for automobile product evaluation. For this reason, we decide not to directly use the attention mechanism and Recurrent Neural Network (RNN) algorithm in the way of running deep learning models on data.

Based on the analysis above, in this paper, we propose a series of methods for feature construction, feature fusion, implicit aspect extraction and sentiment polarity classification. We train and evaluate our model on an automobile field online review dataset, the experimental results demonstrate that the proposed approach is effective for aspect-based sentiment classification, and it outperforms approaches without data-based feature, which proves that our methods of data-based feature construction and features fusion are meaningful for sentiment analysis tasks.

Since the traditional classifiers are usually feature driven, it's significant to construct reasonable and useful features. Existing sentiment analysis methods usually focus on text-based features but not data-based features. Our statistical results on datasets show that data-based features can reveal the relation within data, so we propose a method to construct statistical-based features and fuse them with other features.

2 Approach

As has been mentioned above, the dataset we use is quite particular, thus we had to preprocess the source data and convert the data to standard format. From the sample format shown in Table 1 we can see that the review sample consists of review text together with many attributes. We utilize these fine-grained attributes to construct data-based features, and the review text will be decomposed into fine-grained comment samples for different aspects. The corpus we use is constructed by the data from https://www.autohome.com.cn. Based on the form submission requirements of the online review platform, users need to comment and score on the fixed eight aspects of a car. For this reason, we define eight aspect words according to the platform: space, power, control, fuel consumption, comfort, appearance, interior decoration, and cost performance. The source review text has corresponding labels of aspects for every sentence except for three special clips, which are labeled as "most satisfied aspect", "most unsatisfied aspect" and "why buy this car". These three labels cannot reveal the opinion target explicitly, and the corresponding review fragments usually don't contain explicit aspects, that is why we propose an extract approach to distinguish implicit aspects. After identifying the corresponding aspect words for all review fragments, we cut the source samples into smaller training samples according to different aspects. That being said, we will employ aspect-level sample together with corresponding score to train eight classifiers for eight aspects.

Table 1. The sample data

Attributes	Content
Title	The big star with the powerful side leakage
Car type	Sunray; 2017; 1.9T; Short axle, passenger vehicle
Car purchase location	Huaxi, Guiyang, Guizhou
Purchase time	2018/1/1
Price	11.88
Purpose of purchase	Long distance freight transportation
Publication time	2018/1/11
Terminal type	iPhone
Pageviews	2850
Approval amount	10
Comment amount	3

[Most Satisfied Aspects] The noise is low, the fuel consumption level is general, the power is good, the space is big, the seat is comfortable, the air conditioning gives strength

[Most Unsatisfied Aspects] It's not easy to buy the hub cover without aluminum alloy hub

[Space] 100 kg of body in the front row is not particularly crowded. **Score: 5**

[Power] Although it is a 2.0 engine, the body has a weight of more than 3 tons, but the power is sufficient. **Score: 3**

[Control] The car body will not be very floating when running on the highway. It is heavy, but it feels very light. **Score: 4**

[Fuel Consumption] At present, about 12 L/100 km. **Score:4**

[Comfort] This car is very comfortable for travelling. **Score: 5**

[Appearance] Good sheet metal, beautiful appearance. **Score: 5**

[Interior Decoration] General workmanship. **Score: 2**

[Cost Performance] Good value for money. **Score:4**

[Why buy this car] Large space and strong carrying capacity

2.1 Source Data Preprocessing

Since it's difficult to extract sufficiently useful information from short text, and some meaningless features may disturb the performance of models, we filter out short reviews. As shown in Fig. 1, we deprecated reviews with fewer than two hundred words.

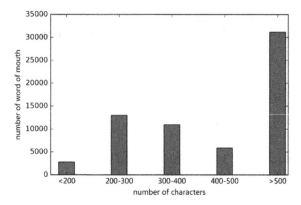

Fig. 1. The length of the word-of-mouth comments

To determine the sentiment polarity of each aspect sample, we map the sample polarity of score in [0, 1] to negative, the sample polarity of score in [2, 4] to neutral, and the sample polarity of score 5 to positive.

2.2   Implicit Aspect Extraction

As has been introduced above, implicit aspects need to be extracted. We calculate the similarity between the word embedding and predefined aspects vector, respectively. We choose the word with the greatest similarity as the candidate word, and select the candidate with the highest frequency as the implicit aspect of the sentence. The extraction process is as follows:

for every word ($word_i$) in sentence:

$$asp_i^w = \arg \max sim_{aspect_j}(word_i, aspect_j), j = 1, 2, \ldots, J \tag{1}$$

then the implicit aspect word can be calculated as follows:

$$asp^s = \arg \max_{asp_i^w} count(asp_i^w), i = 1, 2, \ldots, I \tag{2}$$

where $word_i$ is the embedding of word within the sentence, $aspect_j$ represents the vector of predefined aspect words. sim is the cosine similarity calculation function, where $count$ is the counting function.

2.3   Feature Extraction

Embedding Feature. We construct sentence embedding feature by taking the average of the word embedding, which is to add up the word embedding of each word in the sentence and divide by the number of words in the sentence. The calculation method is as follows:

$$vec^s = \frac{\sum_{i=1}^{N} vec_i^w}{N} \tag{3}$$

where N represents the number of words in the sentence, vec_i^w is the word embedding and vec^s is the sentence embedding feature.

Text-Based Features. In this paper, twelve features are constructed as text features, which including the number of words, the number of total characters, the number of non-repeated words, the number of stop words, the number of punctuation marks, the number of nouns, the number of verbs, the number of adjectives, the number of adverbs, the number of pronouns, the number of positive words and the number of negative words.

In order to rationalize each text feature, all text features in this paper are normalized. Formulated as follows:

$$feature = \frac{feature_{vec}}{N_w} \tag{4}$$

where $feature_{vec}$ is the original representation of text features, N_w is the number of words in sentence.

Data-Based Features. Many valuable information is usually hidden behind big data. Thus, we mine the hidden association information in the data as a data-based feature.

Figure 2 shows the relationship between the purchase location and the aspect sentiment polarity. Here "tier" means city level. The higher the level is, the higher the city's economic level and population size are. Since some of the reviewers' information is incomplete, the city to which they belong is defined as "unknown city". Figure 3 shows the relationship between the access terminal type and aspect sentiment polarity.

It can be clearly seen from Fig. 2 that the sentiment polarity of unknown city users tends to be more negative. And from Fig. 3 we can recognize that the sentiment polarity of iPhone users is more negative than that of other type. Through the above

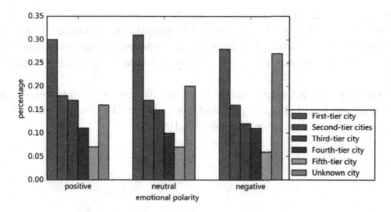

Fig. 2. Sentiment polarity percentage of users from different levels citys

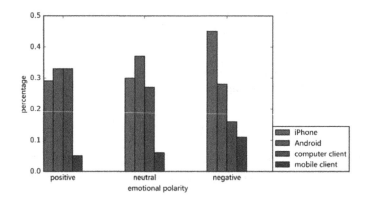

Fig. 3. Sentiment polarity percentage of users from different terminal type

statistics, it can be concluded that there is a certain correlation between some data based features and sentiment polarity, for this reason, we extract the purchase month, purchase city, purchase purpose, purchase time, price, pageview amount, point of praise, the number of comments and terminal type as data-based features.

2.4 Feature Fusion and Classifier

Previously, we have considered the construction of features from different aspects. To utilize these features efficiently, we mosaic embedding features, text-based features and data-based features as final feature, whose form is vector. Since we decide to employ traditional classifiers, we selected Support Vector Machine (SVM), Random Forest, and eXtreme Gradient Boosting (XGBoost) for experimental comparison.

3 Experiments

3.1 Dataset and Embeddings

The dataset we use is obtained from the website "automobile home". This dataset has 35,116 samples as training samples, and 8,773 samples as test sample. Aspect words include space, power, control, fuel consumption, comfort, appearance, interior decoration and cost performance, sentiment polarity is divided into positive, negative and neutral.

We use Google's open source toolkit word2vec to train the word embedding model on the dataset presented above. Specifically, we choose SkipGram model, where the window size is 5 and the vector dimension is 100.

3.2   Evaluation Indicators

In this paper, precision rate (Micro_P), recall rate (Micro_R) and F1 score (Micro_F1) are used as evaluation indicators, as shown below:

$$Micro\_P = \frac{\sum_{i=1}^{n} TP_i}{\sum_{i=1}^{n} TP_i + \sum_{i=1}^{n} FP_i} \tag{5}$$

$$Micro\_R = \frac{\sum_{i=1}^{n} TP_i}{\sum_{i=1}^{n} TP_i + \sum_{i=1}^{n} FN_i} \tag{6}$$

$$Micro\_F1 = \frac{2 * Micro\_P * Micro\_R}{Micro\_P + Micro\_R} \tag{7}$$

where n is the number of opinion aspects.

3.3   Experimental Results and Analysis

Table 2 shows the performance comparison of our method with the methods which employ single or two features only. From Table 2, we can clearly observe that the method we proposed which combine embedding feature, text-based feature and data-based feature together get the better result on F1 score, both individual aspect and overall performance. The results demonstrate that the feature construction method considering data-based feature is helpful for improving the classifier performance.

Table 2. Comparison of sentiment classification methods on multi-features

Aspect word	Our method	Single feature mean value	Two features mean value
	Micro_F1	Micro_F1	Micro_F1
Space	0.75	0.72	0.73
Power	0.66	0.58	0.63
Control	0.67	0.64	0.66
Fuel consumption	0.66	0.61	0.64
Comfort	0.67	0.59	0.64
Appearance	0.74	0.72	0.73
Interior decoration	0.63	0.53	0.60
Cost performance	0.73	0.71	0.71
Overall	**0.69**	0.64	0.67

Table 3 shows the performance comparison of different classifiers. From the result comparison of XGBoost, Random Forest and SVM, we can observe that XGBoost performs better than other two models, and the F1 score on different aspect words is more stable, which shows that XGBoost has better robustness.

Table 3. Comparison of classifier performance

Aspect word	Our method	SVM	RF
	Micro_F1	Micro_F1	Micro_F1
Space	0.75	0.71	0.70
Power	0.66	0.49	0.61
Control	0.67	0.62	0.64
Fuel consumption	0.66	0.61	0.59
Comfort	0.67	0.52	0.61
Appearance	0.74	0.71	0.72
Interior decoration	0.63	0.37	0.61
Cost performance	0.73	0.71	0.62
Overall	**0.69**	0.59	0.64

4   Conclusion

The method proposed in this paper is based on the characteristics of domain-specific texts and is not a simple combination of existing methods. Aiming at the problem that the existing emotion classification methods don't take data-based features into consideration, this paper proposes a multi-feature Chinese domain sentiment analysis method, and uses the data from "Car Home" website to construct corpus. To solve the problem of implicit aspect word extraction in training corpus, this paper adopts the method of word vector similarity calculation. In terms of feature extraction, this paper integrates data-based features, sentence embedding features and text-based features into a richer feature from the comment text for classifier training. The experiments show that the fusion of multi-features is obviously better than single feature or pairwise features without data-based feature, and prove that XGBoost can get better performance on online review dataset used in this paper, compared with other traditional classifiers. In the future, we will try to extract aspects without predefined words and look for other characteristics to conduct experiments.

References

1. Wang, W., Pan, S.J., Dahlmeier, D., Xiao, X.: Coupled multi-layer attentions for co-extraction of aspect and opinion terms. In: AAAI, pp. 3316–3322 (2017)
2. He, R., Lee, W.S., Ng, H.T., Dahlmeier, D: An unsupervised neural attention model for aspect extraction. In: Proceedings of the 55th Annual Meeting of the Association for Computational Linguistics (Long Papers), vol. 1, pp. 388–397 (2017)
3. Hu, X., Bing, L., Lei, S., et al.: Double embeddings and CNN-based sequence labeling for aspect extraction (2018)
4. Ma, D., Li, S., Zhang, X., Wang, H.: Interactive attention networks for aspect-level sentiment classification. In: Proceedings of IJCAI, pp. 4068–4074 (2017)
5. Fan, F., Feng, Y., Zhao, D.: Multi-grained attention network for aspect-level sentiment classification. In: Proceedings of the 2018 Conference on Empirical Methods in Natural Language Processing, pp. 3433–3442 (2018)

6. Li, L., Liu, Y., Zhou, A.Q.: Hierarchical attention based position-aware network for aspect-level sentiment analysis. In Proceedings of the 22nd Conference on Computational Natural Language Learning, pp. 181–189 (2018)
7. Taboada, M., Brooke, J., Tofiloski, M., et al.: Lexicon-based methods for sentiment analysis. Comput. Linguist. **37**(2), 267–307 (2011)
8. Pu, X., Wu, G., Yuan, C.: Exploring overall opinions for document level sentiment classification with structural SVM. Multimed. Syst. **25**, 21–33 (2017)

A Seq2seq-Based Approach to Question Answering over Knowledge Bases

Linjuan Wu[1,2], Peiyun Wu[1,2], and Xiaowang Zhang[1,2(✉)]

[1] College of Intelligence and Computing, Tianjin University, Tianjin 300350, China
{wulinjuan1997,wupeiyun,xiaowangzhang}@tju.edu.cn
[2] Tianjin Key Laboratory of Cognitive Computing and Application, Tianjin, China

Abstract. Semantic parsing, as an essential approach to question answering over knowledge bases KBQA), transforms a question into query graphs for further generating logical queries. Existing semantic parsing approaches in KBQA mainly focus on relations (called local semantics) with paying less attention to the relationship among relations (called global semantics). In this paper, we present a seq2seq-based semantic parsing approach to improving performance of KBQA by converting the identification problem of question types to the problem of machine translation. Firstly, we introduce a BiLSTM-based named entity recognition (NER) method to extract all classes of entities occurring in questions. Secondly, we present an attention-based seq2seq model to learn one type of a question by applying seq2seq model in extracting relationships among classes. Finally, we generate templates to adopt more question types for matching more complex questions. The experimental results on a real knowledge base Chinese film show that our approach outperforms the existing template matching model.

1 Introduction

Question answering over knowledge bases (KBQA) is a task that a natural language question can be accurately and concisely answered over a knowledge base (KB) by understanding the intention of the question [9]. Due to the advent of many large-scale KBs such as Yago [16], Freebase [7], and Wikidata [20], KBQA has become a popular way for humans to access KBs [10]. A big challenge of KBQA is extracting the whole semantics of questions and capturing intentions of users since the semantics of natural language questions are often intricate and obscure in practical. As a result, it is crucial to extract the semantics of questions.

The critical components in QA require the capability of understanding the question and the context in which the question is generated [2]. KBQA computes answers to natural language questions based on existing knowledge bases [3]. Identification problem of question types is a key to QA [1].

Semantic parsing, as an essential class of KBQA approaches, focuses on constructing a semantic parsing tree or equivalent query structure (called *query*

X. Wang et al. (Eds.): JIST 2019, CCIS 1157, pp. 170–181, 2020.
https://doi.org/10.1007/978-981-15-3412-6_17

graph) that represents the semantics of questions. Semantic parsing based approaches effectively transform questions into logical queries where the reliability of logical querying can ensure the correctness of answering questions even better for complex questions [4, 21].

Many KBQA are focusing on how to identify types of questions, and adopting dependency tree or Convolution Neural Network (CNN)-based classification. *Dependency tree approach* in [18], converting the dependency tree into a problem graph, the essence is to extract the information from the problem. Extract the problem features that help find the answer and delete the unimportant information. The performance relies on the settings and effects of the operation on the dependency tree. *CNN-based classification approach* has been used to QA [14], but there are many types of question, so the implementation of multi-classification models is the key to question type identification. [5] uses the CNN and GRU models to achieve multi-category of sentences. After that, [13] also uses a CNN-based approach to improve the multi-classification problem in a multi-label text classification task.

We consider that the question type identification and machine translation tasks have two similar characteristics as follows:

They are all N to M relationship. In machine translation, a word can be translated into multiple words with the same or similar meaning. Multiple similar words may also be translated the same one. Similar to this task, a question in question type identification can have multiple expressions to make it a different type of question.

They all depend on context. Machine translation is not a simple word-by-word translation. It is also necessary to combine the meaning of the context to improve the sentence structure and achieve a more accurate translation effect. In question type identification, we also need to understand the problem expression, rather than a simple keyword, but context associations.

Hence, it is interesting to apply machine translation approach to identify types of questions [22], which is based on a complicated representation of training sets.

In this paper, based on seq2seq model [17], we present an approach to identification of question type, and the experiments show that our approach significantly outperforms the existing template matching model for KBQA. The main contributions of this paper are summarized as follows:

- We introduce a BiLSTM-based named entity recognition method to extract all classes of entities occurring in questions.
- We present an attention-based seq2seq model to learn one type of a question by applying seq2seq model in extracting relationships among classes.
- We generate templates to adopt more question types for matching more complex questions.

The remainder of this paper is structured as follows: Next section presents our approach in details. Section 3 presents experiments and evaluations. Section 4 discusses related work. Finally, we summarize our work in Sect. 5.

2 Our Approach

In this paper, we introduce an overview of our approach, and the overview framework of our model is shown in Fig. 1.

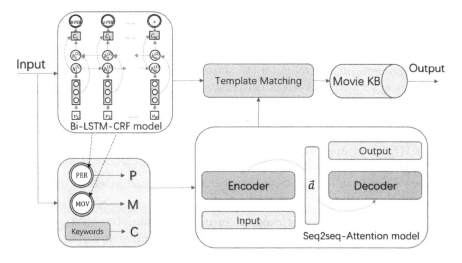

Fig. 1. The overview framework of our model

2.1 Named Entity Recognition

The key to getting the information in our KB and identifying the type of question is to identify the named entities. So we use the deep learning model to achieve NER for the accuracy of recognition.

The Bi-LSTM-CRF model [12] is currently the most mainstream in NER technology (see Fig. 2), which is include the embedding layer, Bi-LSTM layer and CRF layer. In our model, the tag of the named entity uses the BIO sequence annotation mode, marking the person name as PER and the movie name as MOV. Bi-LSTM learns the probability that each word will generate a certain type of tag, and CRF learns the constraints between tags. The training set of the model comes from the corpus of the labelled People's Daily plus the annotated corpus generated using named entities in our KB.

We use a bi-directional LSTM network to capture the context. The output of the Bi-LSTM layer is passed to a CRF layer that produces a probability distribution over the tag sequence using the dependencies among labels of the entire sequence. In order to find the best sequence of labels for an input sequence, the Viterbi algorithm is used as follows:

$$y^* = \text{argmax}_{y \in \mathbf{y}(o)} P(y|o; \mathbf{W}, b) \tag{1}$$

where

$$P(y|o; \mathrm{W}, b) \propto \exp(\sum_{i=1}^{w} \mathrm{W}_{y_{i-1}, y_i}^{T} o_i + b_{y_{i-1}, y_i}).\tag{2}$$

Here $\mathrm{W}_{y_{i-1}, y_i}$ and b_{y_{i-1}, y_i} are model parameters (weight vector and bias) corresponding to the neighboring labels (y_{i-1}, y_i). For training a CRF model, we estimate model parameters W and b from a training dataset $D = \{x^{(j)}, y^{(j)}\}_{j=1}^{N}$ by maximizing the log-likelihood given by:

$$L(\mathrm{W}, b) = \sum_{j=1}^{N} \log p(y^{(j)}|o^{(j)}; \mathrm{W}, b).\tag{3}$$

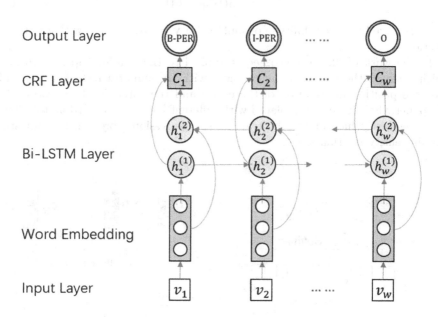

Fig. 2. The model of Bi-LSTM-CRF

2.2 Question Type Identification

Seq2seq is a general-purpose encoder-decoder framework that can be used for machine translation [8], text summarization, conversational modelling, and more.

We use the LSTM model to realize the basic encoder-decoder. Considering that problem attribute recognition has a significant impact on template matching, we apply an attention mechanism to improve the precision (see Fig. 3).

In the Encoder-Decoder framework, an encoder reads the input a sequence of vectors $\mathbf{x} = (x_1, \cdots, x_n)$, into a vector c, which present context vector. The

c_i is computed as a weighted sum of these hidden state h_j, and the weight α_{ij} of each hidden state h_j is computed by the following equation:

$$\alpha_j = \frac{\exp(e_{ij})}{\sum_{k=1}^{n} \exp(e_{ik})} \tag{4}$$

where the score function about how well the inputs around position j and the output at position i match is defined as follows:

$$e_{ij} = \text{score}(d_{i-1}, h_j).$$

The d_i is the hidden state of decoder. Then we string up the t-th c_t and d_t as the input of the last hidden layer of the decoder defined as follows:

$$d_t = \tanh(W_c[c_t; d_t]) \tag{5}$$

and normalized the probability of output vector $\mathbf{y} = (y_1, \cdots, y_m)$ with a softmax function.

In the work of [22], the seq2seq is applied to the relationship recognition, which replaces the entity in the problem with the uniform identifier $\langle e \rangle$, and adds the position information of the entity and the entity in the question. In this paper, the entities are replaced with different identifiers according to different categories, which makes the training set expression more concise, but still contains entity information.

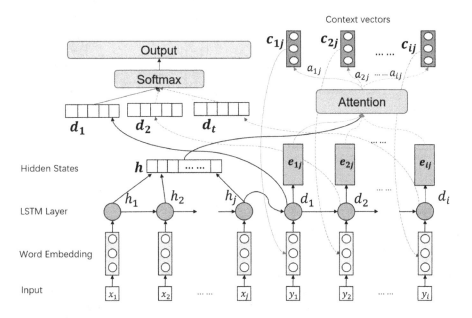

Fig. 3. The model of seq2seq-Attention

2.3   Template Matching

Once the question type is identified, we can match different problem templates based on the types. We use the rule as a class *Rule*. The problem template is the object of the class, which includes the attributes of the problem template: the matching *condition* and the *action* after the problem template is matched. The matching *condition* is equivalent to the addition of the components of the natural language question. According to the SPARQL query, we classify four query templates (Fig. 4).

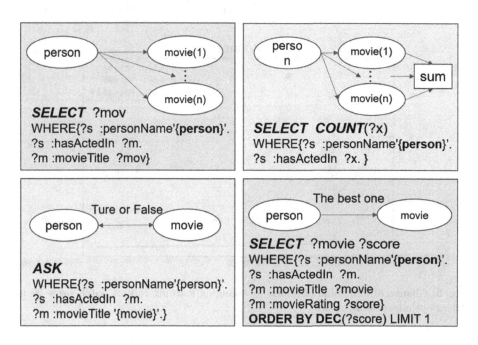

Fig. 4. The four types of query template

3   Experiments and Evaluation

Our Chinese film knowledge includes information on 88,662 actors and 65,633 movies. Refer to [11], we collected 436 valid questions by questionnaire to form our training and test sets. The training set we used was 336 randomly selected from 436 natural questions. The remaining 100 questions are used as test sets.

Three parts of the experiments are shown as follows:

NER. In our system, the experiment of NER is mainly the parameter adjustment of the model. And we compared two optimization algorithms with a small learning rate(lr), then we adjust the batch-size value for experimentation (see Table 1). We choose the batch-size = 20 that gets the best results, and continue

Table 1. Experimental results obtained by adjusting the batch-size value at $lr = 0.0001$ in Adam and AdaGrad optimization algorithm.

Optimization algorithm	Batch-size	lr	FB1
Adam	20	0.0001	96.08
	50	0.0001	95.28
	100	0.0001	82.14
AdaGrad	20	0.01	94.03
	50	0.01	93.27
	100	0.01	92.54

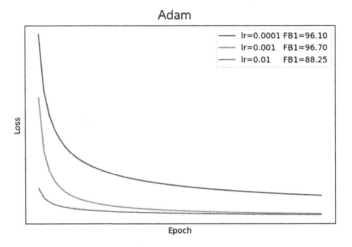

Fig. 5. Change of loss value obtained by changing learning rate at batch-size = 20 in Adam optimization algorithm.

our experiment to obtain the transformation of the loss value as shown in Figs. 5 and 6 in Adam and AdaGrad optimization algorithms, respectively. Under Adam optimization algorithm, we got the NER model with the best F1-score of 96.7.

Question Type Identification. Question type is mainly the form of the answer that the question hopes. We set twenty templates of types and SPARQL (see Tables 2 and 3). The first step of identifying the type of question is to process the input question. That is to replace named entities and keywords with class name or uniform identifiers in natural question. Table 4 gives a summary of all conversion tags.

Then, we trained the seq2seq model and the seq2seq-Attention model separately. The test accuracy of seq2seq-Attention reached 98%, which has 10% higher than only-seq2seq (Table 5).

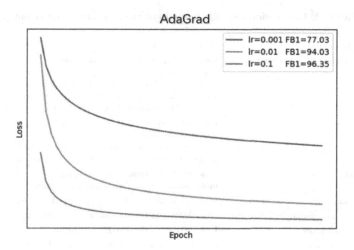

AdaGrad

——	lr=0.001 FB1=77.03
——	lr=0.01 FB1=94.03
——	lr=0.1 FB1=96.35

Loss

Epoch

Fig. 6. Change of loss value obtained by changing learning rate at batch-size = 20 in AdaGrad optimization algorithm.

Table 2. Conversion tags for named entities and keywords.

Attribute template	SPARQL template
The movies that an actor acted in	Rule(attribute_num=1.1, condition= person_entity + Star(Any(), greedy=False) + movie + Star(Any(), greedy=False), action=QuestionSet.has_movie_question)
The movies that two actors acted in together	Rule(attribute_num=1.2, condition= person_entity + Star(Any(), greedy=False) + person_entity + Star(Any(), greedy=False) movie + Star(Any(), greedy=False), action= QuestionSet.has_cooperation_question)
A certain type of movies an actor acted	Rule(attribute_num=1.3, condition= person_entity + Star(Any(), greedy=False) + genre | (genre + movie) + Star(Any(), greedy=False), action=QuestionSet. has_specific_type_movie_question)
Actors who acted in a movie	Rule(attribute_num=1.4, condition = movie_entity | actor + Star(Any(), greedy=False) + actor | movie_entity + Star(Any(), greedy=False), action=QuestionSet.has_actor_question)
Directors who directed a movie	Rule(attribute_num=1.5, condition= movie_entity | director + Star(Any(), greedy=False) + director | movie_entity + Star(Any(), greedy=False), action= QuestionSet.has_director_question)

Template Matching. According to Chinese film knowledge base and question types, we set twenty templates to match, which is more than existing templates in Template Matching QA. The template matching test is relatively simple. Under the premise of accurate attribute recognition, our template matching accuracy

Table 3. Conversion tags for named entities and keywords (Cont.).

Attribute template	SPARQL template
Types of movie that an actor has acted in	Rule(attribute_num=1.6, condition= person_entity + Star(Any(), greedy=False) + category + Star(Any(), greedy=False) + movie + Star(Any(), greedy=False), action= QuestionSet.has_movie_type_question)
Types of a moive	Rule(attribute_num=1.7, condition= movie_entity + Star(Any(), greedy=False) + category + Star(Any(), greedy=False) action=QuestionSet.movie_category_question)
Release data of a movie	Rule(attribute_num=1.8, condition= movie_entity + Star(Any(), greedy=False) +
Score of a movie	movie_basic_info + Star(Any(), greedy=False), action=
Introduction of a movie	QuestionSet.has_movie_basic_info_question)
Birthday of an actor	Rule(attribute_num=1.11, condition=
Constellation of an actor	person_entity + Star(Any(), greedy=False) +
Place of birth of an actor	person_basic_info + Star(Any(), greedy=False)
introduction of an actor	action=QuestionSet.has_movie_basic_info_question)
Number of movies that an actor acted in	Rule(attribute_num=2.1, condition= person_entity + Star(Any(), greedy=False) + several + Star(Any(), greedy=False) action=QuestionSet.has_quantity_question)
Number of movies that two actors acted together	Rule(attribute_num=2.2, condition= person_entity + Star(Any(), greedy=False) + person_entity + Star(Any(), greedy=False) + several + Star(Any(), greedy=False), action= QuestionSet.has_cooperation_num_question)
Number of a certain type movie that an actor has acted	Rule(attribute_num=2.3, condition= person_entity + Star(Any(), greedy=False) + several + Star(Any(), greedy=False) + genre | (genre + movie) + Star(Any(), greedy=False) action=QuestionSet.has_cooperation_num_question)
Did an actor act in a movie?	Rule(attribute_num=3.1, condition= person_entity + Star(Any(), greedy=False) + movie_entity + Star(Any(), greedy=False) action=QuestionSet.is_actor_in_movie_question)
Did an actor act a certain type of movie?	Rule(attribute_num=3.2, condition= person_entity + Star(Any(), greedy=False) + genre | (genre + movie) + Star(Any(),greedy=False) action=QuestionSet.is_sometype_person_question)
The best movie an actor has acted in	Rule(attribute_num=3.2, condition= person_entity + Star(Any(), greedy=False) + best + Star(Any(), greedy=False) action=QuestionSet.has_best_work_question)

rate reached 100% in the 100 test sets we collected. The accuracy is improved by 27% compared to the method of implementing QA with a separate template (Table 6).

Table 4. Conversion tags for named entities and keywords.

Word in question	Tag
Name entity of person	P
Name entity of movie	M
Keyword about movie type	C

Table 5. Accuracy comparison of seq2seq model with or without Attention

Model	The right number	Accuracy rate
seq2seq	88	88%
seq2seq-Attention	98	98%

Table 6. Accuracy comparison of our model and separate template matching method

Model	The right number	Accuracy rate
Template matching	73	73%
NER-seq2seq-Attention-Template	100	100%

4 Related Works

There are some KBQA works in a restricted domain. [15] discussed that restricted domains need to deal with complex problems and provide opportunities for complex analysis of text sources and issues. They also discussed that restricted domains provide comprehensive ontology and domain resources to help find the answers more easily. [19] proposed a model-based approach to adapt the question and answer system to the restricted domain. They believed that to answer questions in real-world scenarios effectively, the QA system can be changed from an open domain to a restricted domain. [6] proposed a framework for restricted domain question Answering System using advanced NLP tools and software. This framework can be used to develop a QA System for extracting exact and precise answer from restricted domain textual data set.

5 Conclusions

In this paper, we present a seq2seq-based approach to identify question types by reducing to machine translation so that we can improve the performance of KBQA. Our approach can overtake the limitation of those dependency-tree-based approaches in processing words (possible entities) outside of dictionaries. Moreover, our approach can support multiple types of questions built on multiple-classification, where neural network-based approaches are not always good at it. In this sense, our approach provides an alternative way to identify question types effectively in KBQA. In the experiment, we show that our approach can outperform the existing template matching approach in a Chinese film knowledge base. Furthermore, we would like to extend our proposal to other domain knowledge bases, even open knowledge bases.

Acknowledgments. This work is supported by the National Key Research and Development Program of China (2017YFC0908401) and the National Natural Science Foundation of China (61972455). Xiaowang Zhang is supported by the Peiyang Young Scholars at Tianjin University (2019XRX-0032).

References

1. Walker, A.D., Alexopoulos, P., Starkey, A., Pan, J.Z., Gómez-Pérez, J.M., Siddharthan, A.: Answer type identification for question answering. In: Qi, G., Kozaki, K., Pan, J., Yu, S. (eds.) JIST 2015. LNCS, vol. 9544, pp. 235–251. Springer, Cham (2015). https://doi.org/10.1007/978-3-319-31676-5_17
2. Aneeze, A., Ishwari, K., Karunaratne, H., Mallawarachchi, Y., Nugaliyadde, A., Sudheesan, S.: Advances in natural language question answering: a review. CoRR, abs/1904.05276 (2019)
3. Bao, J., Duan, N., Zhou, M., Zhao, T.: Knowledge-based question answering as machine translation. In: Proceedings of ACL 2014, pp. 967–976 (2014)
4. Berant, J., Chou, A., Frostig, R., Liang, P.: Semantic parsing on freebase from question-answer pairs. In: Proceedings of EMNLP 2013, pp. 1533–1544 (2013)
5. Nam, J., Kim, J., Loza Mencía, E., Gurevych, I., Fürnkranz, J.: Large-Scale Multi-label Text Classification — Revisiting Neural Networks. In: Calders, T., Esposito, F., Hüllermeier, E., Meo, R. (eds.) ECML PKDD 2014. LNCS (LNAI), vol. 8725, pp. 437–452. Springer, Heidelberg (2014). https://doi.org/10.1007/978-3-662-44851-9_28
6. Biswas, P., Sharan, A., Malik, N.: A framework for restricted domain question answering system. In: Proceedings of ICICT 2014, pp. 613–620 (2014)
7. Bollacker, K.D., Evans, C., Paritosh, P., Sturge, T., Taylor, J.: Freebase: a collaboratively created graph database for structuring human knowledge. In: Proceedings of SIGMOD 2008, pp. 1247–1250 (2008)
8. Cho, K., et al.: Learning Phrase representations using RNN encoder-decoder for statistical machine translation. In: Proceedings of EMNLP 2014, pp. 1724–1734 (2014)
9. Christina, U., John, M., Philipp, C.: Ontology-based interpretation of natural language. Comput. Linguist. 41(2), 347–350 (2015)
10. Cui, W., Xiao, Y., Wang, H., Song, Y., Hwang, S., Wang, W.: KBQA: learning question answering over QA corpora and knowledge bases. PVLDB 10(5), 565–576 (2017)
11. Diekerma, A., Yilmazel, O., Liddy, E.: Evaluation of restricted domain question-answering systems. In: Proceedings of ACL 2004, pp. 2–7 (2004)
12. Huang, Z., Xu, W., Yu, K.: Bidirectional LSTM-CRF models for sequence tagging. CoRR, abs/1508.01991 (2015)
13. Kurata, G., Xiang, B., Zhou, B.: Improved neural network-based multi-label classification with better initialization leveraging label co-occurrence. In: Proceedings of ACL2016, pp. 521–526 (2016)
14. Lei, T., Liu, D., Shi, Z., Yang, L., Zhu, F.: A novel CNN-based method for question classification in intelligent question answering. In: Proceedings of ACAI 2018, pp. 541–546 (2018)

15. Molla, A.D., González, J.: Question answering in restricted domains: an overview. Comput. Linguist. **33**, 41–61 (2007)
16. Suchanek, F.M., Kasneci, G., Weikum, G.: Yago: a core of semantic knowledge. In: Proceedings of WWW 2007, pp. 697–706 (2007)
17. Sutskever, L., Vinyals, O., Le, V.: Sequence to sequence learning with neural networks. In: Proceedings of NIPS 2014, pp. 3104–3112 (2014)
18. Van Durme, B., Yao, X.: Information extraction over structured data: question answering with freebase. In: Proceedings of ACL 2014, pp. 956–966 (2014)
19. Vila, K., Mazón, J., Ferrández, A.: Model-driven adaptation of question answering systems for ambient intelligence by integrating restricted-domain knowledge. In: Proceedings of ICCS 2011, pp. 1650–1659 (2011)
20. Vrandecic, D., Krötzsch, M.: Wikidata: a free collaborative knowledgebase. Commun. ACM **57**(10), 78–85 (2014)
21. Yih, W., Chang, M., He, X., Gao, J.: Semantic parsing via staged query graph generation: question answering with knowledge base. In: Proceedings of ACL 2015, pp. 1321–1331 (2015)
22. Yue, W., Richong, Z., Cheng, X., Yongyi, M.: The APVA-TURBO approach to question answering in knowledge base. In: Proceedings of COLING 2018, pp. 1998–2009 (2018)

Building Knowledge Graph Across Different Subdomains Using Interlinking Ontology for Biomedical Concepts

Kouji Kozaki[1](✉) , Tatsuya Kushida[2,3] , Yasunori Yamamoto[4] ,
and Toshihisa Takagi[3,5]

[1] Osaka Electro-Communication University, Osaka, Japan
kozaki@osakac.ac.jp
[2] RIKEN BioResource Research Center, Ibaraki, Japan
tatsuya.kushida@riken.jp
[3] National Bioscience Database Center, Japan Science and Technology Agency,
Tokyo, Japan
tt@tuins.ac.jp
[4] Database Center for Life Science, Research Organization of Information
and Systems, Chiba, Japan
yy@dbcls.rois.ac.jp
[5] Toyama University of International Studies, Toyama, Japan

Abstract. This paper proposes a method for building knowledge graphs across different subdomains in life science using Interlinking Ontology for Biological Concepts (IOBC). IOBC provides wide range of concepts related to biomedical domains with relationships between concepts across different subdomains. The proposed method obtains some relationships according to interests of the users. Then, it combines these relationships with mappings from related concepts to other RDF datasets and construct new knowledge graphs using them. This paper introduces the building method which consist of 5 steps with some results of trial constructions of knowledge graphs.

Keywords: Knowledge graph · Ontology · Interlinking concepts · Data integration

1 Introduction

Data integrations among multiple domains are important application of semantic web technologies. Many databases, ontologies and thesauri such as MeSH [1], UniProt [2] and Gene Ontology [3] are developed in life science domains for understanding a large variety of life phenomenon. They are developed in various subdomains, which is more specific domains related to life science, such as medical, genetics, protein, biochemistry. To integrate databases across subdomains, it is essential to develop ontologies not only in each subdomain but also across multiple subdomains. Considering developing an ontology across multiple subdomains in life science, Interlinking Ontology for Biological Concepts (IOBC) is being constructed [4, 5]. IOBC includes 80,000 biological concepts such as biological phenomena, diseases, molecular functions, gene

© Springer Nature Singapore Pte Ltd. 2020
X. Wang et al. (Eds.): JIST 2019, CCIS 1157, pp. 182–190, 2020.
https://doi.org/10.1007/978-981-15-3412-6_18

products, chemicals, and medical cares, and approximately 16,000 semantic relationships among concepts in life science domains and concepts including other domains such as earth science and environmental science. It was used as trial for interlinking biomedical concepts through multiple subdomains, and several examples were shown to confirmed that IOBC could be used to construct knowledge graphs for interlinking across different subdomains [6].

This paper aims to generalize the building process of knowledge graphs using IOBC as a method for knowledge graph constructions across subdomains in life science. It is based on wide range of concepts and semantic relationships defined in IOBC. The proposed method could contribute on efficient protype building of new knowledge graphs bridging different subdomains in life science.

The next section outlines IOBC and its use case for knowledge graph constructions. In Sect. 3, a knowledge graph construction method using IOBC is proposed with a concreate example. Section 4 discusses contributions of the proposed method and IOBC with related works in Sect. 5, then Sect. 6 gives concluding remarks with some future works.

2 Interlinking Ontology for Biological Concepts (IOBC)

Interlinking Ontology for Biological Concepts (IOBC), which has previously been referred to as "Refined JST thesaurus" [4], includes approximately 80,000 biological concepts, such as biological processes, diseases, molecular functions, gene products, chemicals, and drugs, as well as approximately 20,000 related concepts, such as basic chemistry [6]. Each concept has labels of both English and Japanese. This ontology is visible and downloadable on the web site[1] through BioPortal [7]. The SPARQL endpoint is also prepared[2]. The IOBC is being constructed for describing relationships among biological concepts. It has been developed from "JST thesaurus" [4] which only

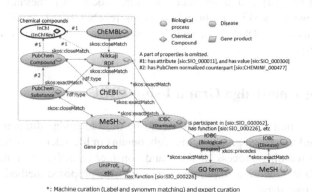

*: Machine curation (Label and synonym matching) and expert curation

Fig. 1. Data schema of the IOBC's KG extended by other data sources [11].

---

[1] http://purl.bioontology.org/ontology/IOBC.

[2] http://lod.hozo.jp/repositories/IOBC.

contains skos:related (RT) as relation types between concepts besides skos:broader, skos:narrower. In order to rigorously describe complicated biological relationships, life science experts and ontologists have subclassified the RT [4]. As a result, the IOBC has 35 relations such as "has function," "has role," "has quality," "precedes," and "is participant in," and approximately 16,000 relationships defined by the subclassified relations. IOBC was used as a trial for finding meaningful relationships among concepts in different categories such as biological processes with diseases, and chemical compounds with diseases [6].

We implemented Lexical OWL Ontology Matcher (LOOM) algorithm [8] for matching the labels of between IOBC concepts and other data sources such as a chemical compound RDF: NikkajiRDF [6] with a SPARQL search. In the case of IOBC and NikkajiRDF, 10,576 NikkajiRDF's chemicals were incorporated into IOBC. Thus, by using the IOBC ontological structure, it was possible to infer information on at least one of the 432 kinds of biological and chemical functions, roles, and chemical involvements in biological phenomena for 5,038 extended chemicals [6]. Inference using the ontology enabled the assignment of more chemical functions, roles, and involvements with biological phenomena, which are unique to IOBC.

Furthermore, we developed knowledge graphs (KGs) from IOBC by performing SPARQL search [4], and we attempted to discover disease-related gene products [9] and disease-related chemical compounds [6] from the KGs. We focused on the relationships between a preceding biological phenomenon (e.g., platelet aggregation) and the succeeding disease (e.g., thromboembolism), and the relationships were described using a property "precedes [xkos:precedes]" in the KGs [9]. We claimed that gene products and chemical compounds, which regulate or promote a biological phenomenon and precede a disease, became potential candidates for disease-related gene products and chemical compounds.

Besides, by performing the LOOM algorithm and expert curation for the purpose of label matching between IOBC, and other data sources such as a chemical compound ontology: ChEBI [10] and a medical controlled vocabulary thesaurus: MeSH [1] (Fig. 1) [11], we found 13 antifibrinolytic drugs [chebi:CHEBI_48675] and Antifibrinolytic Agents [mesh:D000933], and 38 bone density conservation agents [chebi: CHEBI_50646].

3   Building Knowledge Graph Using IOBC

The previous section shows that ICBO could be used to bridge different datasets and construct some knowledge graphs across subdomains in life science. In this section, we generalize the building process of them and consider a method to build knowledge graph using IOBC. Figure 2 shows an overview of the proposed method. It consists of the following five steps;

1. Select concepts which could be bridge different subdomains.
2. Obtain relationships among the selected concepts.
3. Choose some relationships and obtain paths to use construct knowledge graphs.
4. Collect mappings between concepts in paths and other datasets.
5. Construct knowledge graphs using obtained paths and mappings.

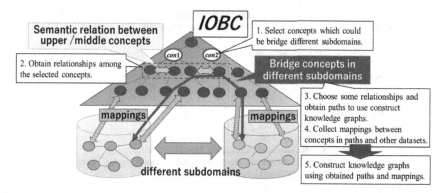

Fig. 2. An overview of the method for Knowledge Graph Building using IOBC.

3.1   Select Concepts Which Could Be Bridge Different Subdomains

An important purpose of data integrations across subdomains is to find candidates of meaningful relationships among several concepts such as relationships among chemical compounds and diseases, diseases and environments.

In this step, the user selects such concepts which could be used to bridge different subdomains. For example, if the user wants to construct knowledge graphs which explain effects of chemical compounds to diseases, two concepts "chemical compounds" and "disease" are selected. The user can select such concepts through browsing the class hierarchy of IOBC and/or keyword search of classes.

3.2   Obtain Relationships Among Selected Concepts

Relationships among the concepts selected in the previous step are obtained by retrieving IOBC. Please note here that relationships defined in IOBC are sparse since IOBC is designed to provide not exhaustive and detailed relationship of all concepts but representative relationships which interlinking different subdomains. Therefore, we should consider wider range of concepts when we obtain relationships. In concreate, we use sub-classes of the selected concepts for retrieving relationships among them.

Figure 3 shows the SPARQL query for obtaining relationships among two concepts *con*1 and *con*2 considering sub-classes of them. In this query, we consider sub-classes of the two concepts within three steps so that the number of sub-classes is not too large. And, we suppose to obtain only semantic relationships such as "has function", "has part", "succeeds", etc. while IOBC includes large numbers of soks:related.

For instance, 303 relationships were obtained using the query when "Inflammation[3]" and "Biological process[4]" were selected. Table 1 partly shows the result of obtained relationships between "Inflammation" and "Biological process".

---

[3] http://purl.jp/bio/4/id/200906082725054443.

[4] http://purl.jp/bio/4/subject/System_cat.

```
prefix rdfs:<http://www.w3.org/2000/01/rdf-schema#>
prefix rdf:<http://www.w3.org/1999/02/22-rdf-syntax-ns#>
prefix iobc:<http://purl.jp/bio/4/id/>
prefix schema:<https://schema.org/>

select  distinct  ?x  ?x_label  ?p  ?p_label  ?y  ?y_label
where{
   BIND ( <con1>  AS  ?con1 )
   BIND ( <con2>  AS  ?con2 )

   { ?x  rdfs:subClassOf  ? con1 . }
     UNION{ ?x  rdfs:subClassOf/rdfs:subClassOf  ? con1 . }
     UNION{ ?x  rdfs:subClassOf/rdfs:subClassOf/rdfs:subClassOf  ? con1 . }
   ?x  skos:prefLabel  ?x_label .

   { ?y  rdfs:subClassOf  ?con2 . }
     UNION{ ?y  rdfs:subClassOf/rdfs:subClassOf  ?con2 . }
     UNION{ ?y  rdfs:subClassOf/rdfs:subClassOf/rdfs:subClassOf  ?con2 . }
   ?y skos:prefLabel ?y_label.

   ?x  rdfs:subClassOf [
         owl:someValuesFrom  ?y ;
         owl:onProperty  ?p ] .
   ?p  rdfs:label  ?p_label .
}
```

Fig. 3. SPARQL query for obtaining relationships among the selected concepts.

Table 1. The obtained relationships between "Inflammation" and "Biological process" (part).

x_label	p_label	y_label
fibrinolytic system	is part of	coagulation and fibrinolytic system
COP9 signalosome	is participant in	cellular signal transduction
latent period	is part of	metabasis
Respiration	has part	expiration
mastocyte	has function	Cell Degranulation
Blood Glucose	is participant in	glycaemic response
heavy metal pollution	precedes	bioaccumulation
Contact Inhibition	precedes	inhibition of multiplication
phytoalexin	has function	biological defense
biohazard	succeeds	microorganism contamination

3.3 Choose Some Relationships and Obtain Paths

The user chooses some relationships obtained in the previous step according to interests of the user. Then, the user obtains paths including the relationships. The paths consist of the selected relationships and sub-classes of the concepts in the relationships. That is, when the user chooses some relationships between *con*1 and *con*2, the paths includes subclasses of *con*1 and *con*2.

3.4 Collect Mappings with Other Datasets

The user collects mappings between concepts in the paths obtained in the previous step with other datasets. If there are no mappings yet, new mappings are made using some mapping methods or tools such as LOOM [8] and the Ontology Lookup Service (OLS)[5] [12] while IOBC contains mappings with Mesh, Nikkaji, and part of some other datasets [6, 11].

3.5 Construct Knowledge Graphs Using Obtained Data

Knowledge graphs are constructed by combining concepts, relationships, paths and mappings. As the result, concepts in different datasets could be bridged through paths obtained from IOBC (see Fig. 2).

Figure 4 shows an example of knowledge graph constructed by the proposed method. It bridges three subdomains Disease, Biological process and Biological substance.

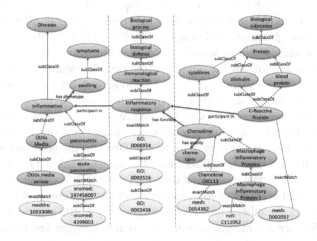

Fig. 4. An example of knowledge graph constructed by the proposed method.

---

[5] https://www.ebi.ac.uk/ols/.

4 Discussions

In order to use ontology for interlinking concepts across subdomains, the ontology should have the following features as requirements;

1. It includes rich relationships between concepts in different subdomains.
2. Semantic relationships (e.g. has function, has role, has quality) are preferable to non-semantic relationships (e.g. related terms, co-occurrence). It is because kinds of semantic relationships could help us to choose meaningful relationships if there are many candidates to consider.

Table 2. The numbers of semantic relationship between concepts across different subdomains (Top 10).

Relationship	# of relationships
has role	806
has function	268
is participant in	197
is function of	194
is part of	134
has part	125
is role of	123
is connected to	69
succeeds	40
precedes	40

As shown in Table 2, we consider that IOBC satisfies the above requirements. It was also confirmed through a trail of knowledge graph construction using IOBC shown in the previous section.

5 Related Works

In life science research domain, there are following major databases. MeSH [1] is a medical controlled vocabulary thesaurus. It comprehensively has information on life science, but don't have direct relationships between concepts in different categories, such as biological processes and diseases. UniProt knowledgebase [2] is a large resource specialized on protein and the associated information. Gene Ontology [3] is one of the most well-known life science ontologies. It consists of three ontologies including biological processes, molecular functions, and cellular components. Each concept contains information on related gene products such as proteins.

However, there are almost no other life science databases, ontologies, and thesauri that have direct links between life science concepts and concepts in different subdomains such like IOBC. It is strong point to use IOBC for the proposed metohd.

Kamdar and Musen present PhLeGrA platform for Linked Graph Analytics in Pharmacology [13]. It integrates four datasets from the LSLOD cloud using query federation. Its target is Pharmacology domain while the platform could be extended to other domains. On the other hands, our methods using IOBC supposed to use for all domains in life science while its main targets are middle/upper level concepts.

6 Concluding Remarks and Future Works

This paper proposed a method for building knowledge graph across subdomains in life science using IOBC. We suppose that IOBC has enough potential to interlink concepts across multiple subdomains and the proposed method support to efficient building of initial knowledge graphs. The feature of IOBC comes from its wide range of concepts derived from JST thesaurus and its semantic relationships curated by domain experts and otologists [4, 5]. Although IOBC consists of only classes (concepts) in the ontology, the propose method constructs knowledge graphs which consists both of classes and individuals (instances) when it integrates datasets which includes individuals.

However, there are some rooms to consider and improve for practical use of the proposed method. The first issue is how to support appropriate concepts, relationships and paths to construct knowledge graphs according to interests and purposes of the user. Sometimes, it is difficult to select them appropriately because the numbers of them are more than thousands according to way of selections. We plan to analyze IOBC in more detail for considering criteria to select appropriate ones in each step.

The second issue is investigating tools to support conducting the method. We are developing some tools to select concepts and relationships of IOBC and to visualize obtained paths. We suppose that it can support the user to select appropriate concepts, relationships and paths to construct knowledge graphs effectively.

Acknowledgments. This study was supported by an operating grant from the Japan Science and Technology Agency and JSPS KAKENHI Grant Number JP17H01789.

References

1. Bodenreider, O., Nelson, S.J., et al.: Beyond synonymy: exploiting the UMLS semantics in mapping vocabularies. In: Proceedings of AMIA Symposium, pp. 815–819 (1998)
2. The UniProt Consortium: UniProt: the universal protein knowledgebase. Nucleic Acids Res. **45**(D1), D158–D169 (2017)
3. Gene Ontology Consortium: Creating the gene ontology resource: design and implementation. Genome Res. **11**(8), 1425–1433 (2001)
4. Kushida, T., et al.: Refined JST thesaurus extended with data from other open life science data sources. In: Wang, Z., Turhan, A.Y., Wang, K., Zhang, X. (eds.) JIST 2017. LNCS, vol. 10675, pp. 35–48. Springer, Cham (2017). https://doi.org/10.1007/978-3-319-70682-5_3
5. Kushida, T., Kozaki, K., Tateisi, Y., et al.: Efficient construction of a new ontology for life sciences by sub-classifying related terms in the Japan science and technology agency thesaurus. In: Proceedings of ICBO 2017, vol. 2137, pp. 1–6. CEUR-WS.org, Newcastle (2017)
6. Kushida, T., Kozaki, K., Kawamura, T., Tateisi, Y., Yamamoto, Y., Takagi, T.: Inference of functions, roles, and applications of chemicals using linked open data and ontologies. In: Ichise, R., Lecue, F., Kawamura, T., Muggleton, S., Kozaki, K. (eds.) JIST 2018. LNCS, vol. 11341, pp. 385–397. Springer, Cham (2018). https://doi.org/10.1007/978-3-030-04284-4_26
7. Noy, N.F., et al.: BioPortal: ontologies and integrated data resources at the click of a mouse. Nucleic Acids Res. **37**(suppl 2), W170–W173 (2009)
8. Ghazvinian, A., Noy, N.F., Musen, M.A.: Creating mappings for ontologies in biomedicine: simple methods work. In: AMIA Annual Symposium Proceedings, pp. 198–202. American Medical Informatics Association (2009)

9. Kushida, T., et al.: Refining JST thesaurus and discussing the effectiveness in life science research. In: Proceedings of 5th Intelligent Exploration of Semantic Data Workshop (IESD 2016, co-located with ISWC 2016), Kobe, pp. 1–14 (2016)

10. Hastings, J., de Matos, P., Dekker, A., Ennis, M., Harsha, B., Kale, N., et al.: The ChEBI reference database and ontology for biologically relevant chemistry: enhancements for 2013. Nucleic Acids Res. **41**(D1), D456–D463 (2013)

11. Kushida, T., Kozaki, K., Kawamura, T., Tateisi, Y., Yamamoto, Y., Takagi, T.: Interconnection of biological knowledge using NikkajiRDF and interlinking ontology for biological concepts: new generation computing. New Gener. Comput. **37**, 525–549 (2019)

12. Jupp, S., et al.: A new ontology lookup service at EMBL-EBI. In: Malone, J. et al. (eds.) Proceedings of SWAT4LS International Conference 2015 (2015)

13. Kamdar, M.R., Musen, M.A.: PhLeGrA: graph analytics in pharmacology over the web of life sciences linked open data. In: Proceedings of the 26th International Conference on World Wide Web, pp. 321–329 (2017)

WPQA: A Gaming Support System Based on Machine Learning and Knowledge Graph

Luwei Wang, Yan Tang$^{(\boxtimes)}$, and Jie Liu

College of Computer and Information, Data Science and Knowledge Engineering Lab,
Hohai University, Nanjing, China
{lwwang,tangyan}@hhu.edu.cn, liujie520@gmail.com

Abstract. Honor of Kings is a multiplayer online battle arena game in which two teams fight with each other with five players controlling five different heroes on each side. By 2017, Honor of Kings has over 80 million daily active players and 200 million monthly active players and was both the world's most popular and highest-grossing game of all time as well as the most downloaded gaming app globally. In this paper, we will introduce a prediction model based on a machine learning algorithm to forecast the victory of Honor of Kings 5V5 game by considering the heroes formation on each side using a gaming history dataset.

Keywords: Mobile Online Game · MOBA · Honor of Kings · Machine learning · Victory prediction

1 Introduction

In recent years, E-Sports has become very popular. The data shows that the actual sales revenue of China's E-sports game market in the first half of 2018 reached 41.79 billion yuan. Every game in such a large market generates a huge amount of data. Honor of Kings is a multiplayer online battle arena (MOBA) mobile game produced by Tencent company. Competitive team battle is the main attraction of this game, in which players can choose various person VS person (PVP) game modes such as 1V1, 3V3, 5V5, etc. Each player controls a single character, known as a hero or a summoner. The condition of victory is to destroy the master crystal of the other team.

According to the official data released by Tencent Inc, the peak concurrent users in Honor of Kings exceeded 1 million, the Honor of Kings official league KPL (King Pro League) has been viewed over 17 billion times, and the Honor of Kings International (Arena of Valor) is selected as one of the demonstration programs at 2018 Jakarta Asian Olympic Games [1].

So far, the researches about MOBA games mainly focus on analyzing player behavior, improving game AI, and predicting game outcomes. However, there is still little research on the game outcome prediction for Honor of Kings. Currently,

© Springer Nature Singapore Pte Ltd. 2020
X. Wang et al. (Eds.): JIST 2019, CCIS 1157, pp. 191–204, 2020.
https://doi.org/10.1007/978-981-15-3412-6_19

88 heroes are available in the present Honor of Kings version. Each hero has unique skills and attributes. In general, heroes in the game can be divided into the following classifications:

- **Archer**: Distance type hero who is good at long range physical damage. Mainly achieve damage through the normal attack.
- **Mage**: Magic type hero. Mainly achieve magic damage through specific spell skills.
- **Assassin**: Explosion type hero can achieve high damage in a concise time; Great threat to Archers and Mages.
- **Support**: Protection type hero who is weak in harming other heroes, provides protection to friendly heroes.
- **Warrior**: Melee type hero who can achieve melee damage while undertaking the damage from the enemy.

The types above are all important roles in one team since each type is supposed to take respective responsibilities. A reasonable collocation of team formation is necessary if a team wants to win the game. In other words, it is vital to choose the right heroes for the team to win the game.

In this paper, we will discuss how to predict game outcome only with the information of chosen heroes on both sides. For the prediction of the game outcome, a large amount of historical game information can ensure a high prediction accuracy. How to improve the accuracy of prediction as much as possible with limited information is a challenging problem. To solve this problem, in this paper, the following work is conducted:

- Analyze the game to determine the features we need and introducing a method for calculating the line-up matching degree and countering degree based on the features.
- Introducing the Honor of Kings win prediction algorithm Rule and Logistics Regression based Win Prediction Algorithm (RLWPA) to predict the outcome of an Honor of Kings matches with only the information of the heroes chosen by both sides.

In addition, win prediction is a part of auxiliary systems of Honor of Kings, the other task is that recommending appropriate equipment to a player to every hero. So we struct a knowledge graph to show counter and pair relation between every two heroes, and appropriate equipment to every hero. The rest of the paper is organized as follows. In Sect. 2, A brief review of the related literature is provided. Section 3 introduces the process of construct a hero's winning rate matrix and how to calculate the matching degree and countering degree between every two heroes, which is necessary for our proposed prediction algorithms. Section 4 demonstrates the experimental results. Finally, Sect. 4 concludes the discussion.

2   Related Work

The current researches on MOBA games outcome mainly focus on DOTA2; there is still little research on the Honor of Kings. Compared with DOTA2, the Honor of Kings has a lower fault tolerance rate, which makes the prediction of the Honor of Kings more difficult.

Conley et al. [2] described a DotA 2 hero recommendation system which depends on a win predictor. It specifies two possible models for win prediction. The first uses Logistic regression with a binary hero feature vector. The second uses K-nearest neighbor classification using a custom weight to specify the distance between teams.

Kalyanaraman et al. [3] described a DotA 2 win predictor. It specifies two possible models for win prediction. The first uses logistic regression with a binary hero feature vector. The second combines this predictor with a genetic fitness metric, weighting each predictor equally in the final prediction.

Semenov et al. [4] introduced using Naive Bayes classifier, Logistic Regression, Gradient Boosted Decision Trees and Factorization Machines to predict the match winner.

Wang et al. [5] used Naive Bayes classifier analyzes the lineups and predict the outcome according to the lineups and gives an improved Naive Bayes classifier.

Kinkade et al. [9] presented two win predictors. The first predictor uses full post-match data and the second predictor uses only hero selection data.

3   Proposed Approach

Our task is to predict the results of the game only with the data of hero formation. It is a pregame prediction without regard for other factors like players' operation skill. In the following parts, we will discuss how to create a predictor model in detail.

3.1   Hero Analysis

Heros Match Relation. Figure 1 shows the hero pair win rate. The abscissa shows hero IDs, while ordinate gives the winning rate. For our experimental data in this article, 88 heroes in the present game version are included, for which we choose different colors to represent. This table provides the matching relation among different heroes. Each hero has different features, and that leads to a different match degree between two different heroes. As a result of the high match degree between two heroes, some heroes can maximize both of their features when they are on the same side. The table explains that the cooperation between two heroes will significantly affect the result of the game, so the choice of heroes for each player should be well-matched to the teammates'. As an example, the top three pairings are (Yixing, Nüwa), (Yixing, Wu Zetian), and (Pei Qinhu, Yang Yuhuan) with win rates of over 70%. Its counterpart is the low winning rate result from the mismatching pairs, such as Genghis Khan and Marco Polo, Ying Zheng and Gan Jiang with Mo Ye, Jiang Ziya and Taoist Taiyi, of which the winning rates are all below 20%. Also, the winning rate among other hero collocations reflects the matching relation to a large extent.

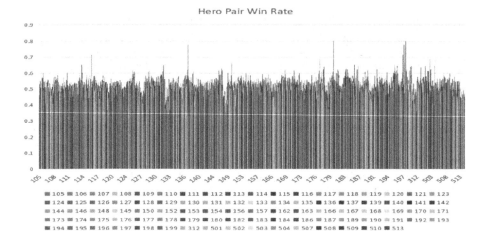

Fig. 1. Hero matching win rate

Heros Counter Relation. Figure 2 shows the hero counter win rate. The abscissa shows hero IDs, while Ordinate gives the winning rate. For our experimental data in this article, 88 heroes in the present game version are included, for which we choose different colors to represent. This table provides the constraint relation among different heroes. When two heroes are in antagonistic position, the difference of their attributes will lead to a state of mutual constraint. Some heroes are restrained by the others due to their specific features. Therefore, it will be easier to gain an advantage in the game if choosing the right hero who can available limit the enemy, thus affect the result of the game. As an example, the top three pairings are (Yixing over Gongsun Li), (Taoist Taiyi over Marco Polo), and (Genghis Khan over Jiang Ziya) with win rates of over 80%. When Gongsun Li meets Yixing, his damage capabilities will be primarily limited by Yixing's spell. When Marco Polo meets Taoist Taiyi, he has to face the risk of getting killed easily by the opposing side, given his short range. Similarly, when Jiang Ziya meets Genghis Khan, his flexibility disadvantage is highlighted compared with Genghis Khan's huger damage and stronger flexibility, which makes Jiang very fragile and easy to fail. Constraint relation among other heroes is also well presented according to their counter win rate.

3.2 Feature Selection

The battle scenes in Honor of Kings are mirror image scenes. That means the maps and operational perspectives of players on both sides are exactly the same. Thus, being on different sides will not affect the winning rate of the game. We now define these two sides as camp α and camp β.

We have analyzed in the article above the importance of matching relation when different heroes are in the same camp. The high matching degree of one side's formation will certainly lead to advantages for the game. Therefore, we

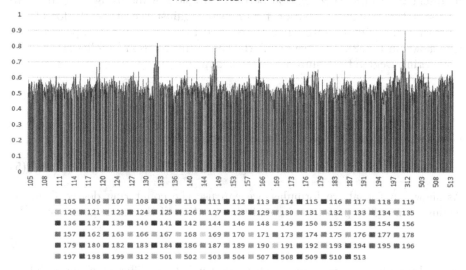

Fig. 2. Hero counter win rate

consider the following features. Let S represent the difference of the matching degree between two sides while using S_α and S_β to represent the two sides' matching degree, respectively. As for S_{ij}, it represents the winning rate when Hero i and Hero j are in the same team (As shown in Fig. 1). Now we define the matching degree of one side as follows:

Matching Degree of Camp α:

$$S_\alpha = \sum_{i\in\alpha} \sum_{j\in\alpha, i\neq j} S_{ij} \tag{1}$$

Matching Degree of Camp β:

$$S_\beta = \sum_{i\in\beta} \sum_{j\in\beta, i\neq j} S_{ij} \tag{2}$$

Then the difference of the matching degree between camp α and camp β can be:

$$S = S_\alpha - S_\beta \tag{3}$$

The main function of this formula is to measure the hero matching degree for both sides. When S is a positive number, Camp α shows a better matching degree; when S is negative, camp β is better.

Countering relation is also mentioned in the article above to be effective in the result of the game when different heroes are in the antagonistic camp. When one side as a whole restrains the other one better, this side will certainly get more advantage in the game. Thus we extract these features as follows. Let C

represent the Countering relation between two sides while using C_α and C_β to represent the constraint relation for one side against the other. As for C_{ij}, it represents the winning rate when Hero i and Hero j are in the opposing team (As shown in Fig. 2). Now we define the constraint relation as follows:

Countering Degree for Camp α against Camp β:

$$C_\alpha = \sum_{i \in \alpha} \sum_{j \in \beta} C_{ij} \tag{4}$$

Countering Degree for Camp β against Camp α:

$$C_\beta = 1 - C_\alpha \tag{5}$$

As shown in the above formulas, we can use the countering degree Camp α against Camp β to present the countering relation of the whole game as:

$$C = C_\alpha \tag{6}$$

With the update of the game, each version will have different changes. These changes will cause some heroes to strengthen or weaken so that each hero will have a different win rate in different versions, and some heroes more suitable the current version will have a higher win rate. If one side chooses more version heroes, it will have more advantages in the game.

We extracted the win rate of all heroes in the current experimental version. Let R represent the difference of total hero win rate between camp α and camp β, while using R_i represent hero i win rate. The camp α total hero win rate can be defined as:

$$R_\alpha = \sum i \in \alpha R_i \tag{7}$$

The camp β total hero win rate can be defined as:

$$R_\beta = \sum i \in \beta R_i \tag{8}$$

The difference between the total hero win rate can be:

$$R = R_\alpha - R\beta \tag{9}$$

3.3   Prediction Model

After determining the features, we consider using the Logistic Regression algorithm to predict the win rate. The process of prediction is to first use the Logistic Regression algorithm and the features we mentioned in the previous section to train the required pre-trained parameters C_p and S_p. Then we send the parameters and the chosen hero data of the game into the prediction function which mainly uses Sigmoid function to predict the result of the game. The whole predict process is reviewed in Algorithm 1.

Algorithm 1. Rule and Logistics Regression based Win Prediction Algorithm (RLWPA)

Input:
   Pretrained parameters C_p and S_p;
   10 Chosen Hero sequence H;
Output:
   Winner;
 1:
 2: C_r=Hero counter win rate list, S_r=Hero pair win rate list;
 3: S_α=camp α Hero pair win rate list[], S_β=camp β Hero pair win rate list[];
 4: C= Hero counter win rate list[];
 5: **for** each $i \in H$ **do**
 6:    **for** each $j \in H$ **do**
 7:       **if** $i \neq j$ and i, j both in camp α **then**
 8:          search S_{ij} in S_r;
 9:          $S_\alpha = S_\alpha$.add(S_{ij});
10:       **end if**
11:       **if** $i \neq j$ and i, j both in camp β **then**
12:          search S_{ij} in S_r;
13:          $S_\beta = S_\beta$.add(S_{ij});
14:       **end if**
15:       **if** $i \neq j$ and i, j in different camp **then**
16:          search C_{ij} in C_r;
17:          $C = C$.add(C_{ij});
18:       **end if**
19:    **end for**
20: **end for**
21: c=sum(C);
22: s=sum(S_α)-sum(S_β);
23: prob=sigmoid(sum($C_p * c, S_p * s$));
24: **if** prob ¿ 0.5 **then**
25:    **return** camp α
26: **else**
27:    **return** camp β
28: **end if**

3.4   Q&A System

Excepting the task of predicting the win rate, we also need to give players advice about equipment selection and show the advantages and disadvantages of the lineup. So we use game data to constructed an Honor of Kings knowledge graph to solve this problem. Figure 3 shows the shape of the knowledge grpah.

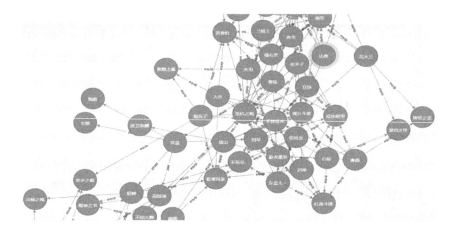

Fig. 3. Knowledge graph

First, we use the previously obtained Heros Match Relation and Heros Countering Relation as relationship, and each hero as entity to consturct a knowledge graph. Specifically, we sort every hero's Heros Match Relation and Heros Countering Relation, then choose the top three match rate as the three most match heroes which these heroes are suitable to be teammates, and top three counter rate as the three most afraid heros which means players should be careful of these heroes in the game. For example, as shown in Fig. 4, Nüwa, Gao Jianli and Liu Bang are the most three match heros to Yi Xing, and Diao Chan, Zhen Ji and Cao cao are Yi Xing's most three afraid heros.

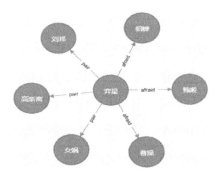

Fig. 4. Knowledge graph: heros relationship

In addition, we counted 100,000 games data. For a certain hero X, we extracted those game which has X in this game and X win the game, and in this game X is the MVP. Then count all equipment used by the hero X in these games, and select 6 types of equipment which are used the most, as the most suitable equipment for the hero. As shown in Fig. 5, we can see Bai Qi most suitble equipments.

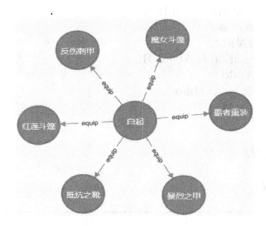

Fig. 5. Knowledge graph: hero suitable equipment

We construct HOK Knowledge Graph to provide Q&A support to the HOK Support System, and our Q&A tasks focus on the following three questions:

- Which equipment should I buy?
- How should I play this hero?
- Which enemy hero I need to be careful in this game?

Our knowledge graph is not yet able to provide us with good answers to the following questions. So we did some work to complete the HOK knowledge graph. In order to answer the question 2 and question 3, we have crawled the information about the HOK from the Internet. We extracted the specific information of each hero from the data. After manual processing, we obtained the play skills of each hero and add it to the HOK knowledge graph. The whole process is reviewed in Algorithm 2.

Algorithm 2. Proccess of HOK Knowledge Grpah Completion

Input:
   IKG: Init Knowledge Graph;
   $INFO$: Text imformation of HOK;
Output:
   NKG:New Knowledge Graph;
1: H = Hero , A = Attributes of Hero
2: **for** each Hi ∈ IKG **do**
3:    Search Hi in $INFO$;
4:    Extract Imformation Ii About Hi;
5:    **for** each j ∈ Ai **do**
6:       **if** Ij not exit in Ai **then**
7:          add Ij into Ai
8:       **end if**
9:    **end for**
10:    Add into IKG;
11: **end for**
12: $NKG = IKG$;
13: **return** NKG

To answer the three questions mentioned above, we first find the corresponding hero in the knowledege graph according to the hero selected by the player. Then, for question 1, we get the corresponding equipment according to the *equip* relationship. For question 2, we get the play skill of the hero which selected by the player according to the *skill* property. For question 3, we get all the enemy heros and sort them by the countering rate of the hero which selected by the player and select the hero with the highest countering rate as a hero which player needs to be careful, furthermore, we also will show the play skill of this hero according to the *skill* property.

4   Experiments and Discussion

Our mainly task is to predict the result of the game only with the data of hero formation. It is a pregame prediction without regard for other factors like players' operation skill. In the following parts, we will discuss how to create a predictor model in detail.

4.1   Data Set

We gathered the competition data of 200,000 games on December 31, 2018, and extracted the following data for each match from the data set:

- All heroes from winning side.
- All heroes from losing side.

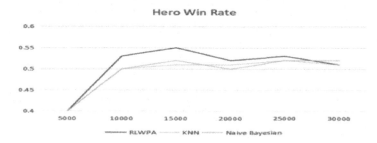

Fig. 6. Feature hero win rate

The matches we have chosen has the following characteristics:

- All the players we choose are high-level ones. The reason for this is that high-level players commonly understand and operate the game better, and better operation level can lead to more clear character features.
- 5V5 game mode. All games are in 5V5 mode rather than 1V1 or 3V3.

4.2 Experiments Results Win Prediction

We separate the data into 50000 training matches and 10000 test matches. Selecting different machine learning algorithms and using different features has a greater impact on the results. As shown in Fig. 6, we use RLWPA as the predictor and using feature Hero Win Rate to test accuracy asymptotically approaches 55% and does not change much with an increase in the training set size, in addition, using KNN accuracy is 52% and Naive Bayesian is 53%.

In Fig. 7, we use feature Pairing and Countering to match the three machine learning algorithms. The results show that using this feature makes the prediction results of the three algorithms significantly improved. Among them, the accuracy of logistic regression is close to 63%, which is 8% higher than the use of feature Hero Win Rate. In addition, KNN and Naive Bayesian have also increased more than 3% and reach 55%. We also tried to combine these two features, but the results showed no improvement in accuracy. As shown in Fig. 8, we can see

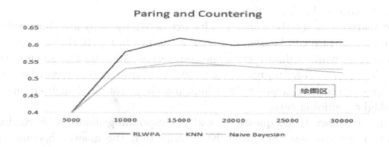

Fig. 7. Feature pairing and countering

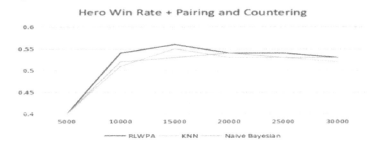

Fig. 8. Feature hero win rate + pairing and countering

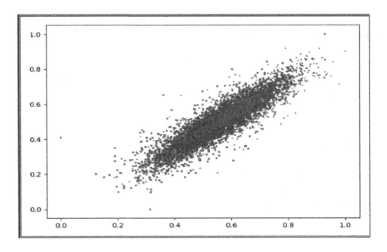

Fig. 9. Scatter plot of game results.

that the results obtained by using this feature to match three machine learning algorithms are nearby 55%.

From the experimental results, the RLWPA was the most appropriate model. The overfitting problem has little effect in this algorithm, and the training accuracy and verification accuracy have a slight difference. The performance of feature selection shows that the performance of the hero Pairing and Countering is the best feature in both algorithms.

The scatter plot of the game results extracted by hero matching rate and hero countering rate can be seen in Fig. 9. As shown in Fig. 9, the abscissa shows matching rate, while ordinate gives the countering rate, and the green dots and the red dots respectively represent each side's winning match. According to this figure, we can see that teams with a high matching rate and high counter rate have a higher winning rate.

Figure 10 shows three questions and corresponding answers. According to the picture we can see that after KG completion the answer becomes more comprehensive. We invited 100 experts to evaluate questions and answers. We

Question	Answer before KG completion	Answer after KG completion
白起应该购买什么装备？	反伤制甲，红莲斗篷，抵抗之靴，暴烈之甲，霸者重装，魔女斗篷	反伤制甲，红莲斗篷，抵抗之靴，暴烈之甲，霸者重装，魔女斗篷
我应该怎么使用白起？	Null	玩法：前期野战阵容刚开始时白起开下路帮敌方与敌方英雄线硬碰硬，黄忠要留意上路为防御团战消失要失时的结合要单兵身更击伤对线2级那就那有小兵能到自己身边，兵品闪身1级就是本身可以给身伤当兵这个时候给上线那与它的来受对霸时的位置，一般对手开身的时候会唤在这方的最后收集团处理手中，这个时候需在这1抵抗块制伤单位置，给帛无法在你例付下一一轮使舰反上后，最后它才抵御承也霸说组织加血。正面：王流庄周应正是辅助，建议庄周辅助射手下来，不建议以庄周带线，至少状态，庄周至2帧1，基本上留2抵抗伤霸木连位，庄周1结带战，开揭直原身2抵给，2抵给有辅助，就是说1信时候应用有两个抵给，这时如不同那射手需配与霸对霸蓝队领块，得到带它日达中的好去 buff一定领队，你只需要现保找我顶心，他的量最金很低，我有己抵抗资清有1枪庄周位，获得一套本强抗疾，差之一一组点2抵给直接杀对面越域抖打击，不需要黄帮射手打红。
白起应该小心敌方哪个英雄？	庄周	王流庄周应正是辅助，建议庄周辅助射手下来，不建议以庄周带线，至少状态，庄周至2帧1，基本上留2抵抗伤霸木连位，庄周1信带战，开揭直原身2抵给，2抵给有辅助，就是说1信时候应用有两个抵给，这时如不同那射手需配与霸对霸蓝队领块，得到带它日达中的好去buff一定领队，你只需要现保找我顶心，他的量最金很低，我有己抵抗资清有1组庄周位，获得一套本强抗疾，差之一一组点2抵给直接杀对面越域抖打击，不需要黄帮射手打红。

Fig. 10. Question and answer

classfied the evaluation of answers as three levels: Agree, Disagree and Neutral. At the same time, we define accuracy as the number of people who Agree on the answers. As shwon in Table 1, the accuracy of the answers is higher than 90%.

Table 1. Expert comments on the answers

Questions	Agree	Disagree	Neutral
Which equipment should I buy?	99%	0%	1%
How should I play this hero?	95%	3%	2%
Which enemy hero I need to be careful in this game?	90%	5%	5%

As shown in Fig. 11, according to the win prediction algorithm and knowledge graph mentioned before, here is the support system we developed. When all

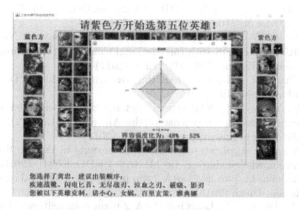

Fig. 11. HOK support system simulator

players have selected their heroes, support system will show the winning rate for both sides. Besides, the system will offer to each player how to choose the equipment and which heroes they need to watch out the most.

5   Conclusion

In this paper, we introduce a prediction model based on a machine learning algorithm to forecast the victory of Honor of Kings 5V5 game by considering the heroes formation on each side using a gaming history dataset. We analyze the Honor of Kings and presents a winning rate prediction model for Honor of Kings according to the characteristics of the game. The model predicts the outcome of the game with only the heroes selection data. The most important part is the feature extraction. We use machine learning algorithms to predict the game outcome. The experimental results show that the Logistic Regression algorithm is most suitable for the winning rate prediction model.

The reason why the prediction accuracy is relatively low may be because the Honor of Kings is a game which the player's skill and the presence of the game will greatly affect the outcome of the game.

Acknowledgments. The work was supported by Key Technologies Research and Development Program of China (2017YFC0405805-04) and Basal Research Fund of China (2018B57614).

References

1. Honor of Kings official website. https://pvp.qq.com/. Accessed 10 Oct 2019
2. Conley, K., Perry, D.: How does he saw me? A recommendation engine for picking heroes in DotA 2. Np, and Web 7 (2013)
3. Kalyanaraman, K: To win or not to win? A prediction model to determine the outcome of a DotA2 match. Technical report, University of California San Diego (2014)
4. Semenov, A., Romov, P., Korolev, S., Yashkov, D., Neklyudov, K.: Performance of machine learning algorithms in predicting game outcome from drafts in DotA 2. In: Ignatov, D., et al. (eds.) AIST 2016. CCIS, vol. 661, pp. 26–37. Springer, Cham (2016). https://doi.org/10.1007/978-3-319-52920-2_3
5. Wang, K., Shang, W.: Outcome prediction of DOTA2 based on Naïve Bayes classifier. In: 2017 IEEE/ACIS 16th International Conference on Computer and Information Science (ICIS), pp. 591–593. IEEE (2017)
6. Song, K., Zhang, T., Ma, C.: Predicting the winning side of DotA2. Technical report, Stanford University (2015)
7. Drachen, A., Yancey, M., Klabajan, D., et al.: Skill-based differences in spatiotemporal team behaviour in defense of the Ancients 2 (DotA 2). In: 2014 IEEE Games Media Entertainment, pp. 1–8. IEEE (2014)
8. Semenov, A., et al. Applications of machine learning in DotA2: literature review and practical knowledge sharing. In: MLSA@ PKDD/ECML (2016)
9. Kinkade, N., Jolla, L., Lim, K.: DotA 2 win prediction. Technical report, University of California San Diego (2015)
10. Agarwala, A., Pearce, M.: Learning DotA 2 team compositions. Technical report, Stanford University (2014)

Combining Concept Graph with Improved Neural Networks for Chinese Short Text Classification

Jialu Liao[1,2], Fanke Sun[1,2], and Jinguang Gu[1,2(✉)]

[1] College of Computer Science and Technology,
Wuhan University of Science and Technology, Wuhan 430065, China
simon@wust.edu.cn
[2] Hubei Province Key Laboratory of Intelligent Information Processing
and Real-Time Industrial System, Wuhan 430065, China

Abstract. With the development of the Internet, network information is booming, and a large amount of short text data has brought more timely and comprehensive information to people. How to find the required information quickly and accurately from these pieces of information is the focus of the industry. Short text processing is one of the key technologies. Because of the sparse and noisy features of short texts, the traditional classification method can not provide good support. At present, the research on short text classification mainly focuses on two aspects: feature processing and classification algorithm. Most feature processing methods only use text literal information when performing feature expansion, which lacks the ability to discriminate the polysemy that is common in Chinese. In the classification algorithm, there are also problems such as insufficient input characteristics and insufficient classification effect. In order to improve the accuracy of Chinese short text classification, this paper proposes a method of Chinese short text classification based on improved convolutional recurrent neural network and concept graph, which achieves better classification results than existing algorithms.

Keywords: Chinese short text classification · Concept graph · Feature processing · Deep learning

1 Introduction

With the coming of mobile Internet era, short text has gradually become the most common form of text, which we call short text. Short texts are mainly produced in scenarios such as bullet-screen interaction, commodity evaluation and news headlines [1]. Enterprises need to understand users' real needs based on these information, so as to launch better services and products. The relevant government departments can also monitor public opinion based on these data. In order to eliminate useless, interference and even error information, we need to correctly use the increasingly mature technology to understand and analyze

© Springer Nature Singapore Pte Ltd. 2020
X. Wang et al. (Eds.): JIST 2019, CCIS 1157, pp. 205–212, 2020.
https://doi.org/10.1007/978-981-15-3412-6_20

these massive data, and obtain valuable information accurately and efficiently. Short text has the characteristics of short text length, large number and large amount of interference information [2], which makes it impossible to provide sufficient context semantics, resulting in the difficulty of extracting effective text features from traditional algorithms for processing long text [3]. Therefore, how to design an effective model to extract the semantic information of short text and improve the classification accuracy of short text is the main challenge. In this paper, based on the characteristics of short text, the feature processing method of conceptual knowledge of word acquisition through concept graph is designed. Combining the advantages of the most popular neural network model, multiple neural network models are combined to improve the feature extraction effect; And from the three levels of characters, words and concepts, a three-channel Chinese short text classification model is constructed to improve the accuracy of short text classification.

The rest of this paper is organized as follows: Sect. 2 will give a brief analysis of current feature processing schemes and short text classification methods; Sect. 3 will introduce the three-channel Chinese text classification model designed in this paper, including how to combine the advantages of existing neural network models to generate an efficient feature extraction network; Sect. 4 will introduce the data set used in the experiment, compare the proposed algorithm with the existing algorithm using short Chinese text, and analyze the experimental results. The fifth section summarizes the work of the full text, and puts forward the prospect of the future research direction of short text feature processing methods and classification methods based on in-depth learning.

2   Research Progress of Text Classification

In the research of classification algorithms, with the deep learning method being applied in large scale in the field of natural language processing, the neural network method can learn from the text to the internal semantic features with the help of big data, and can complete the short text classification task better. Among them, Convolutional Neural Network (CNN) and Recurrent Neural Network (RNN) are the two most popular models in the current short text classification study. For CNN model, Kim [4] combined word vector with convolution neural network at first, and achieved good results in short text sentiment analysis. For RNN model, LSTM is the focus of research. Liang et al. [5] designed a tree structure LSTM with emotional polarity transfer sentiment analysis model.

In recent years, with the continuous development of natural language processing, some new methods have been proposed. Attention mechanism [6], proposed by Google, holds that the results of the model are determined by several or even one key feature, which gives researchers new inspiration. Some researchers apply attention mechanism to short text classification. Er et al. [7] proposed a convolution neural network based on attention pooling, constructed an intermediate vector representation of input text by using parallel LSTM, which was used as the attention weight of the document eigenvector generated by convolution neural network. Finally, the processed text eigenvector was input into the classifier for classification.

Among the feature processing methods based on conceptual graph we know, they are all for English corpus research. How to use knowledge graph to process Chinese short text features, and how to use neural network knowledge to construct an efficient feature extraction model to obtain more semantic knowledge to improve the classification effect of Chinese short text is still a subject that researchers need to continue to explore.

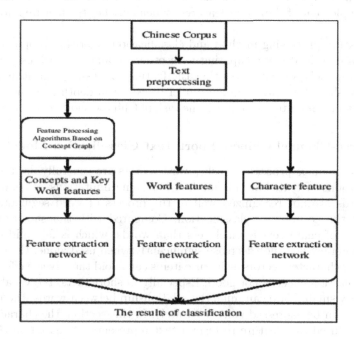

Fig. 1. Overall workflow diagram

3   Constructing Chinese Text Classification Model

3.1   The Process of Chinese Text Classification

The workflow of Chinese text classification is shown in Fig. 1. The research contents are as follows:

1. In order to solve the problem of single feature, this paper proposes a three-channel Chinese short text classification model, which extracts features from three levels: word feature, character feature and concept feature.

2. The Chinese short text classification model designed in this paper is an efficient feature extraction network structure, which combines the advantages of CNN model and Bi-LSTM model, and introduces the attention mechanism to enhance the attention of key words.
3. For the conceptual level features in the model, this paper uses Probase+, a conceptual graph system based on knowledge graph, to obtain candidate concepts of words, and constructs a semantic network from the perspective of the whole text by using concepts and original texts to analyze the correlation between them. In addition, with the help of feature iteration selection algorithm, keywords and concepts suitable for the current context are selected as the complement of short text features, which enriches the feature information of text.
4. The feature processing method and classification algorithm proposed in this paper are verified. By comparing with other popular algorithms and classification models, we can know that the feature processing algorithm and the Chinese short text classification model based on in-depth learning and concept graph can better accomplish the task of Chinese short text classification.

3.2   Three-Channel Chinese Short Text Classification Model

In natural language processing tasks, word vectors are generally used as vector representations of text, but this method has some limitations. If some professional words are not recognized well in the process of word segmentation, it will affect the accuracy of classification. Compared with thousands of words, the number of characters is much less than words, which is fast and efficient, and the accuracy does not decrease significantly when used alone. On the other hand, using character vectors as feature items can avoid the adverse effects when the segmentation effect is not good. Especially in short texts, the vocabulary is usually very small. If we can mine the relationship between words, the meaning of the text can be expressed more accurately. In this section, the character level signal [8] is used as a feature to form a text representation based on character vector features to assist the model to obtain more semantic information.

Whether the commonly used word features or character features mentioned above are processed on the basis of the original corpus [9], but it can not solve the problem of insufficient signals and many interference items provided by the short text itself. In order to solve this problem, it is a common practice to select appropriate feature extension methods to help understand the original semantics, and the method of introducing external knowledge graph is one of the solutions used in this paper. In this section, we will use the feature processing algorithm based on concept graph to get the conceptual set and keyword set of short text from the conceptual level. We hope that these two sets can also be added to text features as conceptual level signals to form a text representation based on conceptual vector features to solve the problem of "polysemy" that most models can't solve.

Based on the above two points, this paper hopes to combine the acquired character signals and conceptual signals to assist the word signals, so that the classification model can get more semantic information. Based on this idea, this paper designs a three-channel short text classification model. By establishing three feature matrices of word vector, character vector and concept vector, they are input into the convolutional recurrent neural network model based on attention mechanism, and their respective features are extracted. Then, the cascade fusion is completed through the full connection layer. Finally, the classifier completes the classification. This multi-channel structure of neural network overcomes the shortcomings of insufficient signals and greater randomness in short text data, and can obtain more abundant short text semantic features. Through the method of multi-feature fusion, the information in text can be obtained more comprehensively, in order to make the model have stronger representation ability for text signals.

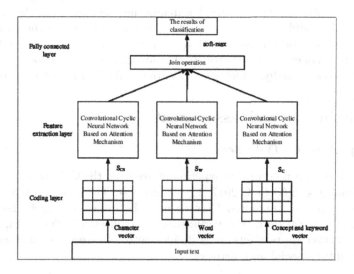

Fig. 2. Three-channel short text classification model

The overall model is shown in Fig. 2. The three-channel model contains three parallel network structures, and their characteristics are computed by parallel computing. The first network deals with character vectors of short text; the second network deals with word vectors; and the third network deals with keywords and concept vectors. The whole model is divided into three layers: coding layer, feature extraction layer and full connection layer. The input module layer and feature extraction layer have one in each channel, and the full connection layer is shared by three channels.

3.3   Feature Processing Based on Concept Graph

Because of the characteristics of short text itself, useful information is very limited, and even there will be many interference words unrelated to the main body of the text, so it is necessary to obtain more semantic signals (e.g concepts) for feature expansion and ambiguity elimination. At the same time, we need to take these signals and the original text as a whole, find the relationship between them, so that they can interact with each other, so as to help the computer obtain the true semantics of the short text to the greatest extent.

This paper uses Microsoft concept graph System Probase+ [10], which can realize the conceptual operation of short text. At present, the core of most conceptual selection work is mapping short text words to candidate concepts in knowledge graph one by one to obtain conceptual words and their probabilities.

The flow chart of feature processing algorithm is divided into three stages: The first stage is feature extension based on Probase+ concept graph. The main work of this stage is to generate candidate concept sets by using words in short text, which can be obtained directly from concept graph system. The second stage is to construct a word-concept semantic network by using the content of word set and candidate concept set. The third stage is to use the constructed semantic network for feature selection calculation and to screen out the final keywords and concepts set. Through this algorithm, the number of effective features increases rapidly, which greatly enriches the feature set of short text.

4 Experiments and Assessment

4.1 Experimental Data Set

The short text data used in this experiment are from the Chinese news headline classification task in NLPCC 2017 [11] shared task. The corpus contains a total of 228,000 manually annotated Chinese news headlines, of which the training set contains 156,000 data, the verification set contains 36,000 data, and the remaining 36,000 are test sets. It is divided into 18 categories, such as sports, tourism, military, social and historical.

4.2 Data Preprocessing

Before the experiment, the data sets need to be processed as follows:

(1) Because the data set is a Chinese corpus, it is necessary to use Jieba tool to segment the whole data set to form a segmented word data set.
(2) We find that the result of deleting stop words in this data set is relatively poor, which means that deleting stop words in very short modeled text may damage the original syntactic structure or even the semantic representation. Therefore, this paper does not perform the operation of deleting stop words in this data set.
(3) Since the classification model designed in this paper contains three channels, the input data of each channel need to be processed.
(4) In order to make the computer understand the text, we need to train the skip-gram model of word2vec tool to get 200-dimensional word vector.

Because of the high dimension of word vector representation, it is necessary to index the characters or words in the data set, replace the words with real numbers, and even the whole text. This method can greatly increase the speed of computer text processing.

4.3   Experimental Analysis

In this experiment, the single-channel classification model with three granularities of characters, words and concepts, the two-channel classification model of characters and words, and the three-channel classification model based on word vector data and concept vector data are used respectively. This experiment is mainly evaluated by Accuracy index.

Table 1. Comparison results of different granularity data

Model	Character vector	Word vector	Concept vector	Character+Word two-channel	Three-channels
CNN	74.02%	76.61%	64.53%	78.08%	79.75%
LSTM	73.56%	75.57%	60.34%	76.60%	79.01%
A-BiLSTM	76.52%	77.63%	65.32%	79.96%	80.34%
CRAN	73.89%	77.01%	66.21%	78.39%	79.83%
C-LSTM	76.83%	78.52%	68.63%	79.78%	81.01%
The model in this paper	78.01%	79.34%	68.01%	80.87%	82.24%

The three-channel method of words, characters and concepts designed in this paper combines the features of word vectors, word vectors and concept vectors, and further overcomes the shortcomings of inadequate signal and large randomness in short text data. By means of multi-feature fusion, more abundant feature information can be obtained, so that the classification model can have enough information for feature extraction in training. From Table 1, it can be seen that the classification model designed in this paper can achieve the best classification results under the conditions of single channel or multi-channel. Compared with the single channel classification method, our method has improved by about 3%, and compared with the double channel classification method of words and characters, the correct rate has increased by 1%–2%, Compared with the mixed model in reference [11], the accuracy is improved by 0.5%. Which proves that the three channel classification method designed in this paper is more effective.

5   Conclusion

With the development of mobile Internet, short text analysis and research has become a hot issue. As a key technology of natural language processing, short text classification has great research value. Traditional text classification methods depend on a large amount of text information, so it is impossible to obtain semantic information by statistical methods. Therefore, this paper mainly studies and improves short text classification from two aspects: feature processing and classification algorithm. Experiments verify the effectiveness of the proposed method.

Acknowledgment. This work was partially supported by a grant from the NSF (Natural Science Foundation) of China under grant number 61673304 and U1836118, the Key Projects of National Social Science Foundation of China under grant number 11&ZD189.

References

1. Zhou, T., Chen, M., Yu, J., Terzopoulos, D.: Attention-based natural language person retrieval. In: Computer Vision and Pattern Recognition Workshops (2017)
2. Yu, B., Zhang, L., School of Management: Chinese short text classification based on CP-CNN. Appl. Res. Comput. **35**, 1001–1004 (2018)
3. Zhang, D., Xu, H., Su, Z., Xu, Y.: Chinese comments sentiment classification based on word2vec and SVM^{perf}. Expert Syst. Appl. **42**(4), 1857–1863 (2014)
4. Kim, Y.: Convolutional neural networks for sentence classification. Eprint Arxiv (2014)
5. Li, S., Yan, Z., Wu, X., Li, A., Zhou, B.: A method of emotional analysis of movie based on convolution neural network and bi-directional LSTM RNN. In: 2017 IEEE Second International Conference on Data Science in Cyberspace (DSC), pp. 156–161 (2017)
6. Yang, Z., Yang, D., Dyer, C., He, X., Smola, A., Hovy, E.: Hierarchical attention networks for document classification. In: Proceedings of the 2016 Conference of the North American Chapter of the Association for Computational Linguistics: Human Language Technologies, pp. 1480–1489 (2016)
7. Zhang, Y., Er, M.J., Wang, N., Pratama, M.: Attention pooling-based convolutional neural network for sentence modelling. Inf. Sci. Int. J. **373**(C), 388–403 (2016)
8. Graves, A., Schmidhuber, J.: Framewise phoneme classification with bidirectional LSTM and other neural network architectures. Neural Netw. **18**(5–6), 602–610 (2005)
9. Wang, J., Wang, Z., Zhang, D., Yan, J.: Combining knowledge with deep convolutional neural networks for short text classification. In: Twenty-Sixth International Joint Conference on Artificial Intelligence (2017)
10. Liang, J., Xiao, Y., Wang, H., Zhang, Y., Wang, W.: Probase+: inferring missing links in conceptual taxonomies. IEEE Trans. Knowl. Data Eng. **29**(6), 1281–1295 (2017)
11. Lu, Z., Liu, W., Zhou, Y., Hu, X., Wang, B.: An effective approach for Chinese news headline classification based on multi-representation mixed model with attention and ensemble learning. In: Huang, X., Jiang, J., Zhao, D., Feng, Y., Hong, Y. (eds.) NLPCC 2017. LNCS (LNAI), vol. 10619, pp. 339–350. Springer, Cham (2018). https://doi.org/10.1007/978-3-319-73618-1_29

Construction of Chinese Pediatric Medical Knowledge Graph

Yu Song[1], Linkun Cai[1,2], Kunli Zhang[1,2(✉)], Hongying Zan[1,2], Tao Liu[1,2], and Xiaohui Ren[1,2]

[1] Zhengzhou University, Zhengzhou, China
ieklzhang@zzu.edu.cn
[2] The Pengcheng Laboratory, Shenzhen, China

Abstract. The knowledge graph is a promising method for knowledge management in the big data era. Pediatrics, as an essential branch of clinical medicine, has accumulated a large amount of medical data. This paper applies the knowledge graph technique in pediatric studies and proposes a method for Chinese pediatric medical knowledge graph (PMKG) construction. The proposed method has a conceptual layer and a data layer. At the conceptual layer we analyze the semantic characteristics of multi-source pediatrics data, formulate the annotation scheme of entity and entity relationship, and extend the traditional triplet form of knowledge graph to a sextuplet form. At the data layer, guided by the annotation scheme, information is extracted from data sources using entity recognition and relationship extraction. Manual annotation, knowledge fusion and other technologies are used to construct a pediatric knowledge graph. The PMKG contains 22,023 entities and 34,434 sextuplets.

Keywords: Pediatrics · Annotation scheme · Knowledge graph

1 Introduction

In the era of big data, knowledge interconnection has gained much attention. Knowledge graph expresses the information of the Internet in a form that is closer to the cognitive world of humans, providing a better way to organize, manage, and understand the vast amount of information on the Internet. Medicine is one of the most widely used vertical fields of knowledge graph. It is also an important domain of the application of Artificial Intelligence (AI). Popular and mature medical knowledge bases include Gene Ontology [2] and SNOMED-CT [9]. The study of medical knowledge graphs started late in China. Yu [13] used a large amount of traditional Chinese medicine (TCM) data, clinical diagnosis and treatment knowledge bases to construct a knowledge graph of TCM. Zhang [14] explored the construction method of ontology-based core knowledge graph of TCM by analyzing the correlation between TCM knowledge and clinical experience. Liu [5] proposed the automatic construction of pediatric knowledge graph from clinical cases based on Naive Bayesian Network.

© Springer Nature Singapore Pte Ltd. 2020
X. Wang et al. (Eds.): JIST 2019, CCIS 1157, pp. 213–220, 2020.
https://doi.org/10.1007/978-981-15-3412-6_21

The above work in existing literature have greatly promoted the development of knowledge graph. However, there are still the following problems: (1) The size of corpus is small, and the use of multiple data sources is not considered. (2) The classification scheme of entity and entity relationship is incomplete. (3) Triplet in traditional knowledge graph cannot fully express complex medical information.

In view of these facts, we take pediatric disease as the focus of this study and propose the pediatric medical knowledge graph (PMKG) construction based on multi-source data fusion.

2   Construction Workflow

This paper does PMKG construction in two parts, a conceptual layer and a data layer. Figure 1 shows the schematic of the PMKG construction.

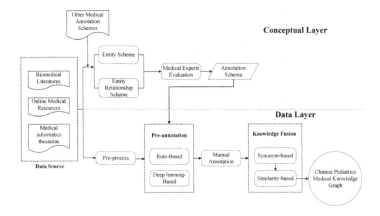

Fig. 1. The Chinese PMKG construction workflow.

The PMKG is built in a top-down approach. First, we analyze medical data and form an annotation scheme of entity and entity relationship under the guidance of medical experts. A man-machine annotation method is used to extract medical knowledge from multi-source texts to build a pediatric corpus. Knowledge fusion is carried out to form the PMKG.

2.1   Data Source

The source of data determines the quality of the knowledge graph and its application scenarios. After comprehensive consideration of the authority, quality, scale and access of the data, we select the following data sources for subsequent work.

Biomedical Literature. We mainly select two kinds of textbooks of pediatrics in Chinese medical schools, Pediatrics [12] and Clinical Pediatrics [8]. The former focuses on the theories while the latter focuses on doctors' clinical practice. The combination of two entirely fits the characteristics of pediatrics. This kind of data mainly describes the pathogenesis, diagnosis, prevention and treatment of pediatric diseases.

Online Resource. The main sources are CDD(China Disease Knowledge Total Database) and BaiDu encyclopedia[1]. These data are good completement to the biomedical literature.

Medical Informatics Thesaurus. These thesauruses include MeSH (Medical Subject Headings) [4], ICD-10 (The International Classification of Diseases, 10th revision) [10], ICD-9-CM-3 [7], ATC (Anatomical Therapeutic Chemical) [1] and SNOMED-CT, which are recommended by domain experts. These data include the classification system and hierarchy of diseases, examinations, etc.

3   Conceptual Layer

We investigate medical corpora annotated in both Chinese and English. With the participation and guidance of doctors and combined with the characteristics of Chinese pediatric data, we define an annotation scheme of entity and entity relationship centered on diseases. There are 9 types of entities and 27 types of entity relationships in the scheme.

3.1   Entity

We reference I2B2 [11] definition of entity type method, and use medical informatics thesauruses to define the scope of medical entity.

Entity Attribute. Attribute in disease-like entity relationship generally refers to the features and parameters of entity. Attribute plays an important role in disease analysis, and knowledge integrated with attribute information is more complete. For example, adjectives such as "acute" and "chronic" often appear in the description of diseases.

Entity Annotation Rules. Medical entity annotation follows three principles: (1) No overlapping annotation. The same string cannot be annotateed as two different entity types. (2) No nested annotation. One entity cannot be inside another entity. (3) No punctuation marks (e.g., commas, periods) and connectives (or, and) if possible.

3.2   Entity Relationship

Entity relationship annotation is expanded on the basis of entity annotation. This paper takes disease as the center to expand the relationship between disease and other entities. We defined 27 different types of disease relationships, which are classified and shown in Table 1.

---

[1] https://baike.baidu.com.

Table 1. Types of entity relationship

Entity1	Relationship type	Entity2
Disease	Typology, Differential diagnosis, Complication, Cause, Transformation	Disease
	Clinical symptom, Clinical sign	Symptom
	Pathogenic site, Involve	Site
	Imaging examination, Pathological examination, Endoscopy, Laboratory examination	Examination
	Drug therapy	Drug
	Operative treatment	Operation
	Prognosis condition, Prognostic survival rate, Prognostic survival time	Prognosis
	Etiology, High risk factors, Genetic factor	Sociology
	Incidence rate, Mortality, Latency, Prevalent area, Prevalent group, Prevalent seasons, Transmission route	Epidemiology

Entity Relationship Attribute. The attribute of entity relationship mainly refers to the restriction condition and explanation of the entity relationship. Such as, the period during which "clinical symptom" occur.

Entity Relationship Annotation Rules. Entity relationships are not limited within a sentence scope. They also include relationships across sentence segments. Only one relationship can be marked between two entities.

3.3   Sextuplet

The triplet representation is the general representation of knowledge graph, which consists of two medical entities with semantic relation and an entity relationship. It is an intuitive representation of medical knowledge. Such (Entity1-Relationship-Entity2).

Therefore, the traditional triplet of knowledge graph is extended to a sextuplet to record disease information as comprehensively as possible. That is, entity and entity relationship can be supplemented with more specific information by adding attribute, which can be expressed as <E1 [Attri1] - R [Attri2]- E2 [Attri3]>. For example, Early-onset neonatal sepsis incidence is very high. For wild case patients, infusions of Cephalosporium is a good choice. This sentence can be represented as <neonatal sepsis [early-onset] - Drug Therapy [wild case patients] - Cephalosporium [infusions]>.

4   Data Layer

The construction of the pediatric knowledge graph mainly involves extracting entities, relationships, and attributes manually or automatically from unstructured data. However, the cost of manual extraction is too high. The automatic extraction of knowledge is a key research direction at present and also the trend of knowledge graph construction in the future.

To reduce the work of manual annotation, a method of man-machine combination is used to improve the speed of annotation and also guarantee the corpus quality. The proposed method has three steps: pre-process, pre-annotation, and manual annotation.

4.1 Pre-process

Due to our diverse sources of medical data, the data formats and encoding schemes are not the same. To satisfy the needs of subsequent multi-source data fusion and annotation, this part mainly includes the following aspects.

Unified Data Format. Our data sources are stored in XML, TXT, HTML, and database files, encoded in UTF8 and GBK. For further annotation work, we first convert these data into TXT and store it in UTF8 format.

Data Cleaning. The online medical text data contains a large amount of information and inevitably has errors, incompleteness, and redundancy. We practice rule-based methods to remove them and improve data quality.

4.2 Pre-annotation

In pre-annotation, rule-based and deep-learning method are applied to automatic annotation of entities.

Rule-Based Method. We use manually defined rules or existing medical dictionaries like the medical informatics thesaurus to match medical entities from data that has been preprocessed. However, there is no complete dictionary of all types of biological entities, and the same word has different entity types in varies of contexts (e.g., jaundice can be a disease or a symptom). Therefore, a rule-based approach alone is not sufficient for entity recognition.

Deep-Learning Method. On the basis of the rule-based method, we use a neural network model based on CNN-LSTM-CRF [3] for medical entity recognition which is pretrained by other medical entity extraction corpus and fine-tuned by the data we have annotated.

We take the fusion of the results of the above two methods as the result of pre-annotation. Comparing with manual annotation results, the accuracy of pre-annotation results is more than 85%, which can effectively reduce manual work.

4.3 Manual Annotation

The construction of the pediatric knowledge graph is inseparable from large-scale annotated corpus, and manually annotated corpus is considered as the gold standard corpus. Through automatic annotation, a part of the entity was well annotated. There are still many problems in the result of automatic annotation, such as error of entity recognition and the matching error resulted from the variants of the entity. Due to these problems, all the automatic annotated entities were imported in the manual annotation system, and manual proofreading and correction were conducted. After the entity annotation was completed, we begin to manually annotate entity relationships and attributes.

Since multiple people annotation at the same time, avoiding mistakes such as annotation error, annotation inconsistency, and leakage of annotation is difficult. In the manual annotation process, we adopt multiple rounds of annotation to ensure the accuracy and consistency of the results. Each text was annotated independently by two annotators, called A and B, and the inconsistencies and uncertainties in the two annotations are later recorded for discussion with medical experts.

4.4   Agreement Metrics

Agreement between annotators is defined in terms of matches and non-matches between the two double-annotation sets created for each document, one set created per annotator. An annotation in one set matches that in the other set if they have the same type, the same word offsets (textual span) and the same attributes. The agreement between double-annotated documents can then be calculated as inter annotator agreement (IAA) [6], as in the following Eq. 1:

$$\text{IAA} = \frac{matches}{matches + non_{matches}} \tag{1}$$

According to statistics, the consistency rate of sextuplets in corpus is 89%.

4.5   Knowledge Fusion

In various data sources, the expressions of multiple entities are diverse. Medical entity abbreviations and mixed expressions in Chinese and English, as well as the ambiguity of the entity's context, lead to the duplication and the discretization of knowledge and other issues.

Entity alignment is the core work of knowledge fusion. Through medical entity alignment, we can better represent the semantic association between different data source entities, to realize multi-source data fusion. In this paper, methods as synonym-based and similarity-based are used to realize the entity alignment between different data source. Specifically, we use the synonym-based approach first and then the similarity-based approach on its results.

Synonym-Based. Create a complete database of synonymous entities to compare different terms in the medical field. For example, a search on the disease synonymous entity comparison library for the disease "小儿哮喘 (infantile asthma)" can get a collection of its synonyms {小儿支气管哮喘, 儿童期哮喘,…}. Also, we have established a synonymy entity comparison library for the symptom, drug, and examination.

Similarity-Based. Entity name plays a vital role in the differentiation of the entity. The relationship reflect the essential characteristics of the entity. Therefore, we mainly consider two features when calculating entity similarity: entity name and entity relationship. The calculation formula is as follows:

$$\text{sim}(e_i, e_j) = a\text{sim}_{\text{Distance}}(e_i, e_j) + (1 - a)\text{sim}_{\text{CommonNB}}(e_i, e_j) \tag{2}$$

Where e_i, e_j represents two entities, $\text{sim}_{\text{Distance}}(e_i, e_j)$ is the text-similarity function of the corresponding entity pairs, we use the edit distance of entity pairs to calculate the similarity. $\text{sim}_{\text{CommonNB}}(e_i, e_j)$ is the structural similarity [15] function of entity pairs. The structural similarity of two entity pairs is obtained by directly calculating the number of identical relationships between two entities, and its formula is as follows:

$$\text{sim}_{\text{CommonNB}}(e_i, e_j) = \frac{1}{K} * |(e_i) \cap \text{NB}(e_j)| \tag{3}$$

$$K = \max(\text{len}(\text{NB}(e_i)), \text{len}(\text{NB}(e_j))) \tag{4}$$

$\text{NB}(e_i)$ is the entity relationship of e_i, the $0 \leq a \leq 1$ is the adjustment parameter of both, and then a similarity threshold value t is set to judge whether the entity matches. Here, we set $t = 0.7, a = 0.7$, which are the best parameters for testing.

At present, we have annotated 504 kinds of pediatric diseases, a total of 2.98 million words. After knowledge fusion, the quantity statistics of annotation entities and entity relationships are presented in Table 2. We randomly sample the merged entities and evaluate them. The average accuracy of entity alignment is above 90%.

Table 2. Entity and relationship statistics

Entity	Before/after the fusion	Relationship type	Num
Diesase	8,779/6,710	Diesase-Diesase	7,960
Symptom	6,884/6,662	Diesase-Symptom	12,218
Site	679/670	Diesase-Site	1,229
Examination	1,764/1,599	Diesase-Examination	2,859
Drug	2,006/1,550	Diesase-Drug	2,950
Prognosis	1,004/1,004	Diesase-Prognosis	1,480
Sociology	3,241/3,060	Diesase-Sociology	4,650
Epidemiology	369/366	Diesase-Epidemiology	515
Total	25,162/22,023	Total	34,434

As can be seen from Table 2, disease, examination and drug have the highest amount of combinations, which due to the fact that many of these medical terms in Chinese are translated from foreign languages, and the forms of translation may be different in varies of bibliographies.

5 Conclusion

This work establishes a Chinese pediatric medical knowledge graph with well-annotated linguistics and high consistency. In the first stage, we construct an annotation scheme centered on pediatric diseases, under the guidance of medical experts. We also extend traditional triplet to sextuplet. In the second stage, during the corpus construction, we use man-machine combination method greatly to reduce the cost of human resources and to effectively guarantee the corpus quality. At present, the Chinese pediatric medical knowledge graph already contains 22,023 entities and 34,434 sextuplets.

This work is formulated with the common pediatric diseases as the core and has certain universality. We believe that this detailed account of our methodology will be beneficial to other researchers contemplating similar exercises.

References

1. ATC, W.: Anatomical therapeutic chemical classification system. WHO Collaborating Center for Drug Statistics (2009)
2. The Gene Ontology Consortium: Gene ontology consortium: going forward. Nucleic Acids Res. **43**(Database issue), 1049–1056 (2015)
3. Li, L., Guy, Y.: Biomedical named entity recognition with CNN-BLSTM-CRF. In: Proceedings of CCL (2017)
4. Lipscomb, C.E.: Medical subject headings (MeSH). Bull. Med. Libr. Assoc. **88**(3), 265 (2000)
5. Liu, P., et al.: HKDP: a hybrid knowledge graph based pediatric disease prediction system. In: Xing, C., Zhang, Y., Liang, Y. (eds.) ICSH 2016. LNCS, vol. 10219, pp. 78–90. Springer, Cham (2017). https://doi.org/10.1007/978-3-319-59858-1_8
6. Neves, M.: An analysis on the entity annotations in biological corpora. F1000Research **3**, 96 (2014)
7. Quan, H., et al.: Coding algorithms for defining comorbidities in ICD-9-CM and ICD-10 administrative data. Med. Care **43**, 1130–1139 (2005)
8. Shen, X.: Clinical Pediatrics. The Peoples Medical Publishing House, Beijing (2005)
9. Stearns, M.Q., Price, C., Spackman, K.A., Wang, A.Y.: SNOMED clinical terms: overview of the development process and project status. In: Proceedings of the AMIA Symposium, p. 662. American Medical Informatics Association (2001)
10. Sundararajan, V., Henderson, T., Perry, C., Muggivan, A., Quan, H., Ghali, W.A.: New ICD-10 version of the Charlson comorbidity index predicted in-hospital mortality. J. Clin. Epidemiol. **57**(12), 1288–1294 (2004)
11. Uzuner, Ö., South, B.R., Shen, S., DuVall, S.L.: 2010 i2b2/VA challenge on concepts, assertions, and relations in clinical text. J. Am. Med. Inform. Assoc. **18**(5), 552–556 (2011)
12. Wang, W., Sun, K., Chang, L.: Pediatrics (2018)
13. Yu, T., et al.: Knowledge graph for TCM health preservation: design, construction, and applications. Artif. Intell. Med. **77**, 48–52 (2017)
14. Zhang, D., Xie, Y., Li, M., Shi, C.: Construction of knowledge graph of traditional chinese medicine based on the ontology. Technol. Intell. Eng **3**(1), 8 (2017)
15. Zou, Y., Ouyang, C., Liu, Y., Yang, X., Yu, Y.: A similarity algorithm based on the generality and individuality of words. In: Lin, C.-Y., Xue, N., Zhao, D., Huang, X., Feng, Y. (eds.) ICCPOL/NLPCC-2016. LNCS (LNAI), vol. 10102, pp. 549–558. Springer, Cham (2016). https://doi.org/10.1007/978-3-319-50496-4_48

EasyKG: An End-to-End Knowledge Graph Construction System

Yantao Jia[✉], Dong Liu, Zhicheng Sheng, Letian Feng, Yi Liu, and Shuo Guo

Huawei Technologies Co., Ltd., Beijing, China
jamaths.h@163.com

Abstract. We present an end-to-end system, called EasyKG, throughout the whole lifecycle of knowledge graph (KG) construction. It has a pluggable pipeline architecture containing the components of knowledge modeling, knowledge extraction, knowledge reasoning, knowledge management and so forth. Users can automatically generate such a pipeline so as to obtain a domain-specific KG. Advanced users are allowed to create a pipeline in a drag-and-drop manner with customized components. EasyKG lowers the barriers of KG construction. Moreover, EasyKG allows users to evaluate different components and KGs, and share them across different domains so as to further reduce the cost of construction.

Keywords: Knowledge graph construction · End-to-end · Pipeline

1 Introduction

Knowledge graph (KG) is a graph structured knowledge base that stores factual information in form of relationships between entities [8]. Typical knowledge graphs include NELL [1], Google's Knowledge Graph [11], Knowledge vault [2], YAGO [12], OpenKN [6] and so on However, the construction of large-scale KGs is labor-intensive in need of the involvement of people with different expertise. For example, building a medical KG requires domain experts like doctors with the knowledge of diseases and symptoms, and software engineers in charge of implementing algorithms to link diseases and symptoms directly from massive electronic medical records [10]. Moreover, building a domain-specific KG is usually time-consuming with multiple steps such as knowledge modeling, data preparation, knowledge extraction, etc. How to glue these steps together is another big challenge since one need to handle different input/output constrains of different algorithms. Therefore, a system easing the construction of KG is imperative.

To lower the barriers of KG construction, we present an end-to-end system, called EasyKG, throughout the whole lifecycle of KG construction. To model the multiple steps in a KG construction process, a pluggable pipeline architecture consisting of components is designed. Each component contains algorithms, if any, and related configurations with respect to specific steps. Then the whole process can be formulated as a directed acyclic graph (DAG) in which components are arranged so that the output of each component is the input of the

© Springer Nature Singapore Pte Ltd. 2020
X. Wang et al. (Eds.): JIST 2019, CCIS 1157, pp. 221–228, 2020.
https://doi.org/10.1007/978-981-15-3412-6_22

next. A friendly GUI aids users to automatically generate a pipeline to obtain a domain-specific KG. In this situation, domain experts without knowledge of algorithms are able to construct a KG in a no-code manner as these algorithms are already encapsulated into reusable components. Furthermore, advanced users can create a pipeline in a drag-and-drop manner with customized components to teach the system to learn a KG.

EasyKG is distinct from existing systems like IBM Watson knowledge studio [4] since it is the first end-to-end system with a pluggable pipeline architecture to construct a KG in a comprehensive manner. In addition, many machine learning platforms are prevalent in recent years, such as Google's Cloud AutoML[1], which provides a suite of general-purpose machine learning products based on the neural architecture search technology [3,13]. Another similar type of systems is the data analytics platform such as KNIME [7], which integrates various machine learning and data mining algorithms through its modular data pipelining concept. Compared with Cloud AutoML and KNIME, EasyKG is carefully designed for KG construction so that users can build KGs efficiently.

2   System Overview

The architecture of EasyKG is shown in Fig. 1. It mainly consists of three layers: KG infrastructure as a cornerstone for high level applications, KG library with a number of algorithms, and KG studio as a user-friendly GUI for KG construction.

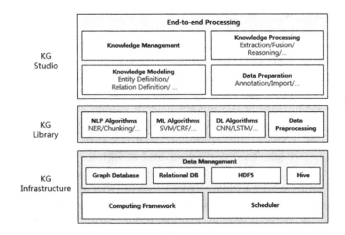

Fig. 1. The EasyKG architecture

---

[1] https://www.blog.google/products/google-cloud/cloud-automl-making-ai-accessible-every-business/.

KG Infrastructure. KG infrastructure is a collection of resources including data management system, schedulers, and computing frameworks. Data management system is composed of graph database, relational database, distributed file system like HDFS, and data warehouse software like Hive. Scheduler like Yarn is responsible for scheduling tasks and resources in a distributed cluster. Computing frameworks like Hadoop MapReduce and Spark provide the ability of parallel computing in a reliable manner.

KG Library. KG library contains a number of commonly used algorithms in natural language processing (e.g., Named Entity Recognizer, Chunking), machine learning (e.g., SVM, CRF), deep learning (e.g., CNN, LSTM) and data preprocessing like data cleaning, data transformation. These algorithms are implemented upon KG infrastructure, and each of them constitutes a component together with its configurations (i.e., input/output/parameter settings). Then the component can be invoked individually via a command line. Advanced users are allowed to import their own algorithms (see Sect. 3.2 for detailed information). EasyKG further encapsulates them to create customized components.

KG Studio. KG studio provides a user-friendly GUI to construct KGs toward different domains in an end-to-end way. Users can import and annotate external data, create components, build a pipeline, and finally generate KGs and evaluate them if necessary. All of them can be shared to other users, and reused by other KG construction. Let us elaborate the steps of KG construction as follows.

(1) Knowledge modeling is the prerequisite of KG construction. A typical KG contains nodes of entities, and edges of relations between entities. In this step, domain experts are supposed to define the schema of a KG, namely, different types of entities and relations, as well as their attributes. The schema is organized as a table or visualized as a graph on which domain experts can further edit.

(2) Data preparation allows users to import their local domain-specific documents containing the data for KG construction to the system, and annotate entities and relations in the documents based on the schema defined in Step 1.

(3) Knowledge processing is the core step for KG construction. It can be divided into three substeps, i.e., knowledge extraction, knowledge fusion and knowledge reasoning. EasyKG has integrated algorithms for each step and encapsulated them into components. A chain of components constitutes a pipeline by which the entire KG construction process is implemented.

(4) Knowledge management is to examine the quality of KGs obtained in previous step. For example, by typing an entity into a search box, an ego network with the query entity as the focal node and a default number of nodes as its neighbours (i.e., 10) is illustrated for users to check the completeness and correctness.

3   The EasyKG System

In this section, two cases are provided to show the KG construction process automatically in an end-to-end manner for ordinary users and advanced users, respectively. Ordinary users directly select one built-in pipeline, while advanced users are supposed to create a pipeline in a drag-and-drop manner with customized components. Let us elaborate each case in the following sections.

3.1   Building a KG by a Built-In Pipeline

In this case, we will elaborate the four steps to build a domain-specific KG of online music (musicKG for short) for ordinary user with a built-in pipeline. For the step of knowledge modeling, users are required to create a workspace to store the Music KG. Then, they are allowed to define entities in terms of entity types (i.e., Song, Singer, Album, etc), entity description, etc., as well as relations between pairs of entities including relation types (i.e., "Sings" between Singer and Song), relation description, etc. The defined musicKG schema can be viewed through a graphical visualizer or a organized table as shown in Fig. 2.

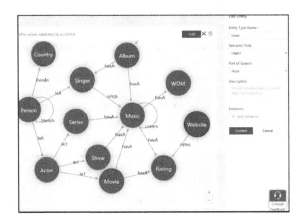

Fig. 2. Knowledge modeling in the whole lifecycle of KG construction

For the step of data preparation, users prepare data for knowledge processing. First, they upload their own data, either structured or unstructured documents. Then as an optional feature, they are encouraged to annotate some documents as training data for future use. If they would like to be the annotators, they select one uploaded document, specify the occurrence of an entity type and relation type in the document, such as Talor Swift as a Singer, and furthermore give some explanations of the annotation as shown in Fig. 3. The explanations can be automatically used to generate knowledge extraction component iteratively. EasyKG also supports annotations in a weakly supervised manner like Snorkel system [9].

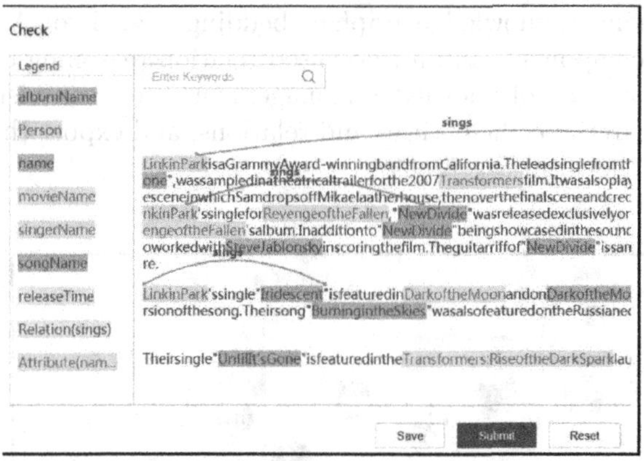

Fig. 3. Data preparation in the whole lifecycle of KG construction

For the step of knowledge processing, a built-in pipeline is selected to construct the musicKG from documents uploaded or annotated in previous steps. Recall that a pipeline consists of one or more components composed of algorithms and its configurations. Different pipelines are used for different knowledge processing tasks, such as knowledge extraction, knowledge reasoning, etc. Suppose that users select a pipeline consisting of named entity recognizer component and relation extraction component for knowledge extraction. Users only need to select the raw document as input of the first component, set corresponding parameters for each component (i.e., types of entities, list of stop words), and then start an extraction task on the cloud. After the task is finished, a KG is generated and automatically stored in a graph database. Figure 4 illustrates one built-in pipeline consisting of three components, namely, CRF-based named entity

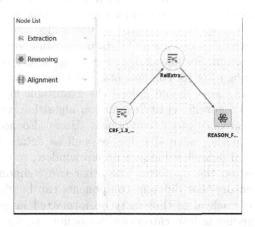

Fig. 4. Knowledge processing in the whole lifecycle of KG construction

recognizer component, knowledge graph embedding (e.g., TransA [5]) based relation extraction component, and a rule-based relation reasoning component.

Finally, for the step of knowledge management, users can visualize, edit the obtained KG, search specific entities and relations, and export the obtained KG as JSON file as shown in Fig. 5.

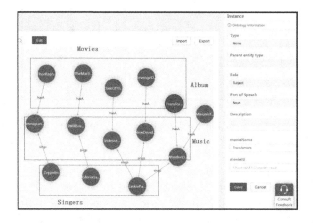

Fig. 5. Knowledge management in the whole lifecycle of KG construction

3.2   Building a KG by a Customized Pipeline

Advanced users (e.g., developers) may have their own algorithms, and prefer to adopt these algorithms in some components during the KG construction process. In this case, we show how to build a KG with a customized pipeline containing entity extraction, relation extraction and knowledge reasoning (e.g., link prediction) components, all of which are created by user's algorithms.

Specifically, knowledge modeling and data preparation are the same as mentioned in previous section. For knowledge processing, users customize a pipeline by creating and configuring its components. For example, to create an entity extraction component, users should upload the executable file (e.g., JAR package) with respect to a specific entity extraction algorithm, then select "entity extraction" as the category of the component. Users also need to specify the command line to run the executable file, as well as details of its arguments such as data type and default value in a popup window, so that the algorithm can be implemented on the platform. The other two components can be created similarly. To ensure that different components can be glued in a pipeline, the input/output of each algorithm must be formatted in advance. Since we have classified components into categories, we define the format for each category. For instance, for relation extraction component, the input contains two parts, i.e., a raw document, and the extracted entities formatted as a JSON file indicating entity type and its position in the document for each entity mention like {"label":{"entities":[{"label":"Singer","pos":[1,12,18],"word":"Talor Swift"}]}}. The output is also a JSON file recording the extracted entity pair and their relation. Likewise, we also have requirements for the format of the input/output of entity extraction and knowledge reasoning components. Next, users can assemble a pipeline using the customized components in a drag-and-drop manner. More precisely, via the GUI, users only need to drag the components to a panel, and draw arrows between components to form a pipeline, followed by setting the input and output of this pipeline. Note that the arrangement of the components of a pipeline should comply with the natural order of the steps when building a KG. After building this customized pipeline, users can run this pipeline to generate a KG as a task (never-ending if necessary), and manage it as described before. Moreover, users can monitor the progress of a running pipeline and further check the performance of the components. For example, suppose that one has created a customized component called "hmm" for entity extraction, and he/she runs a pipeline containing hmm for 5-fold cross-validation with the input of raw corpus of recently published entertainment news together with annotated ground truth of entities mentioned in the corpus. Figure 6 depicts the precision, recall and F1 score of the component. It can be seen that the precision of the uploaded component is about 0.9, and the F1 score is about 0.8. Noted that uses can further fine-tune the component until the performance is satisfactory.

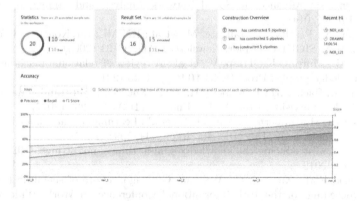

Fig. 6. Monitoring the customized pipeline

4   Conclusion

We presented an end-to-end system EasyKG throughout the whole lifecycle of KG construction. It has a pluggable pipeline architecture containing the components of knowledge modeling, data preparation, knowledge extraction, knowledge reasoning, knowledge management and so forth. A friendly GUI aids users to automatically generate a pipeline and finally obtain its corresponding domain-specific KG. So far, EasyKG has supported 300+ customers to build their own KGs on the cloud with millions of entities and tens of millions of relations.

References

1. Carlson, A., Betteridge, J., Kisiel, B., et al.: Toward an architecture for never-ending language learning. In: Twenty-Fourth AAAI Conference on Artificial Intelligence (2010)
2. Dong, X., Gabrilovich, E., Heitz, G., et al.: Knowledge vault: a web-scale approach to probabilistic knowledge fusion. In: Proceedings of the 20th ACM SIGKDD International Conference on Knowledge Discovery and Data Mining, pp. 601–610. ACM (2014)
3. Elsken, T., Metzen, J.H., Hutter, F., et al.: Neural architecture search: a survey. J. Mach. Learn. Res. **20**(55), 1–21 (2018)
4. Gliozzo, A., Ackerson, C., Bhattacharya, R., et al.: Building Cognitive Applications with IBM Watson Services: Volume 1 Getting Started. IBM Redbooks, New York (2017)
5. Jia, Y., Wang, Y., Lin, H., et al.: Locally adaptive translation for knowledge graph embedding. In: Thirtieth AAAI Conference on Artificial Intelligence, pp. 992–998. AAAI (2016)
6. Jia, Y., Wang, Y., Cheng, X., et al.: OpenKN: an open knowledge computational engine for network big data. In: Proceedings of the 2014 IEEE/ACM International Conference on Advances in Social Network Analysis and Mining, pp. 657–664. IEEE Press (2014)
7. Melchior, A., Peralta, E., Valiente, M., et al.: KNIME: the Konstanz information miner. ACM SIGKDD Explor. Newslett. **11**(1), 26–31 (2006)
8. Nickel, M., Murphy, K., Tresp, V., et al.: A review of relational machine learning for knowledge graphs. Proc. IEEE **104**(1), 11–33 (2015)
9. Ratner, A., Bach, S.H., Ehrenberg, H., et al.: Snorkel: rapid training data creation with weak supervision. Proc. VLDB Endow. **11**(3), 269–282 (2017)
10. Rotmensch, M., Halpern, Y., Tlimat, L., et al.: Learning a health knowledge graph from electronic medical records. Sci. Rep. **7**(1), 5994 (2017)
11. Singhal, A.: Introducing the knowledge graph: things, not strings. Official Google Blog, May 2012
12. Suchanek, F.M., Kasneci, G., Weikum, G.: Yago: a core of semantic knowledge. In: Proceedings of the 16th International Conference on World Wide Web, pp. 697–706. ACM (2007)
13. Zoph, B., Le, Q.V.: Neural architecture search with reinforcement learning. In: Proceedings of 5th International Conference on Learning Representations (2017)

Author Index

Printed in the United States
By Bookmasters

Printed in the United States
By Bookmasters